IMAGES
of America

EUCLID CREEK

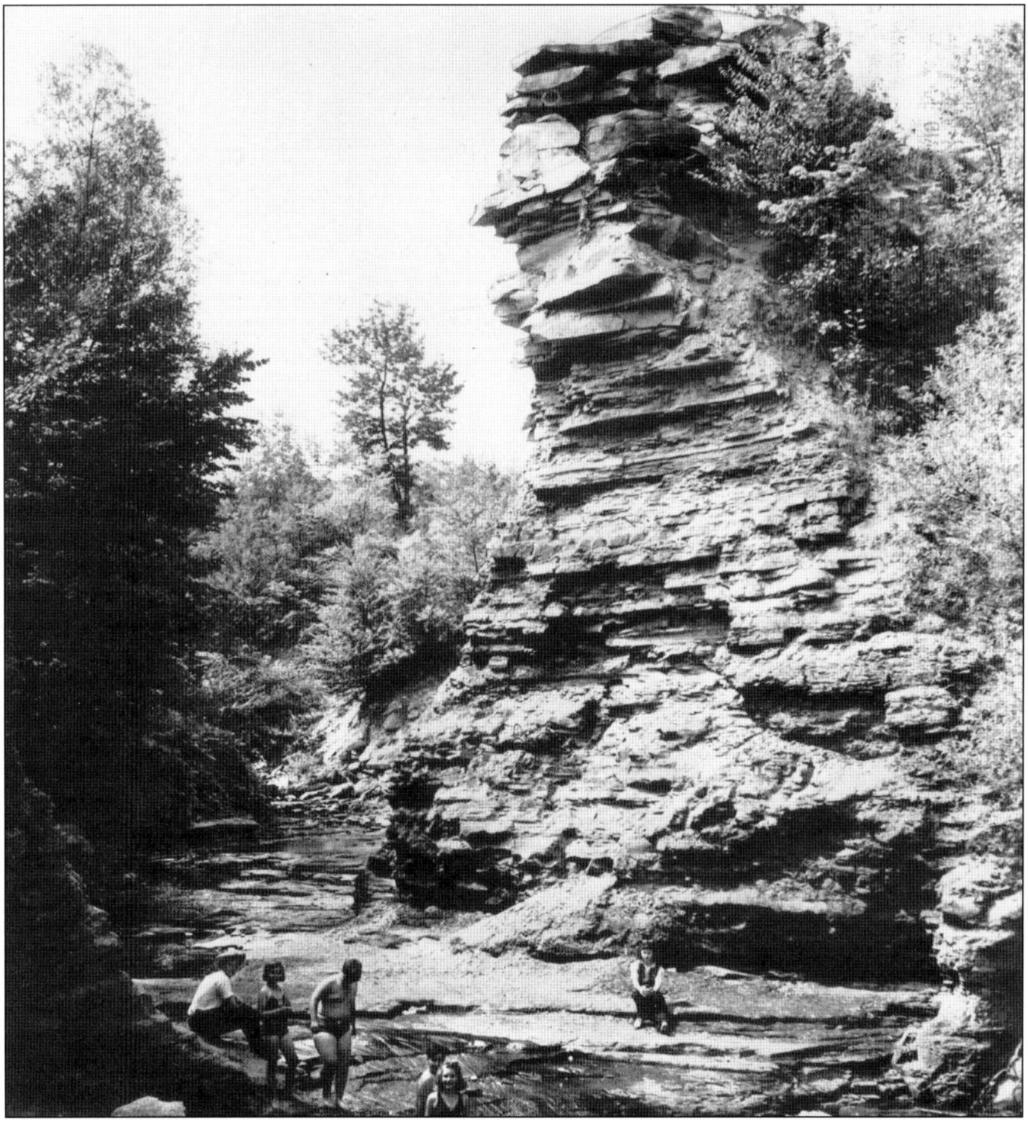

CATHEDRAL ROCK. This unique outcrop of Euclid bluestone (top) and Bedford shale lies just north of the Monticello bridge in the Euclid Creek reservation. Youths gallivanted here in the summer of 1953. (Cleveland Public Library, Photograph Collection.)

IMAGES
of America

EUCLID CREEK

Roy Larick
with Bob Gibbons and Edward Siplock

ARCADIA
PUBLISHING

ISBN 978-0-7385-3953-9

Published by Arcadia Publishing
Charleston SC, Chicago IL, Portsmouth NH, San Francisco CA

Printed in the United States of America

Library of Congress Catalog Card Number: 2005926265

For all general information contact Arcadia Publishing at:
Telephone 843-853-2070
Fax 843-853-0044
E-mail sales@arcadiapublishing.com
For customer service and orders:
Toll-Free 1-888-313-2665

Visit us on the Internet at www.arcadiapublishing.com

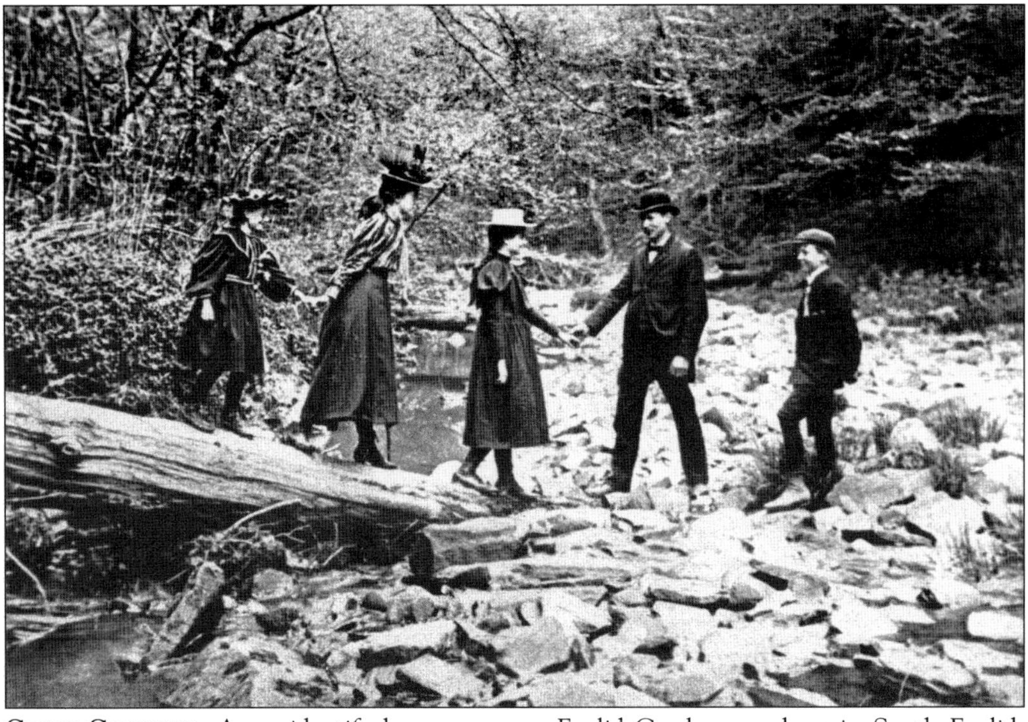

CRICK CROSSING. An unidentified group crosses Euclid Creek somewhere in South Euclid, sometime before 1900. New England settlers pronounced the word *creek* as "crick." Our stream was known as "Euclid crick" or as "the big crick." The rough, angular rocks may be waste material washed downstream from a small quarrying operation. (SEHS.)

Contents

ACKNOWLEDGMENTS

The historical images published herein have come, with great courtesy, from institutional and personal archives. We have enjoyed collaborating with archivists who show passion in making local history accessible. The captions identify contributors by name or by institutional acronym:

CCA	Cuyahoga County Archives
CMNH	Cleveland Museum of Natural History
CPL	Cleveland Public Library, Photograph Collection
CSU	Cleveland State University, the *Cleveland Press* Archives
EHS	Euclid Historical Society
HCGL	Historical Collections of the Great Lakes, Bowling Green University
MTHS	Mayfield Township Historical Society
JEHC	Jesse Earl Hyde Collection, Case Western Reserve University
NARA	National Archives and Records Administration
NHS	Nottingham Historical Society
RFPA	Richard Fleischman Partners Architects Inc.
RMC	Rose-Mary, the Johanna Grasselli Rehabilitation and Education Center
SEHS	South Euclid Historical Society
SMHT	Sisters of the Most Holy Trinity
SMSJ	Sisters of Mount St. Joseph of St. Mark
UHA	University Hospitals Archives
USC	Ursuline Sisters of Cleveland archives
WRHS	Western Reserve Historical Society

For technical support, we thank the Cuyahoga County Planning Commission, the Cuyahoga Soil and Water Conservation District, and the Euclid Historical Society. Finally, we have thrived on the patience, support, and outright tolerance of our loved ones (Patrice, Deb, and Priscilla) and on the enthusiasm of the Friends of Euclid Creek.

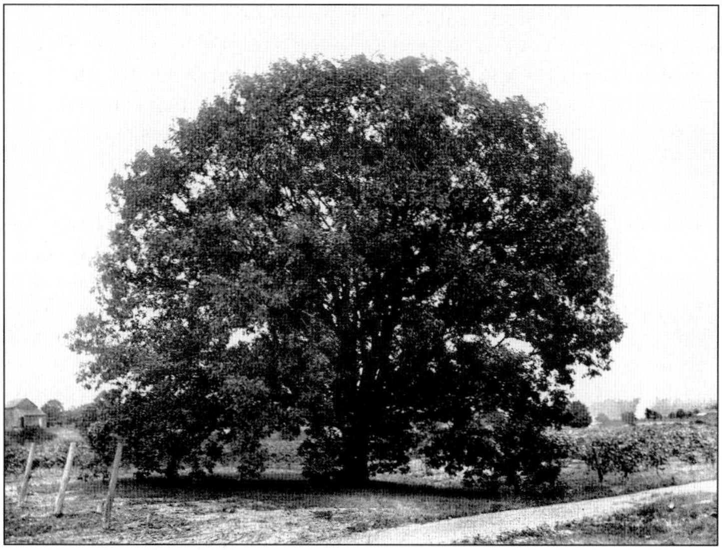

VOORHEES OAK. In 1804, Abraham Voorhees settled 200 acres straddling Euclid Creek near the current Nottingham Filtration Plant. Looking northwest on July 20, 1899, the land gently descends toward Lake Erie. The oak, shown here to honor the strength of our local history archives, had grown in a cleared area, never to be pruned or foraged. Vineyard row-end stakes are visible on either side of the tree. (EHS.)

INTRODUCTION

Euclid Creek begins with the premise that natural landforms connect people in important ways and that landforms are, therefore, an informative and entertaining way to organize local history. The Euclid Creek watershed is one such landform that has subtly linked residents living and traveling within it for more than two centuries. The watershed itself is the area drained by Euclid Creek, currently covering 11 municipalities. The stream has one set of sources about 12 miles from Lake Erie in Pepper Pike, Beachwood, and a corner of Shaker Heights. Another set lies in Mayfield Heights, Highland Heights, and Willoughby Hills. Headwater streams flow south and west, respectively, to coalesce into west and east branches. The branches converge just above Euclid Avenue, at Highland Road. A single, narrow channel then takes Euclid Creek across the lake plain to its mouth at current Wildwood Park.

The watershed has focused natural and cultural life for millennia. Animals, plants, and sediment constantly wash downstream. Numerous lake fish forge their ways upstream in search of protected spawning grounds. Humans have traveled the channels since prehistoric times. Native Americans chose to follow the ridgelines running parallel to major and minor branches. In that the east and west branches converge perpendicular to each other, the ridgeline trails formed a grid system of paths.

Euro-American settlers conveniently appropriated the prehistoric trails as the basis for our county roads. During the 1800s, men and women worked the land along the old trails; the goals were to feed themselves locally and take advantage of a growing regional economy for cash earnings. They turned trees into houses, churches, and schooners; they quarried stone for distant markets and planted vineyards for table and bottle. In recent times, watershed residents have sought ease of movement for automobiles as we pursue life ways nearly oblivious to the land and water under our feet. All manner of recent development has tended to fill in the valleys and flatten the ridges. Nevertheless, the old pathways have made and kept their mark. The watershed's original landforms and landscapes still subtly guide our lives.

Euclid Creek uses historical photographs to show how the stream has influenced life and how residents have transformed the stream. Transportation is the framework. The chapters divide up watershed history by transportation mode. The chapters show how people have arrived to the watershed and have traveled across it. The technology of the vehicle is celebrated: schooners, wagons, trains, and automobiles. However, it is the imprint of the transport channel on the landscape that bursts forth in the photographs: footpaths, wagon tracks, rail beds, county roads, and interstate highways.

Euclid Creek emerged out of flooded basements. By the late 1990s, rampant development had made the entire watershed prone to flash flooding. Residents were fuming. Beginning in 2001, three Euclid Creek partners came together on flooding. One was the Euclid Creek Watershed Council: nine mayors collaborating on a storm-water abatement plan. Partner two was a spirited advocacy group—the Friends of Euclid Creek—that rose around more general environmental issues. Partner three arrived when the Cuyahoga County Soil and Water Conservation District hired a Euclid Creek watershed coordinator, essentially to work with the two other groups. In 2003, the partners began a watershed action plan to revitalize the Euclid Creek's biology, chemistry, and natural habitat. The Cuyahoga County Planning Commission and the Ohio EPA also contributed to the plan, which was published in the summer of 2005.

Larick and Gibbons are Friends of Euclid Creek members. *Euclid Creek* grew directly from their efforts to provide a cultural resource inventory for the action plan. Upon realizing the wealth of archived images, they proposed an Images of America volume on the watershed. In preparing the book, archives relating to all watershed municipalities have been searched. The archives have yielded wonderful images for lost ways of life on Euclid Creek, including shipbuilding, quarrying, and winemaking. Others record a heretofore unrecognized 20th-century watershed life way: specialized caregiving on streamside campuses.

Euclid Creek shows two sides to Euclid Creek's historical life ways. One side has consciously used and respected local landforms in work and play. Such endeavors have included vine growing, estate building, and streamside caregiving. The other side has unconsciously transformed landforms with little regard to intrinsic value. These endeavors have included quarrying, railroading, and the building and using of interstate highways. *Euclid Creek* documents these two sides of history in a watershed whose existence has been nearly forgotten. The result is a handbook of images showing all manner of change across the years. May the handbook form a good basis for appreciating the past and for leading Euclid Creek toward more sustainable development during the next two centuries.

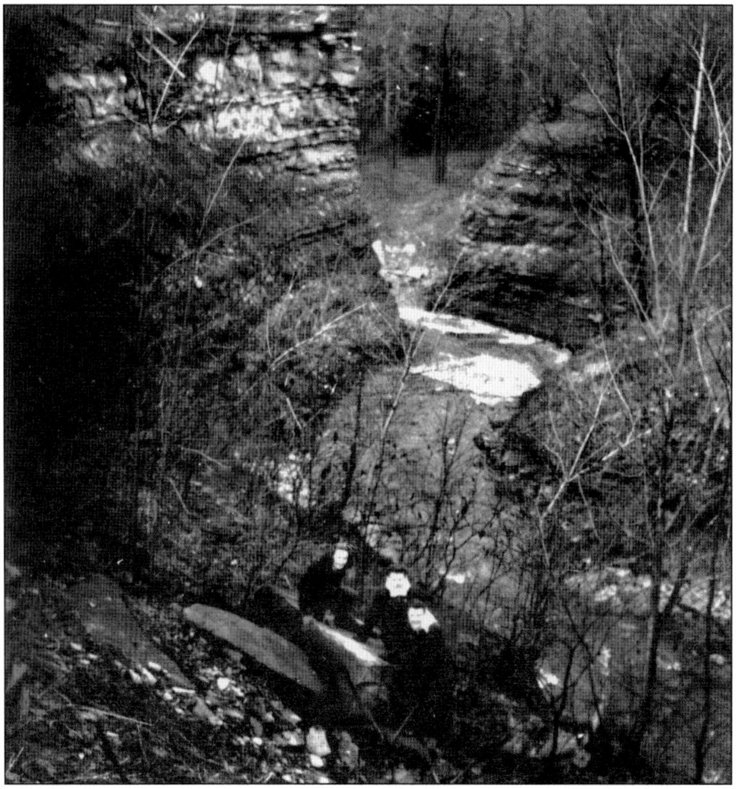

WELCHES WOODS. Twins Eva and Theresa Yost and sister-in-law Eunice Kelley Yost pose in Welches Woods during the winter of 1945. With much of the watershed still unpaved, creek flows were generally more constant and clear. In the early 19th century, surnames were written variably. We find, for example, Welch and Welsh. Surnamed landmarks, such as Welches Woods, did not display modern possessive orthography. (EHS.)

One

NATURAL SETTING

The sandstone and shale layers underlying the Heights—the layers visible in the Euclid Creek gorges—represent the Paleozoic era, which came well before dinosaurs roamed the earth. Vertebrates were already the highest life form, but all were primitive and confined to the seas. The Paleozoic seascape was inconceivably different from anything known on earth today. The Euclid Creek bedrocks were laid down 350 to 400 million years ago in a shallow tropical sea. At that time, northeastern North America and northern Europe were joined via the British Isles, and this entire landmass lay near the equator. The local sea resembled the present Gulf of Mexico, but much larger and warmer and teeming with primitive fish.

At any moment, the water might have been somewhat turbid, the result of warm heavy rains washing fine mud down large rivers. The sediment built up over the millennia to become the shale so prominent in Euclid Creek's cliff faces. However, the rivers occasionally flushed out sand, which settled out to become sandstone beds. Two such beds lie under the Heights, one high and one low. Mid-19th-century geologists and quarrymen named the lower bed "Euclid bluestone." The upper bed, with its more prominent outcrops on Cleveland's southwest side, was called "Berea sandstone."

As the present continents took shape, all the old rocks were slowly pushed up from the sea. Our region came to lie on the western flanks of the grand Appalachian Plateau. The Appalachian Mountains were much higher then; they resembled the current Rocky Mountains. As in the current Rockies, uplift brings erosion. Heavy tropical rains and stream flows took massive amounts of earth out to the Atlantic Ocean. Euclid Creek did not yet exist.

By about 3 million years ago, a large east-flowing river had carved out the current Erie basin and the rest of the Great Lakes watershed. This "Erigan River" had a number of large lateral tributaries, including the lower course of the Cuyahoga. The confluence of the two ancient rivers was situated well out in current Lake Erie. The general relationship can be seen in the curve of Lake Erie's south shoreline. Euclid Creek still did not exist.

By 1.6 million years ago, the Great Lakes basin received the first of numerous ice advances. Each advance brought a thin veneer of glacial till, the yellow-brown clay that is difficult to garden and sticks to our feet when wet. Each advance spread till over the old rocks only to be washed away by the floods coming with glacial retreats. Beginning about 20,000 years ago, the last advance brought the till we walk on today. By about 14,000 years ago, the last retreating ice spawned Euclid Creek. Quickly this stream pierced the sandstones and shale from the Heights to Lake Erie. Today we love the gorges and waterfalls that reflect a brief moment in a long natural history.

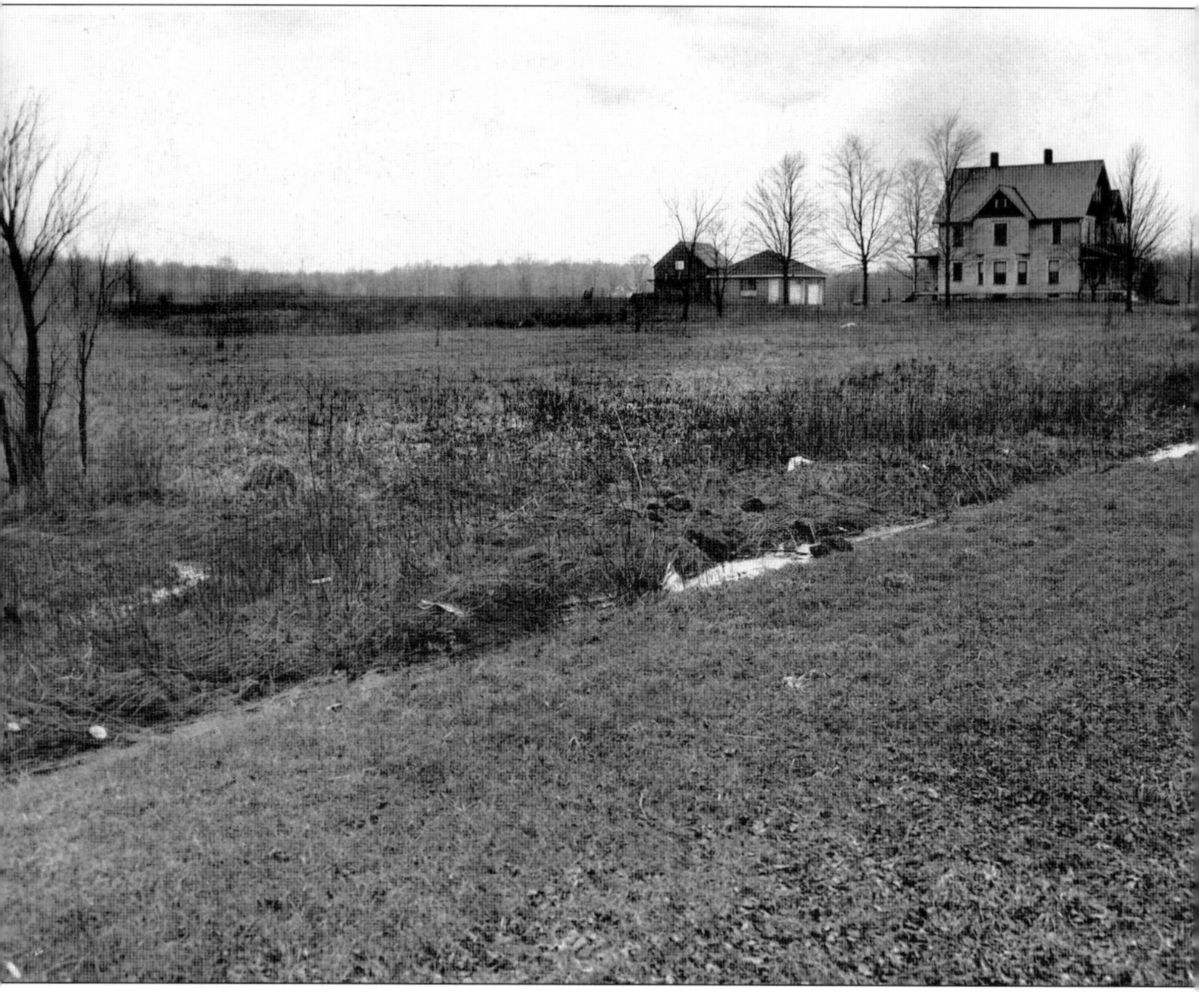

APPALACHIAN PLATEAU. Euclid Creek's headwaters drain the northern edge of the Appalachian Plateau in Pepper Pike, Beachwood, and a corner of Shaker Heights. The relatively flat terrain sits atop resistant beds of Berea sandstone. Neither glacial advances nor creek floodwaters have penetrated these beds on the southern Heights. This 1947 photograph looks southwest from Mayfield Road, just east of Lander. The house was built about 1895. (MTHS.)

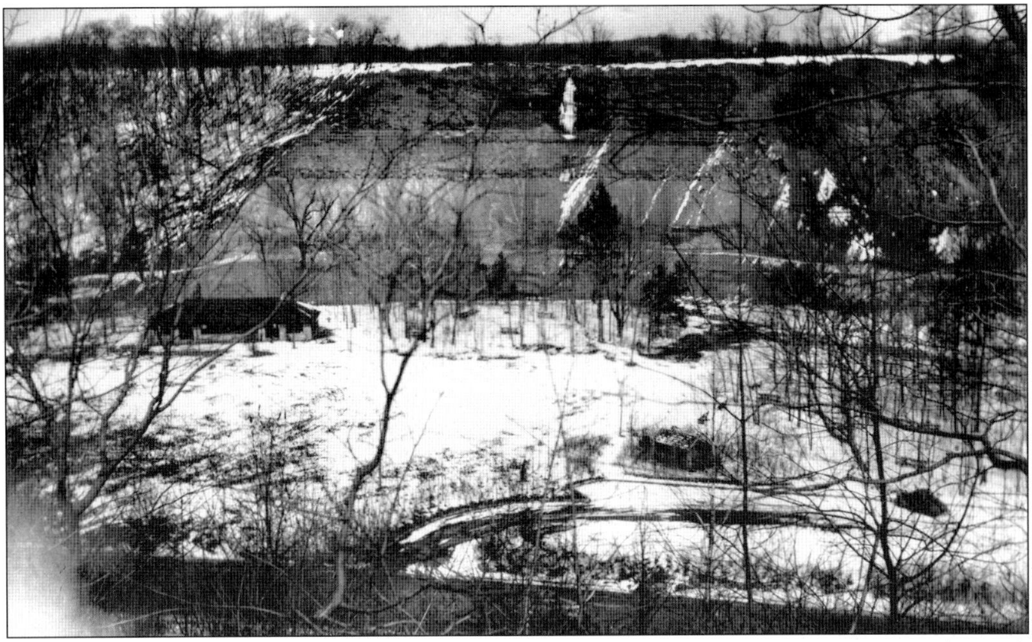

EUCLID BLUESTONE. The Euclid bluestone is a hard, buff-gray sandstone bed lying just beneath the ground surface in the northern Heights communities. Soft shale lies under the bluestone. The bluestone bed caps the Portage escarpment above Euclid Avenue, from Cedar Hill to Richmond Road. Along this ridge, Euclid Creek cut directly through bluestone and shale to form its gorges. (EHS.)

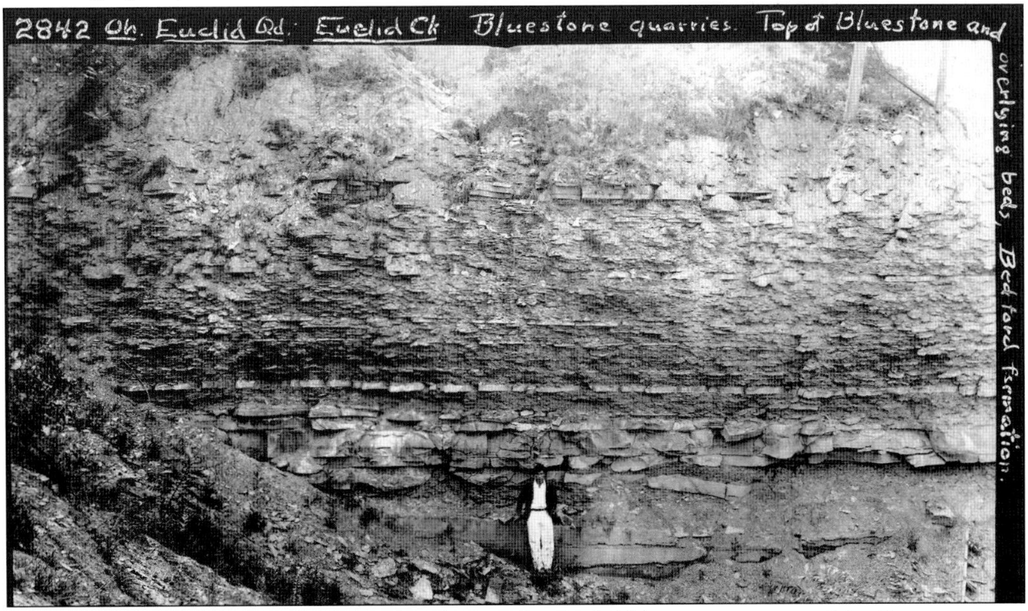

BLUESTONE OUTCROP. In geological parlance, the Euclid bluestone is part of the Devonian-age Bedford Formation. Layering in the Bedford alternates between shale and sandstone. In and around Euclid Creek, the bluestone layers are massive enough to have had market value for a brief period. This 1934 photograph shows the layering in an abandoned Euclid Creek quarry. A geology student poses to give scale. (JEHC.)

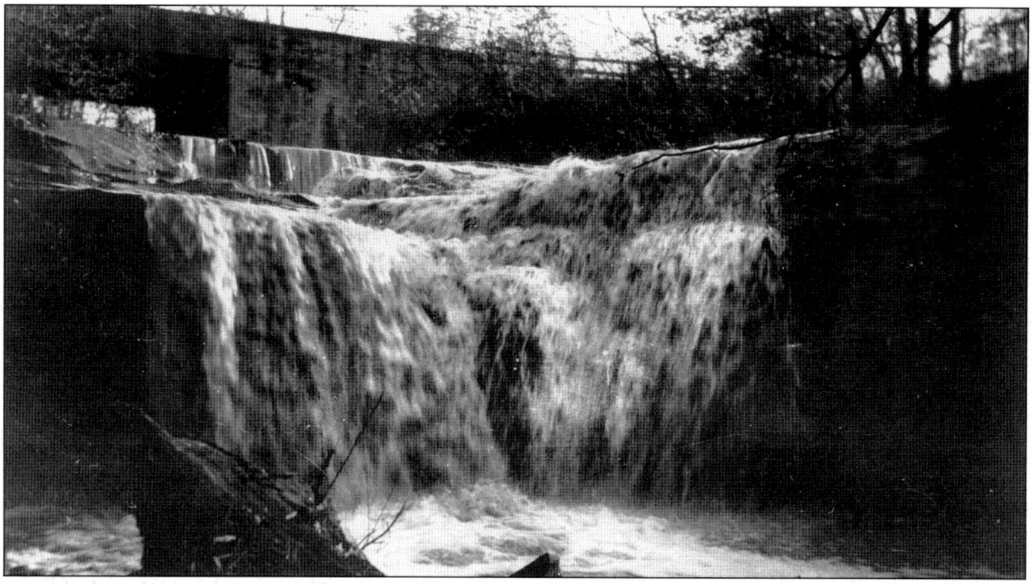

EUCLID FALLS. Euclid Creek's west branch cuts through the bluestone at Anderson and Green Roads. In 1797, Connecticut Land Company surveyors Charles Parker and Joseph Landon saw this locale as a potential site for water-powered milling. In the early 1800s, the area became known as Euclid Falls and had a small settlement. By the 1870s, the economic interest shifted to quarrying, and the settlement name became Bluestone. (SEHS.)

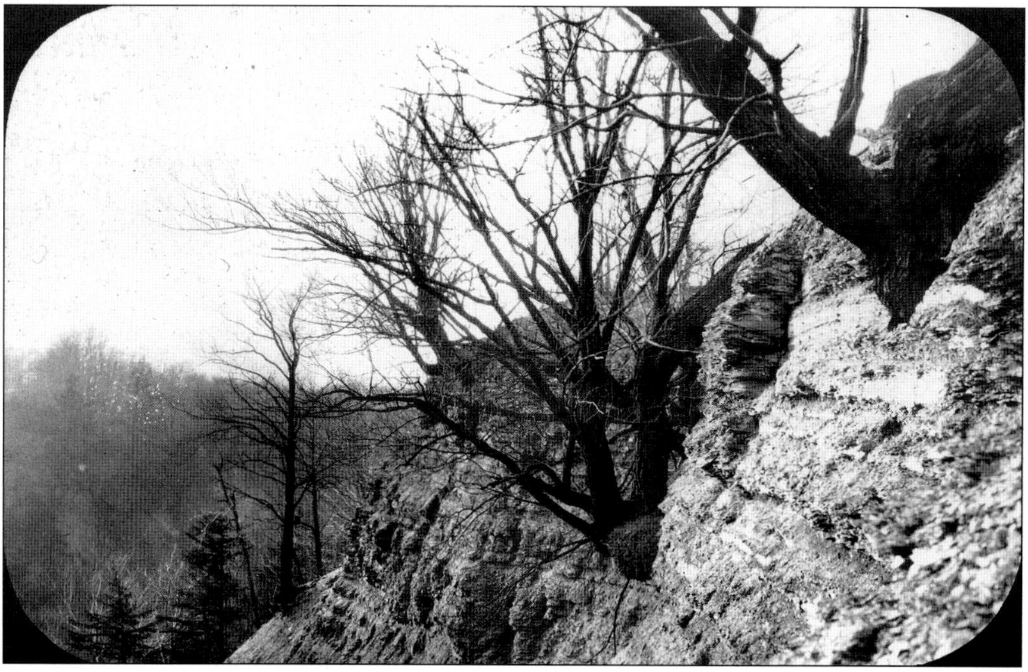

THE GORGES. Prof. Jesse Earl Hyde was a Western Reserve University geologist from 1915 until his death in 1936. He shot and collected thousands of geological landscape photographs. Ohio stream geology was a favorite topic. A score of Euclid Creek images from the 1920s and 1930s have survived. This image shows a seemingly bottomless west branch gorge near the current Welsh Woods recreation area. (JEHC.)

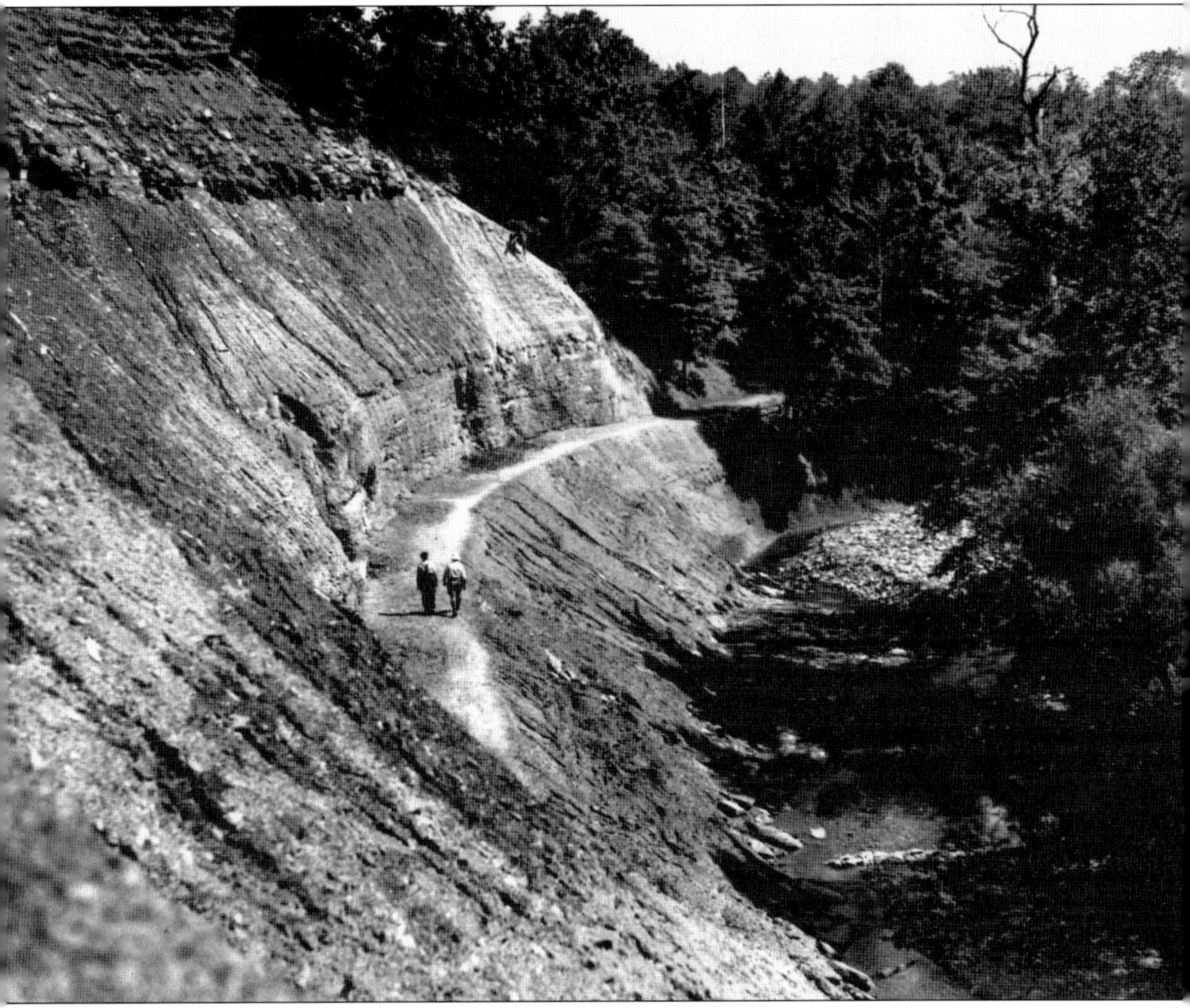

SHALE. A number of shale formations underlie the Euclid bluestone. The shale is weak compared with the sandstone and especially prone to freeze-thaw disintegration. Once creek waters break through the sandstone, they make quick work of the shale. This 1936 photograph shows a new footpath cut in the Chagrin shale, below Welches Woods. The path was dug as part of the Civilian Conservation Corps (CCC) Camp Euclid program directed through the National Park Service. (CPL.)

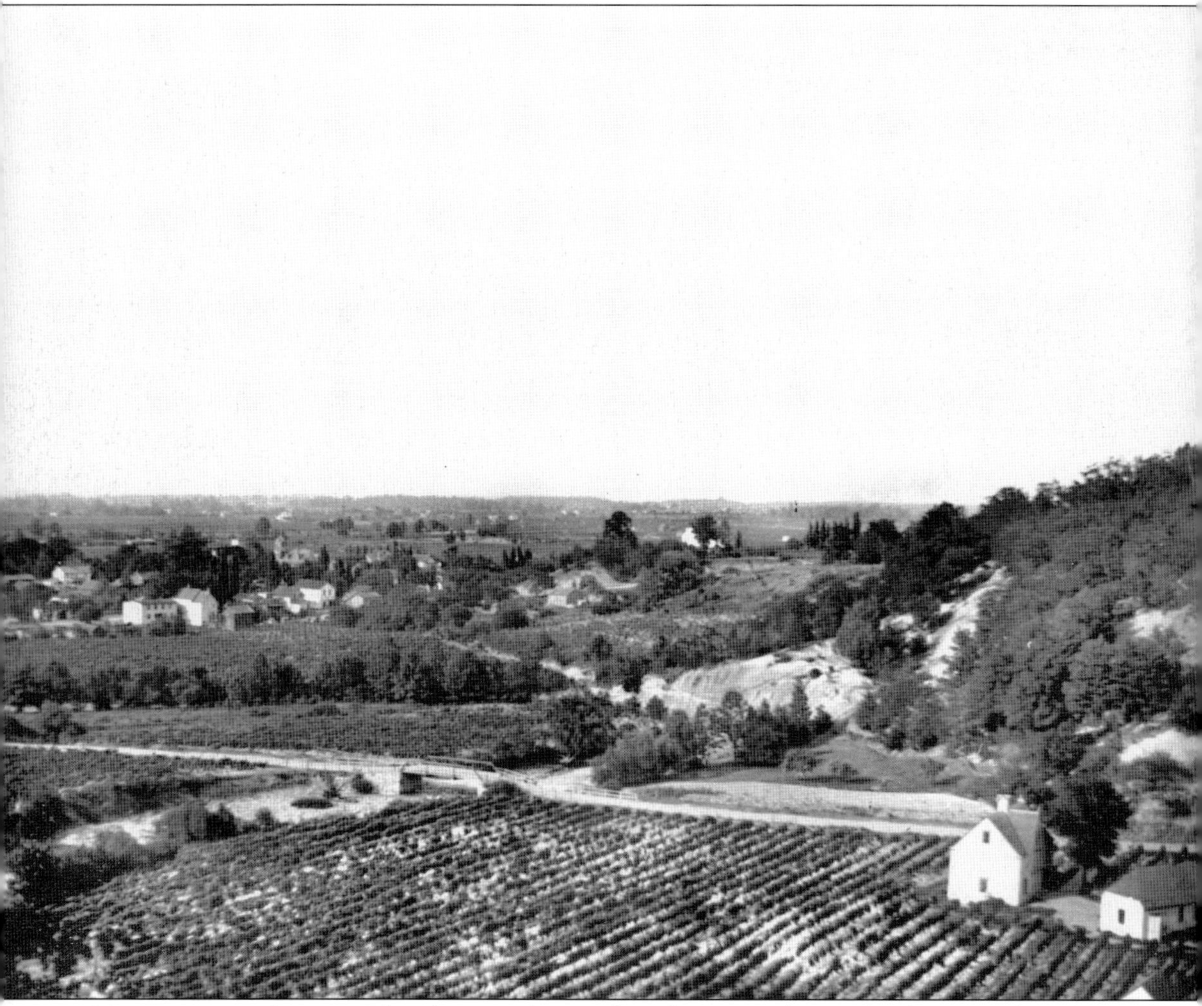

MOUTH OF THE GORGES. This photograph was taken about 1890 from Ridge (current Glenridge) Road. We view northeast to Chardon Hill and beyond to the lake. Here the east and west branches join before issuing north to the lake plain. Much of this area was deforested in 1890 for lumber and agriculture. Vineyards cover the floodplain. (WRHS.)

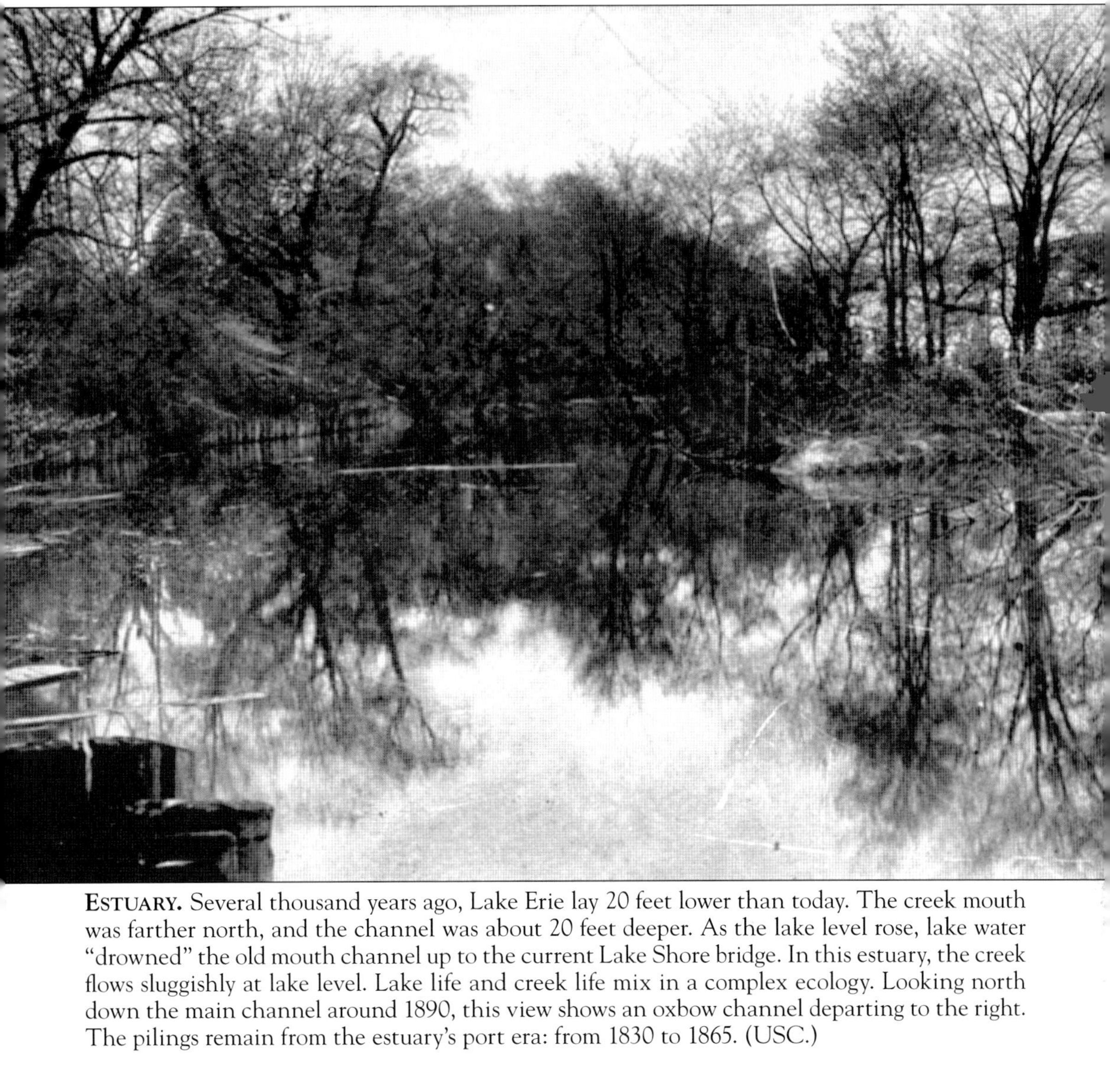

ESTUARY. Several thousand years ago, Lake Erie lay 20 feet lower than today. The creek mouth was farther north, and the channel was about 20 feet deeper. As the lake level rose, lake water "drowned" the old mouth channel up to the current Lake Shore bridge. In this estuary, the creek flows sluggishly at lake level. Lake life and creek life mix in a complex ecology. Looking north down the main channel around 1890, this view shows an oxbow channel departing to the right. The pilings remain from the estuary's port era: from 1830 to 1865. (USC.)

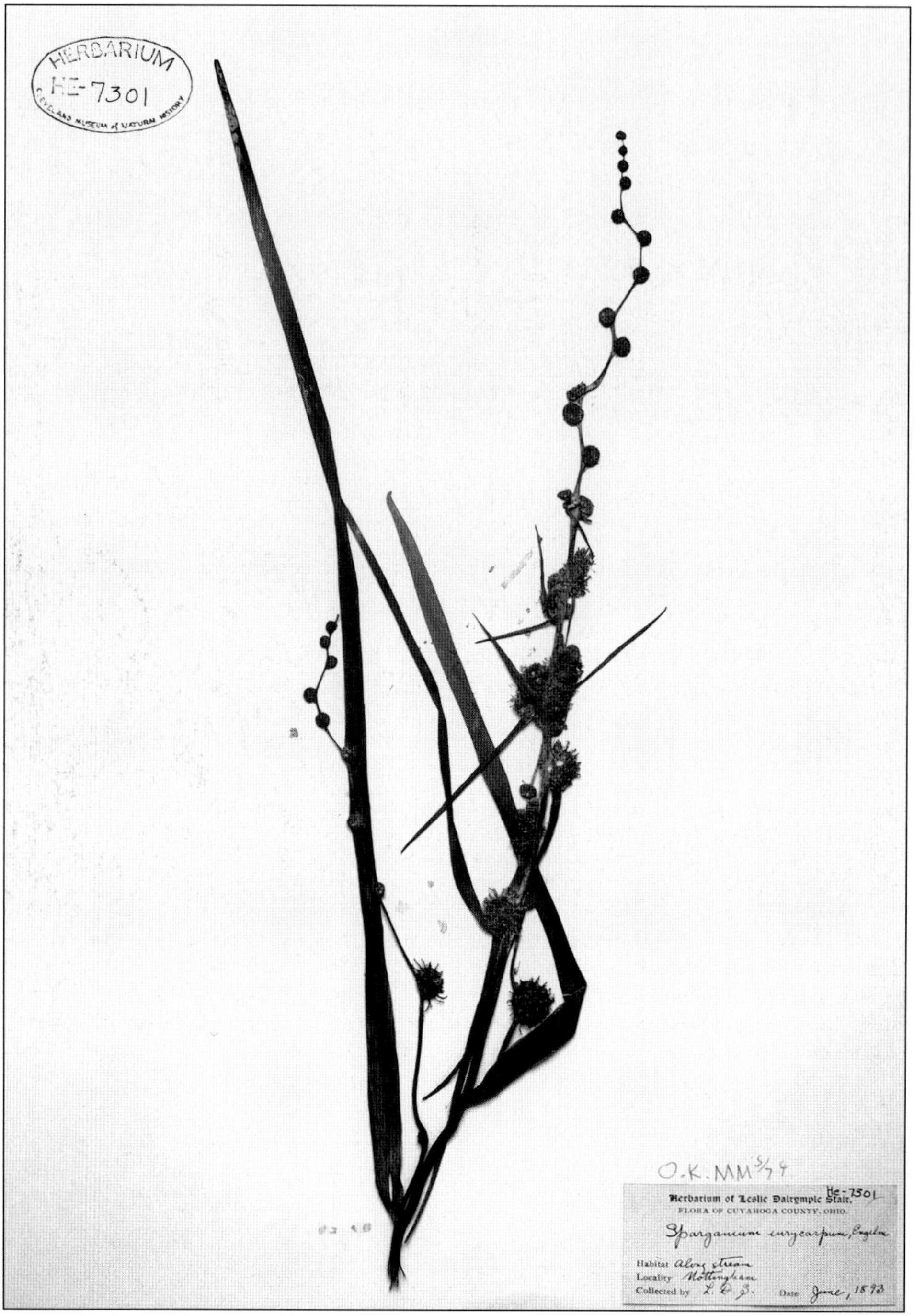

GREATER BUR-REED. Leslie Dalrymple Stair actively collected native plants in the Cleveland region during the late 1800s. The Euclid Creek estuary was one of his haunts. Here, in June 1893, Stair collected this specimen of greater bur-reed (*Sparganium eurycarppum*), which was a common northern Ohio wetland plant. Now it is nearly eradicated from our lake shore marshes, replaced by purple loostrife and narrow-leaf cattail. In general, the plants and animals living in and around Euclid Creek have changed immensely through time. (CMNH.)

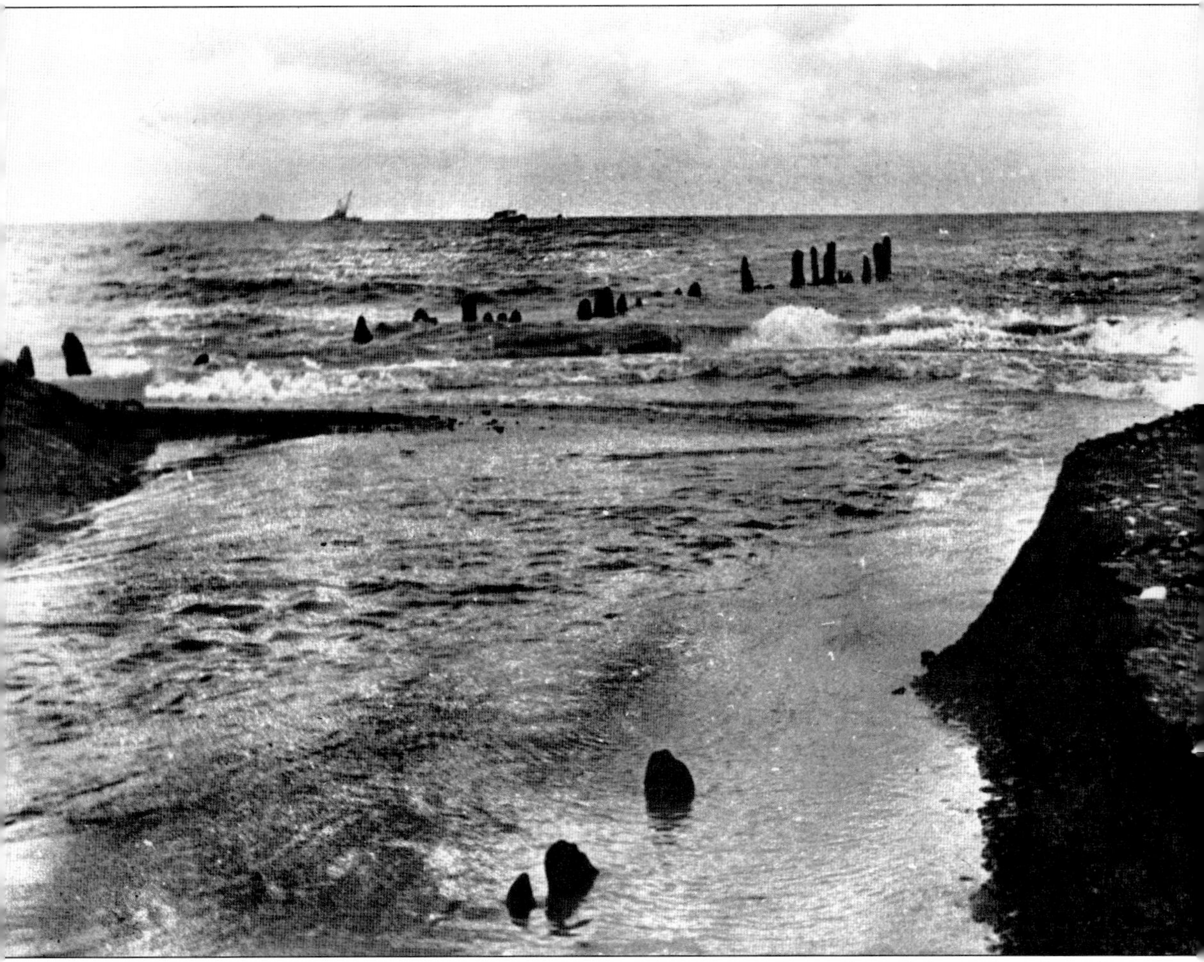

Lake Erie. Prevailing west winds give Lake Erie a strong easterly swell. Euclid Creek's silt and clay discharge is washed away immediately. Sand, nevertheless, does accumulate to form a barrier bar across the mouth. The bar protects the estuary from the direct onslaught of waves. The creek provides a quiet harbor—if a boat can get through the bar. This photograph was taken in 1947 at the start of construction for the Nottingham water intake. (WRHS.)

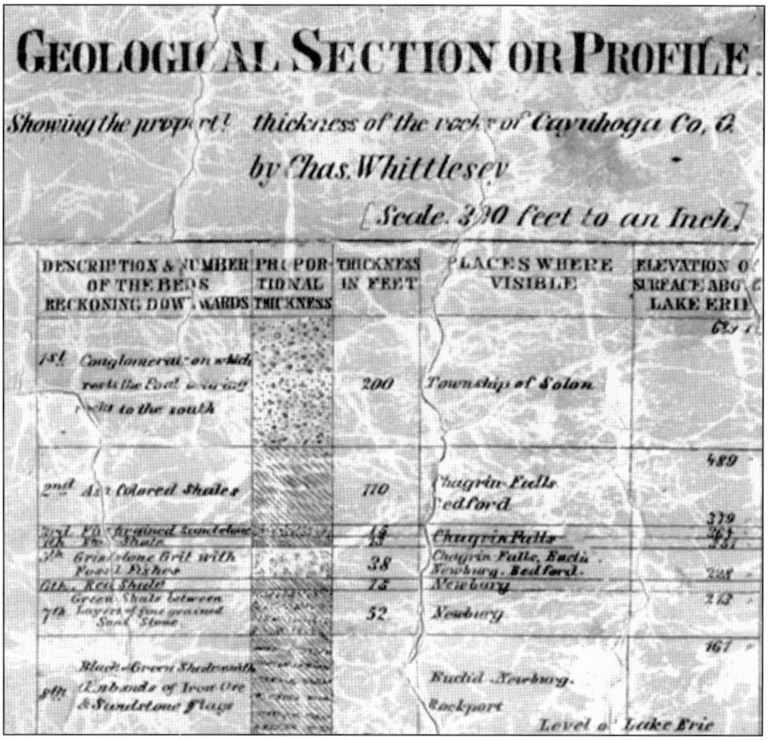

Earth Resources. Clevelander Col. Charles Whittlesey was a national pioneer in geology and archaeology. He began studying Cuyahoga County rocks in the 1830s with an eye toward economic utility. Whittlesey was the first to identify the sandstone bed later called Euclid bluestone. On this uniquely preserved 1858 geological profile, Euclid bluestone is the 38-foot-thick bed lying 228 feet above Lake Erie. (MTHS.)

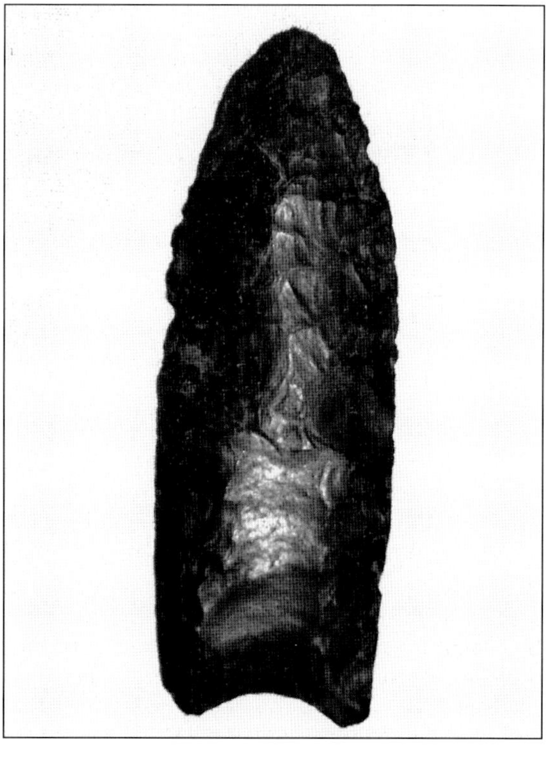

Fluted Point. Humans entered the southern Great Lakes as glaciers retreated about 10,000 years ago. Fluted points were part of their sophisticated means for hunting Ice Age mammals, including mammoth, mastodon, horse, and bison. Debate continues as to whether these peoples were or were not the ancestors of historical Native Americans. This point was found near the Monticello bridge. (Roy Larick.)

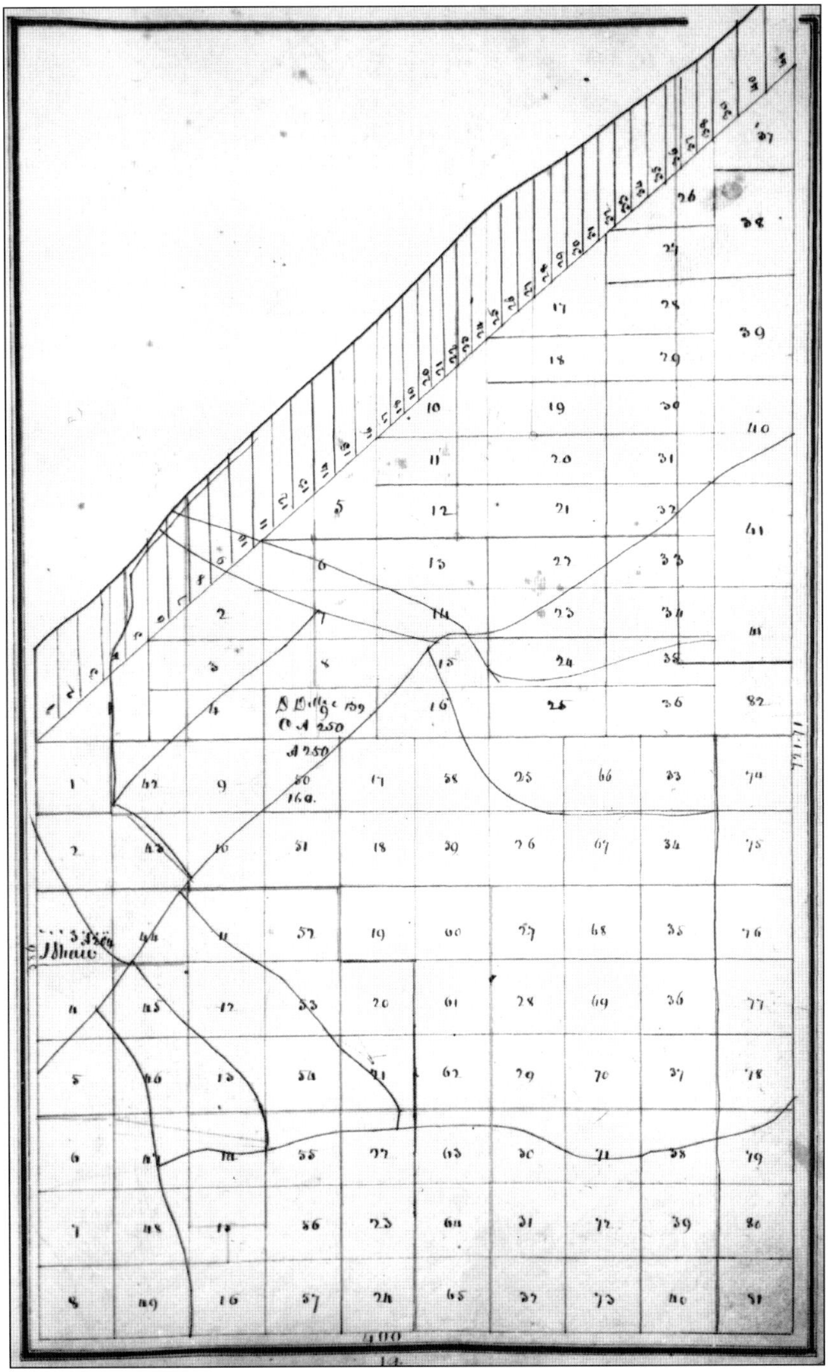

PREHISTORIC TRAILS. One of the original Euclid Township survey maps traced two kinds of prehistoric trails. Beach ridge trails ran parallel to Lake Erie. Current Lake Shore Boulevard, St. Clair Avenue, and Euclid Avenue follow these trails. Gorge rim trails ran up to the Heights. Rim trails lay on both sides of Euclid Creek. Current Nottingham, Dille, and Highland Roads follow the southwest rim trail. Current Neff and Chardon Roads follow the northeast rim. These two crossed the main beach ridge trail (Euclid Avenue) in rectangular tracts 14 and 15. (WRHS.)

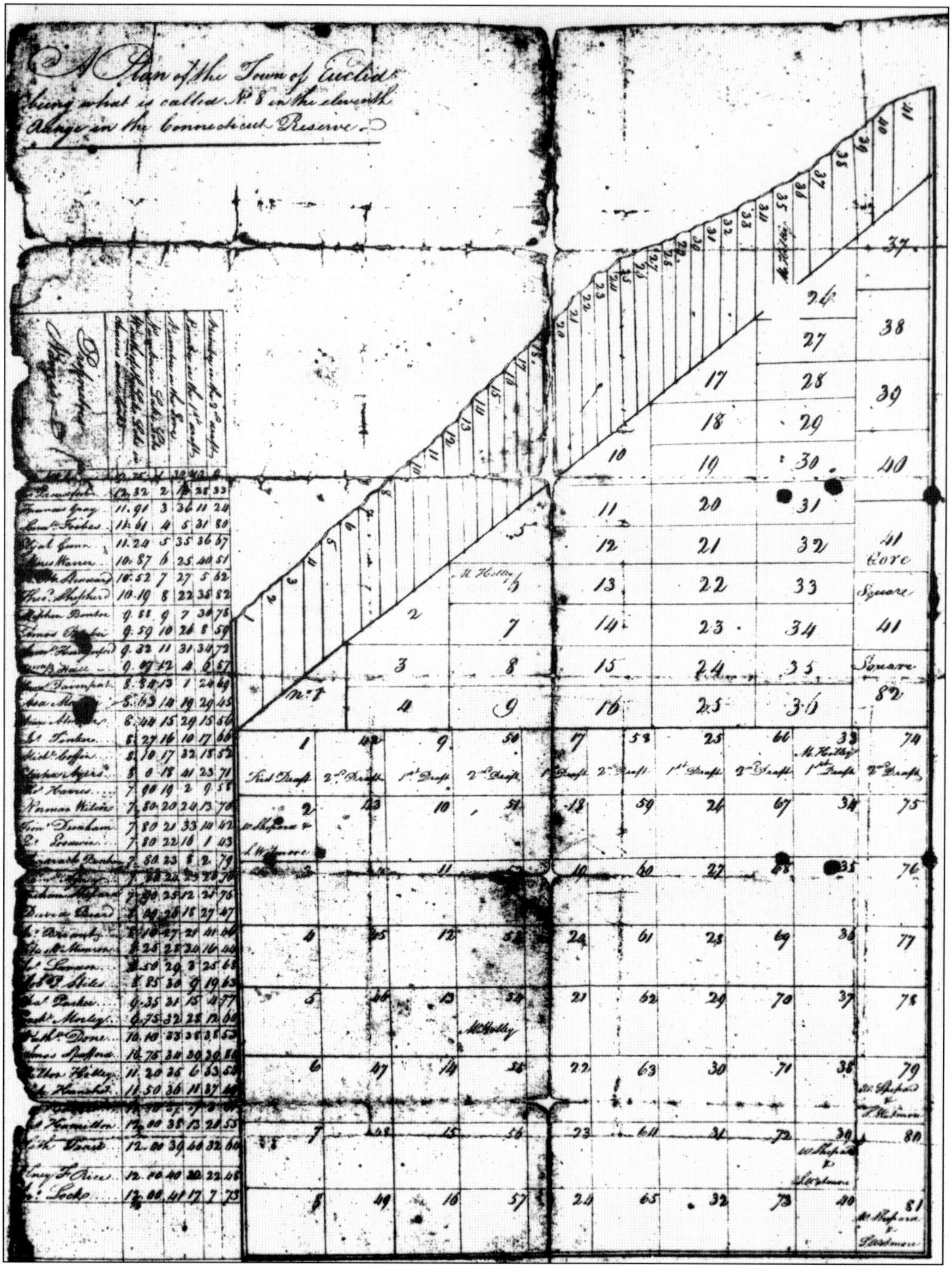

PROTESTORS' LOTS. On September 30, 1796, 41 protestors in Moses Cleaveland's survey crew contracted to purchase Euclid Township, the largest survey unit in the Western Reserve. The group divided the township up equally among themselves, each man receiving four lots totaling 545 acres. This plan lists the protestors' names and their assigned lots. Each allotment covered one narrow lake lot, one rectangular lot on the lake plain, and two square lots on the highlands. (WRHS.)

Two

WALKING AND SAILING 1796–1852

In September 1796, Moses Cleaveland completed his initial Connecticut Western Reserve survey. It was a troubled month as most of the field crew had threatened not to return in 1797. The survey season had been plagued with chronic hunger, mosquito fever, and dysentery. The men were fed up. To resolve the crisis, Cleaveland created the reserve's largest township just east of the capital settlement, and he offered it at a reduced price to the 41 protestors on his crew. The men took the deal and named their township Euclid after the classical Greek inventor of geometry, the surveyors' mathematics.

Euclid Township happened to straddle a sizeable watercourse. Among the streams encountered during survey, this one would be called a big creek. Sailing back eastward on Lake Erie in October 1796, the protestors crossed the mouth of the township stream and named it Euclid Creek. In June 1797, the protestors surveyed Euclid Township. The men ran 250 miles of survey lines to give each stakeholder lots on the lakeshore, plain, and highland. The cleared survey lines left a cardinal grid of transport channels across the watershed.

Alas, the Euclid protestors lost their initiative and gave up on the settlement plan. By 1802, the Connecticut Land Company resurveyed the township and gave the land back to its eastern investors. While the protestors were not the watershed's first settlers, their 1797 survey lines proved useful to the men and women who did make their home here. The first real settlers used these channels to take them where the prehistoric trails did not go. Combining the trails and the survey lines, the pioneers had, by about 1810, the basic county road system that served until the coming of the interstates in the early 1960s.

Three other features drew settlers to Euclid Creek. First, waterfalls on the main and headwater branches provided mill sites for processing wood and grain. Second, the Cleveland-Buffalo Road (current Euclid Avenue) crossed Euclid Creek at a deep chasm. Businesses catering to arrested travelers quickly grew at "Euclid Creek village." Third, with its lake access, the Euclid Creek estuary saw the watershed's earliest industrial development. By 1820, clay was being imported to establish a stoneware kiln, and by 1840, a shipyard was launching two-masted schooners.

The New England settlers who chose to live near Euclid Creek were generally of middle-class means. While they did not bring wealth to the watershed, they did import stylish ways for building houses. Most early dwellings were built on the Cape Cod house design, which dated to the mid-1600s throughout New England. The early Capes were squat dwellings with the roof eaves down low on the front door and window lentils. After about 1790—when New Englanders began moving west—the eaves were moved up a few feet to provide a true half-story on the upper floor. This is sometimes called the "temple" form of dwelling common in Federal and Greek Revival trim. Early-19th-century New Englanders also set "wings" off the sides of their Capes, a fashion derived from Italian Renaissance architect Andrea Palladio. Winged, or Palladian, temple Capes were very handsome and were the first permanent dwellings to be seen across the watershed.

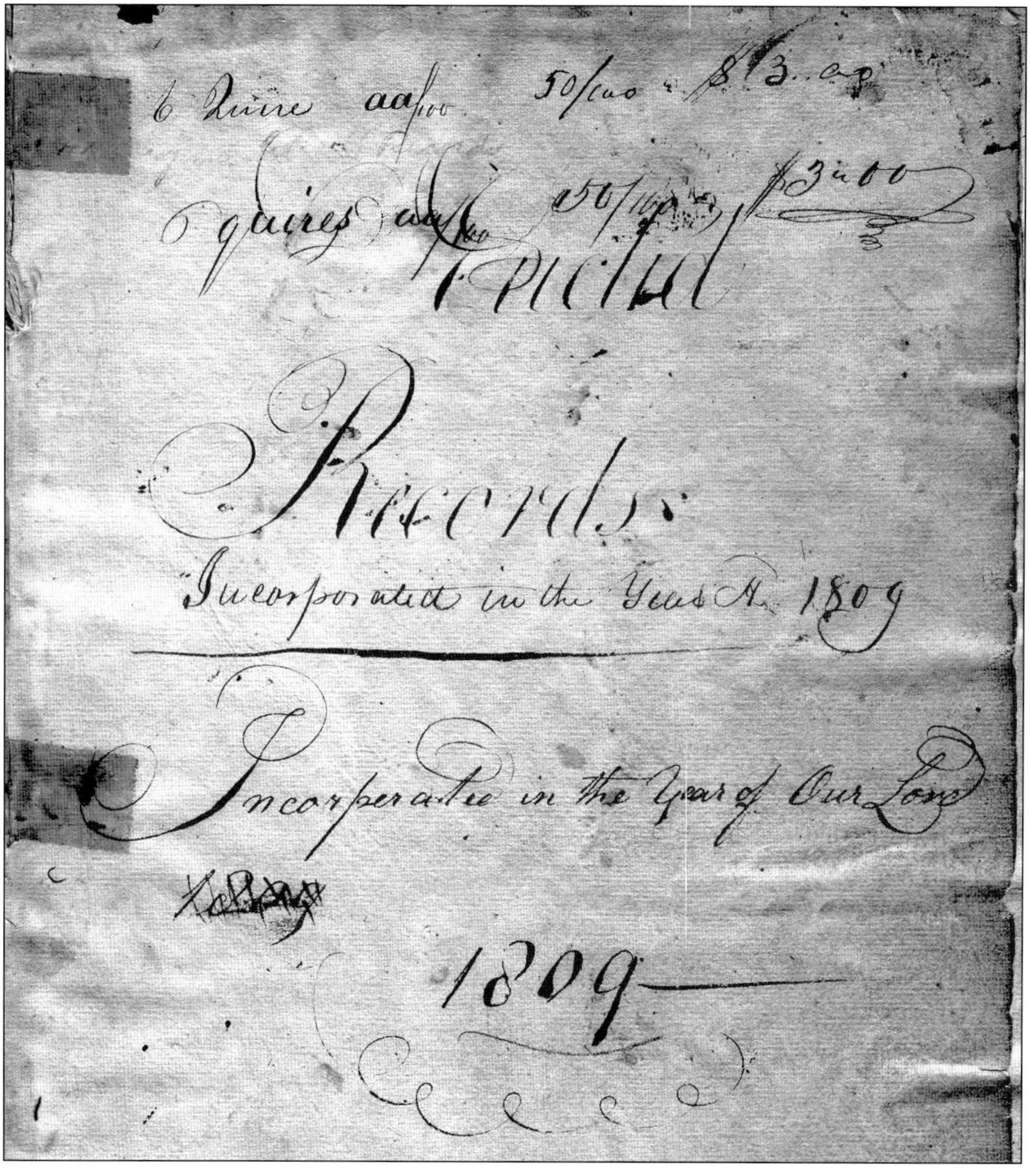

EUCLID RECORDS. On April 2, 1810, most Euclid Township residents gathered for the first election and to inscribe the *Euclid Records*. For the next 111 years, the minutes of all meetings were duly placed behind this cover sheet. The name Dille appeared frequently in the *Records*. The members of the David Dille Jr. family were the watershed's first permanent settlers. They bought two surveyors' lots on the Buffalo Road (Euclid Avenue) in 1797 and settled them in 1803. The Dilles were civic-minded, gregarious, hospitable, intelligent, and prolific. They intermarried with many of Cleveland's prestigious early families. Had our stream been named for a pioneer family, it would certainly be called "Dilles Crick." (EHS.)

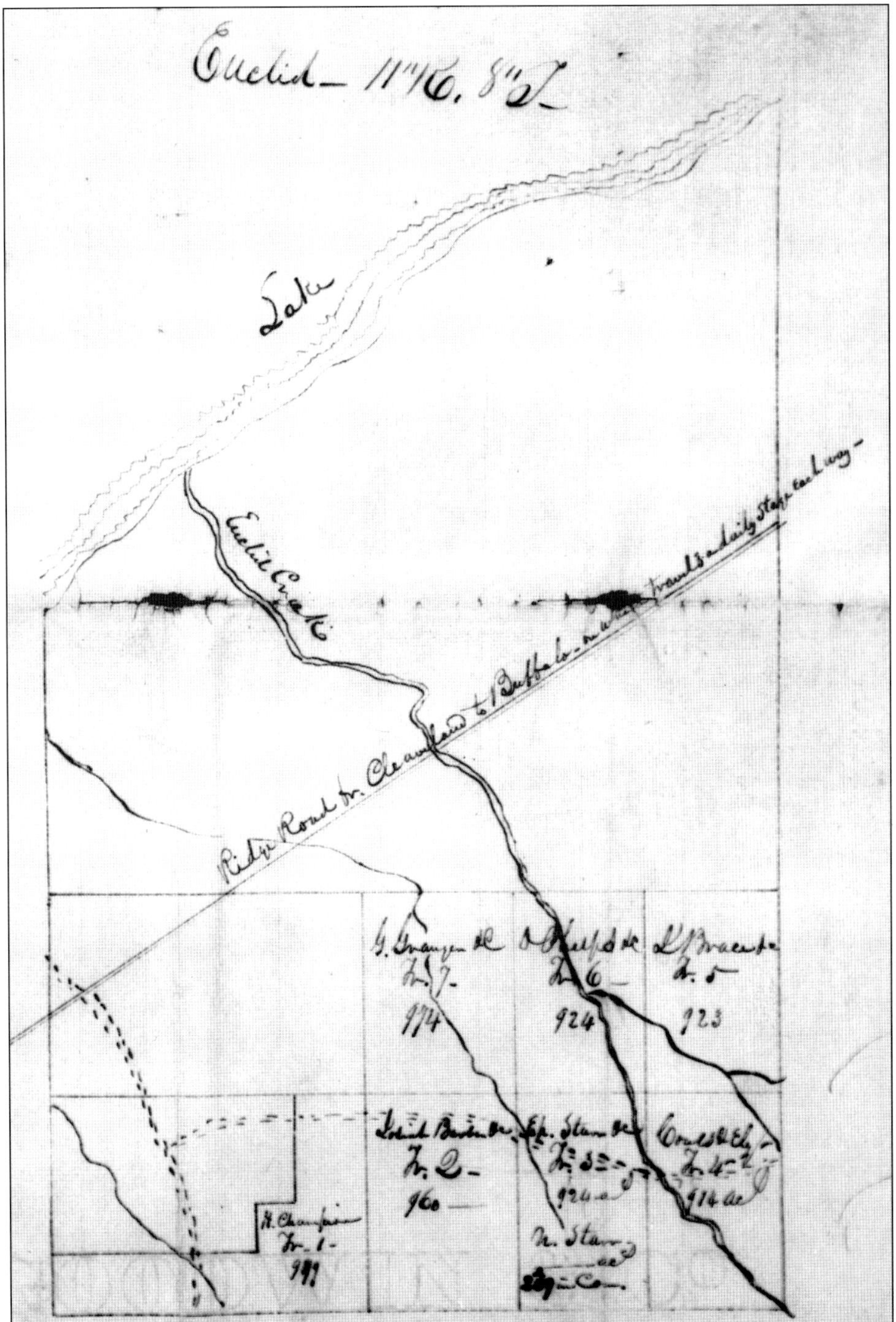

EUCLID CREEKS. Seen here is the earliest map, about 1815, to depict Euclid Township's major watercourses: Euclid Creek, Nine Mile Creek (mid-left), and Dugway Brook (far left). Two prehistoric trails (broken lines) are also shown: Lee Road (north to south) and Mayfield Road (east to west). The Buffalo Road legend reads, "Ridge Road fr. Cleaveland to Buffalo—on which travels a daily stage each way." (WRHS.)

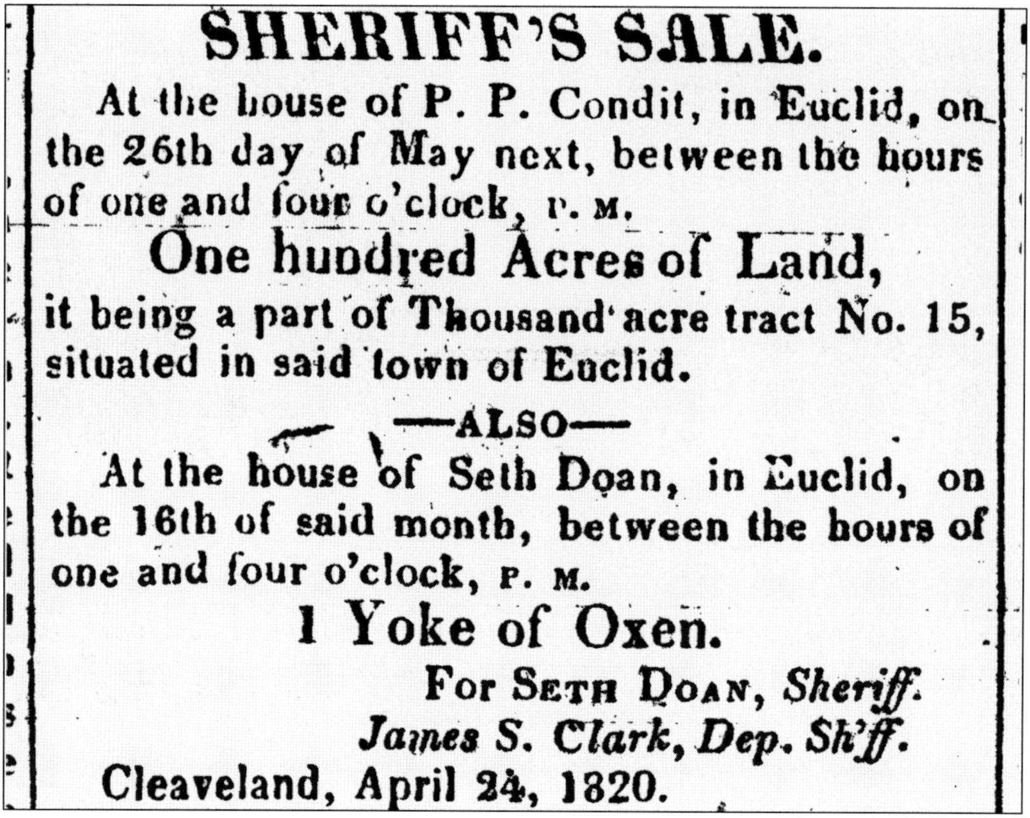

SHERIFF'S SALE.

At the house of P. P. Condit, in Euclid, on the 26th day of May next, between the hours of one and four o'clock, P. M.

One hundred Acres of Land,

it being a part of Thousand acre tract No. 15, situated in said town of Euclid.

—ALSO—

At the house of Seth Doan, in Euclid, on the 16th of said month, between the hours of one and four o'clock, P. M.

1 Yoke of Oxen.

For SETH DOAN, *Sheriff.*

James S. Clark, Dep. Sh'ff.

Cleaveland, April 24, 1820.

FARMERS' INN. In 1814, Paul P. Condit established the first inn within the watershed. It was on the Buffalo Road, currently at 19351 Euclid Avenue. In the later 19th century, it was called the Farmers' Inn. The inn was the site of many official public events, including sheriff's sales. (The *Herald*, April 25, 1820.)

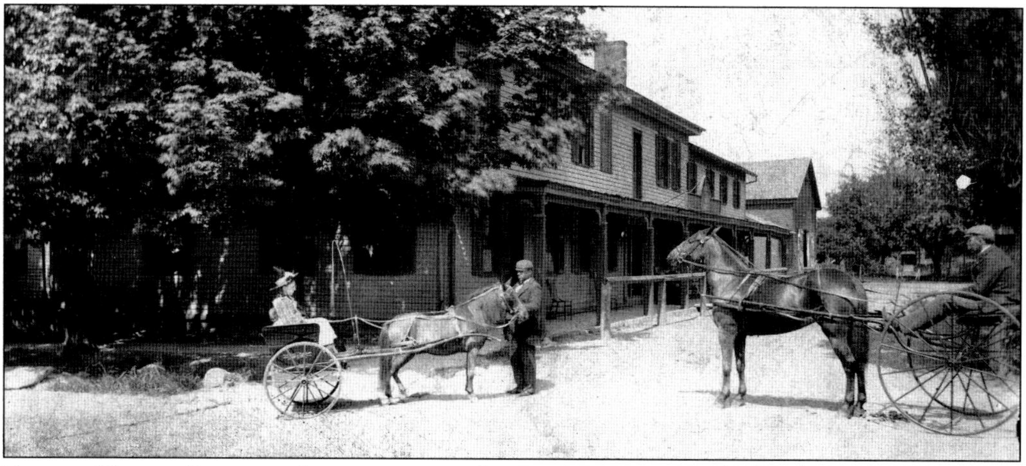

EUCLID HOUSE. For more than a century, the northeast corner of Chardon Road and Euclid Avenue held an inn to refresh the traveling public and locals. Abraham Farr built the first structure in 1815, which became known as the Euclid House. C. E. Fenner rebuilt the house in the 1840s and then sold it to Lewis A. Korf, the proprietor at the time of this photograph. (EHS.)

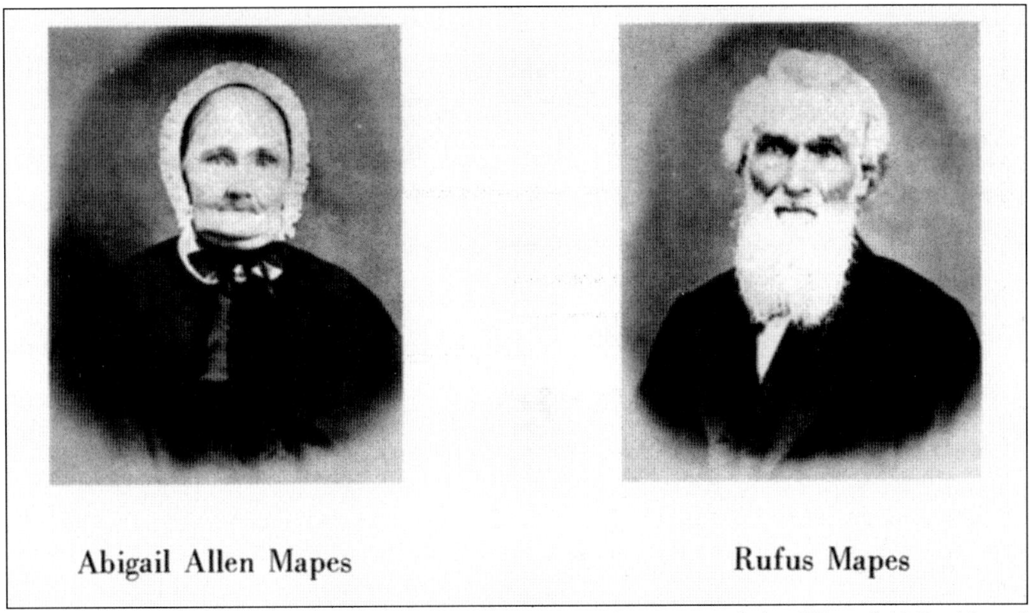

MAPES FAMILY. Rufus Mapes was a Connecticuter and veteran of the War of 1812. Abigail Allen, a descendant of Ethan Allen, was a Mainer and a nurse. The couple married in 1816 and then immigrated to the Highland Heights area of Mayfield Township in 1818. The couple had 17 children. (MTHS.)

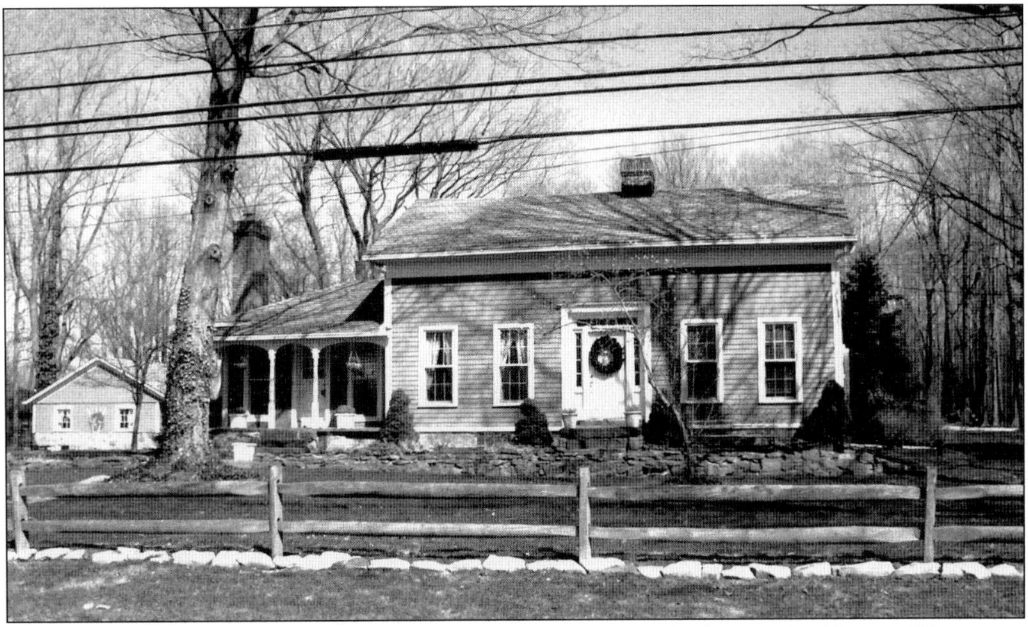

MAPES HOUSE. Around 1830, the Mapes family built this evolved Cape Cod house. The center chimney hearkens back centuries, while the bold Greek Revival front entrance was typical of the 1830s. The parlor wing—with its tall windows, chimney, and arcaded porch—was a later Colonial Revival–style addition. (Roy Larick.)

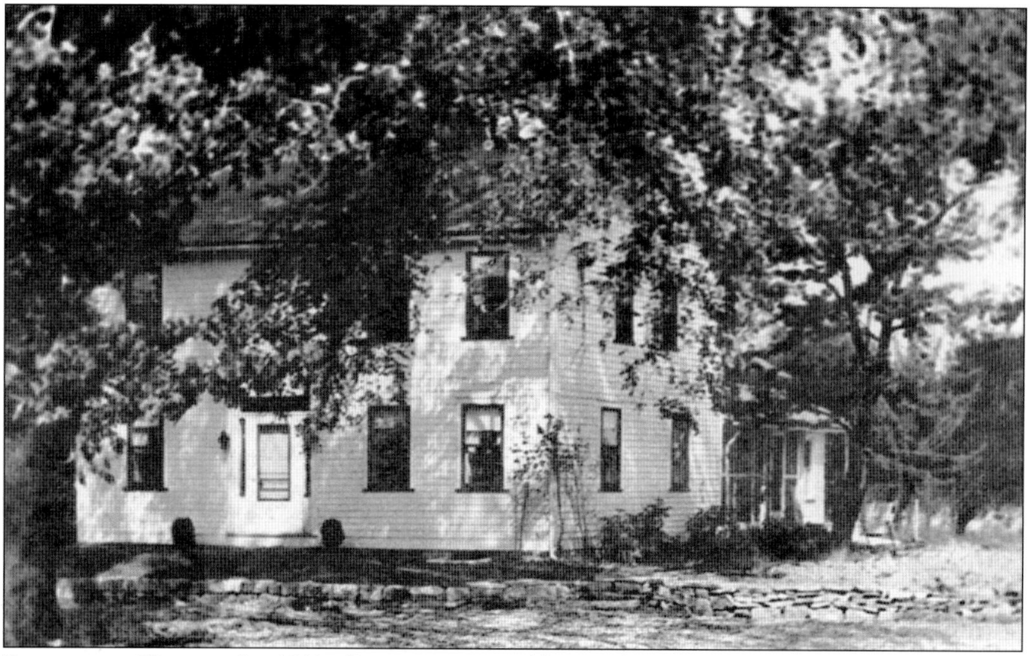

RICHMOND HOUSE. In 1814, Connecticuter Elihu Richmond bought a substantial Euclid Township tract north of the original Highland Road survey line. Like most Western Reserve pioneers, Richmond immediately built a hewn-log dwelling. However, while most settlers built their permanent home alongside, Richmond chose to upgrade his cabin. The result is that this vernacular Greek Revival façade contains the probable oldest standing structure in the Euclid Creek watershed. (*Golden Anniversary*.)

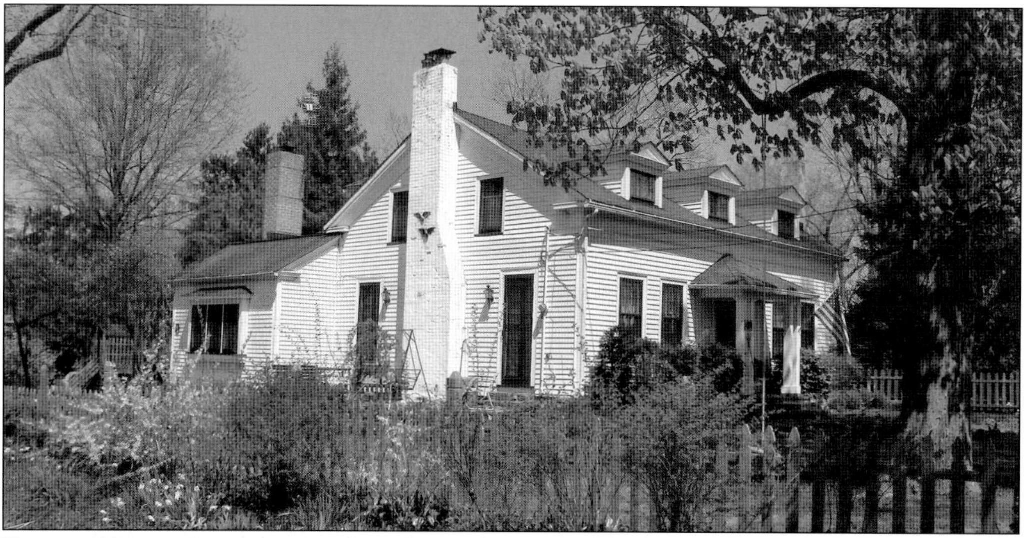

PELTON HOUSE. Connecticuter Jonathan Pelton moved his family to Euclid Township in 1814. He bought Abraham Bishop's sawmill and quarry at current Richmond and Chardon Roads, an area that became known as Peltons Corners. Midway between Peltons Corners and Euclid Creek village, Jonathan built this evolved Cape Cod house around 1820. The house has been modified and expanded for nearly two centuries and was designated a City-of-Euclid Landmark in 2004. (Roy Larick.)

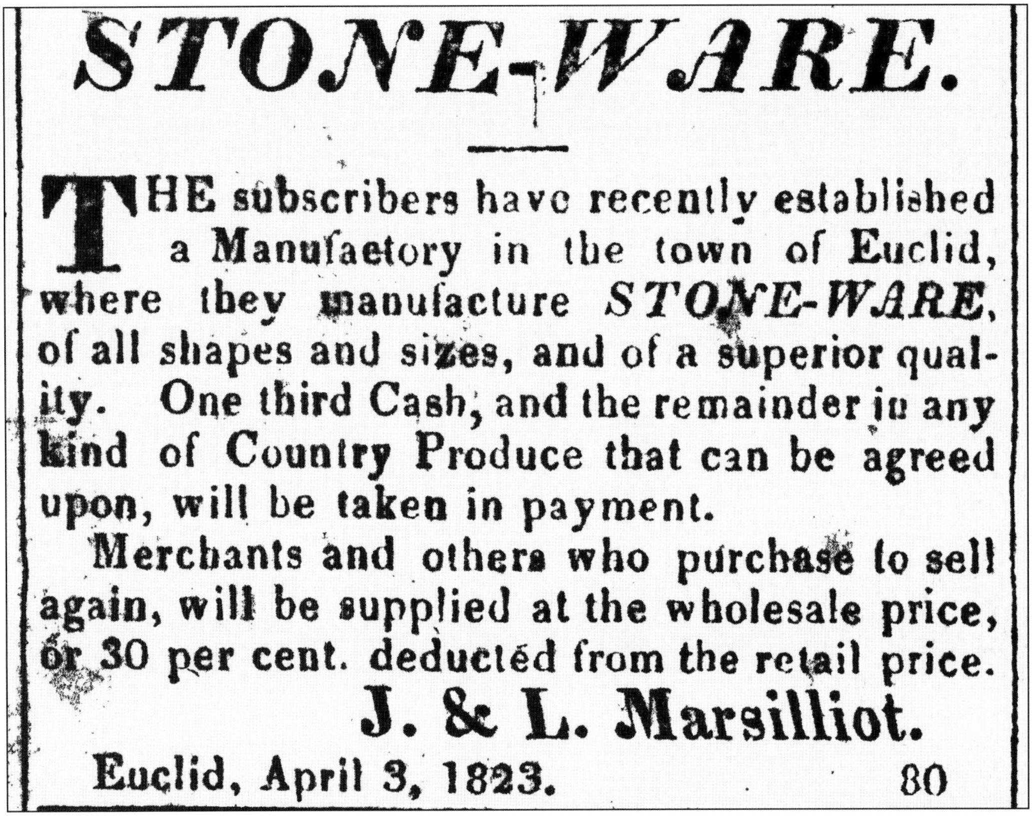

STONE-WARE.

THE subscribers have recently established a Manufactory in the town of Euclid, where they manufacture STONE-WARE, of all shapes and sizes, and of a superior quality. One third Cash, and the remainder in any kind of Country Produce that can be agreed upon, will be taken in payment.

Merchants and others who purchase to sell again, will be supplied at the wholesale price, or 30 per cent. deducted from the retail price.

J. & L. Marsilliot.

Euclid, April 3, 1823. 80

EUCLID POTTERY. In 1823, Jacob and Leonard Marsilliot, father and son of Huguenot and Native American origin, established a stoneware kiln at the mouth of Euclid Creek. Leonard ran the kiln until the mid-1830s, when William Treat established a shipyard on the site. Leonard and two sons later owned and operated a freight schooner out of Euclid Creek. (The *Herald* April 23, 1823.)

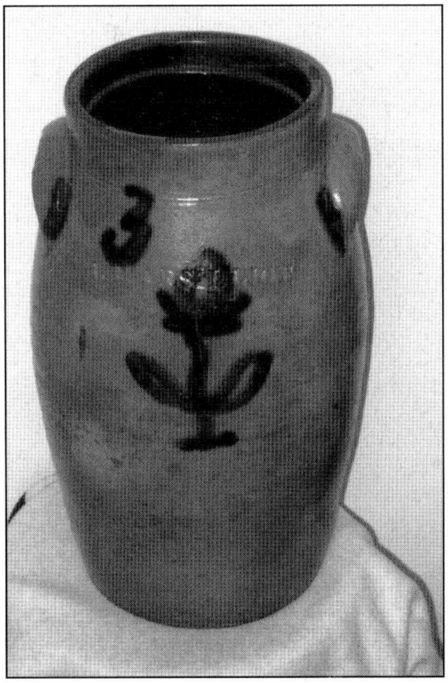

MARSILLIOT CROCK. Several examples of Marsilliot stoneware survive, including this flawless three-gallon crock or churn, impressed with "L. Marsilliot." A rare cobalt glaze produced the "3" (gallons) and the floral design. The flower is typical of potters working in the Mogadore-Ravenna area, where high-quality clay deposits gave rise to a substantial early stoneware industry. The Marsilliots imported clay from Ravenna and probably itinerant potters as well. (Bob Gibbons.)

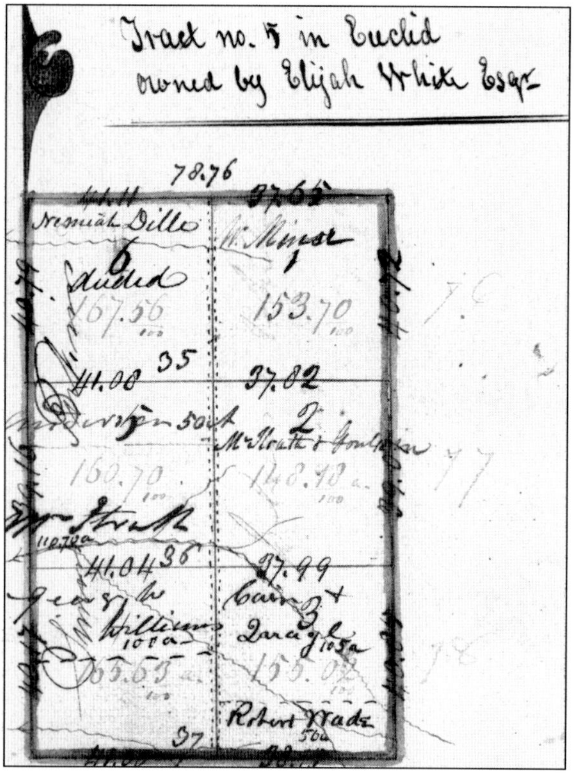

TRACT NO. 5. This detail of Euclid Township Tract 5 (1,000 acres in current southern Richmond Heights and northern Lyndhurst), drawn around 1825, is unique in showing small headwater tributaries to Euclid Creek west branch. The holdings of White, Dille, and Miner gave rise to well-known county roads in Euclid and Mayfield Townships. The plan displays the cartouche of Gen. Simon Perkins, legendary Connecticut Land Company land agent. (WRHS.)

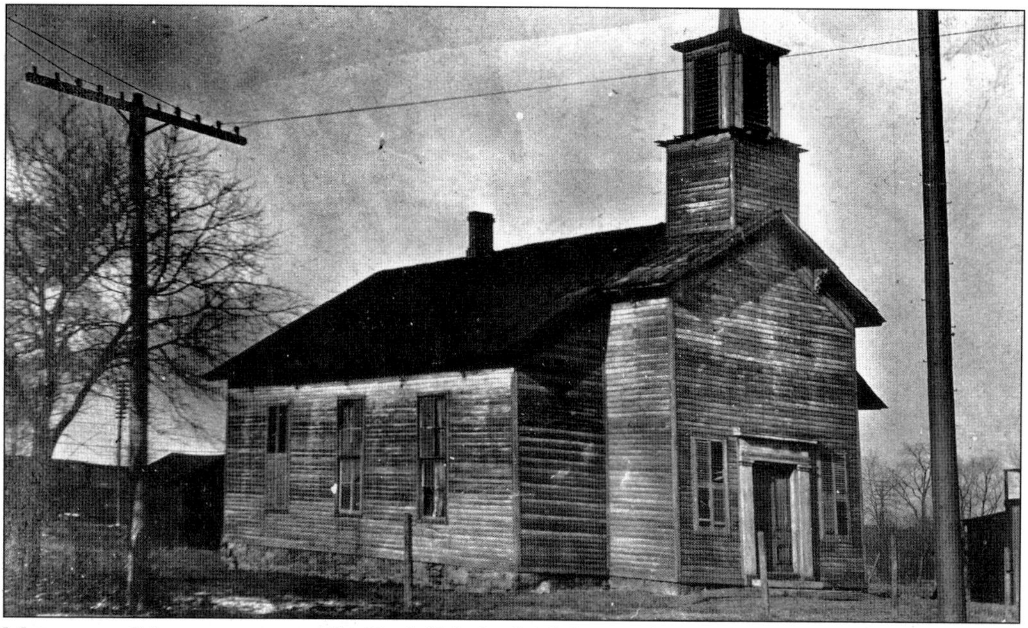

METHODIST MEETINGHOUSE. The Euclid Methodist Meeting (society) built a small meetinghouse around 1829 on the Buffalo Road at Green. The building was moved to Euclid Creek village around 1840. By 1867, this one appeared at 18391 St. Clair Avenue in Nottingham; it may incorporate an earlier doorway. In 1892, the society built the Nottingham Methodist Church at 18306 St. Clair, and the old one was demolished. (NHS.)

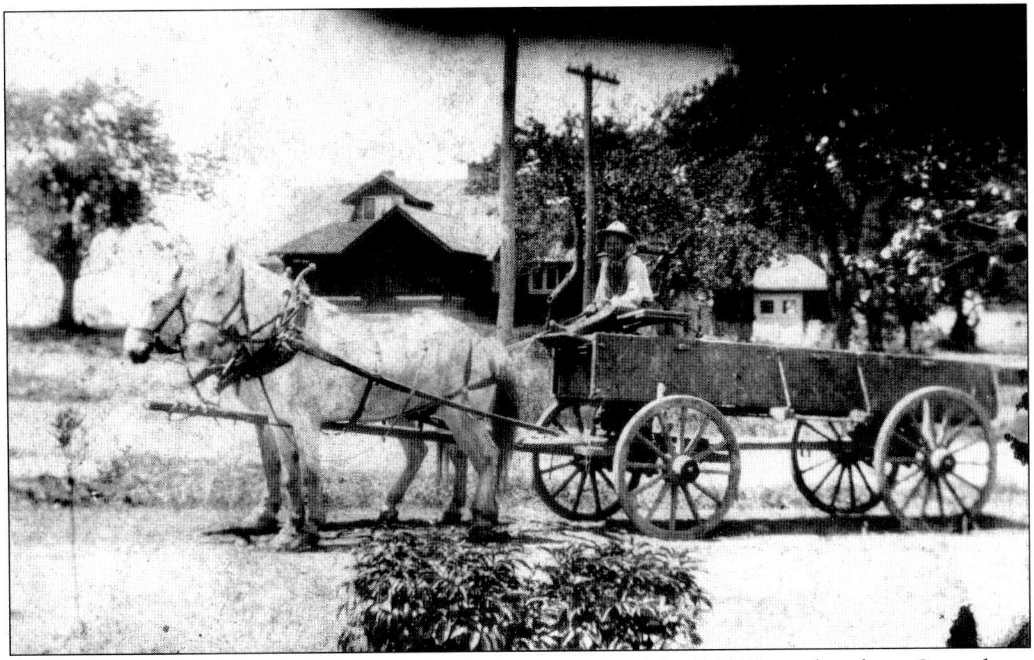

WHITINGS CORNERS. In 1831, George Whiting arrived to Mayfield Township from Onondaga, New York. He settled on the State Road (now Mayfield) near a survey line soon called Whiting Road (now Lander). For a century, this was known as Whitings Corners. Around 1890, the Linnert family bought the southeast corner. Looking south on Lander about 1920, this view shows the Linnert work wagon in its last days of use. (MTHS.)

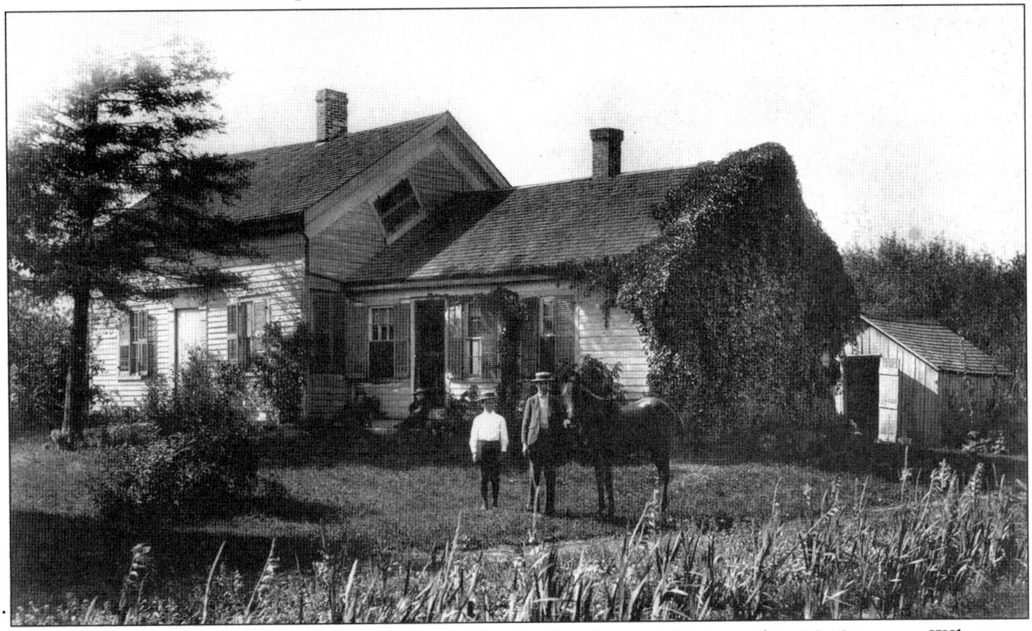

BRAINARD HOUSE. The Brainard family built this house during the 1840s near Whitings Corners. On the left, a small main block retains its Cape Cod structure and form. At right, a kitchen wing has its own doorway and flanking windows for copious light. The tilted window was common on the wing end of a small Cape. (MTHS.)

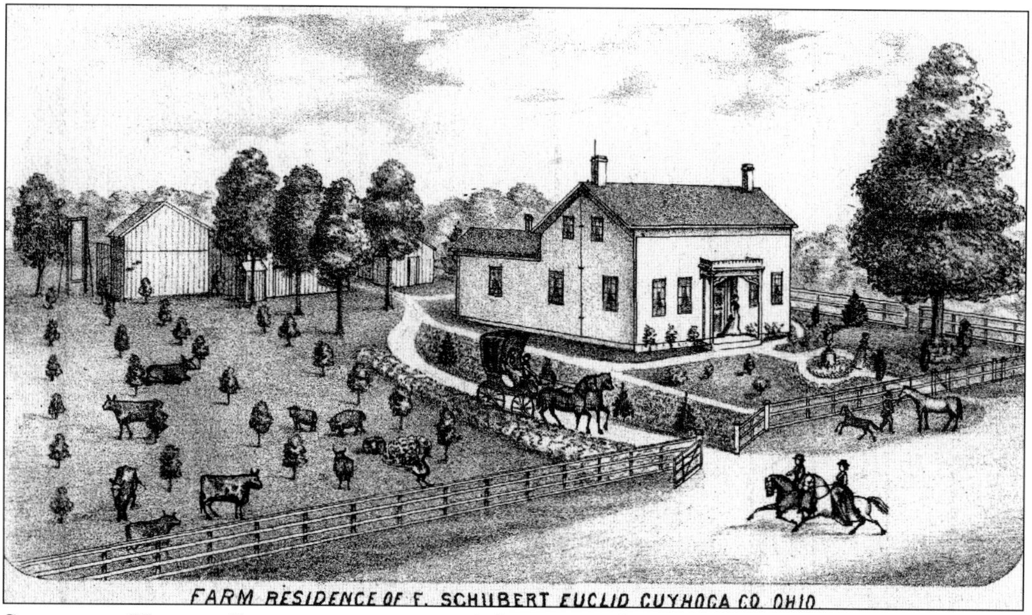

SCHUBERT HOUSE. German immigrants of the 1860s, the Frank Schubert family purchased this farm and house on the west side of Richmond Road, just north of current Ridgebury. The Schuberts tended vineyards, orchards, and gardens. To the left of the house, the gardens descend toward a Euclid Creek headwater stream. (Lake, 1874.)

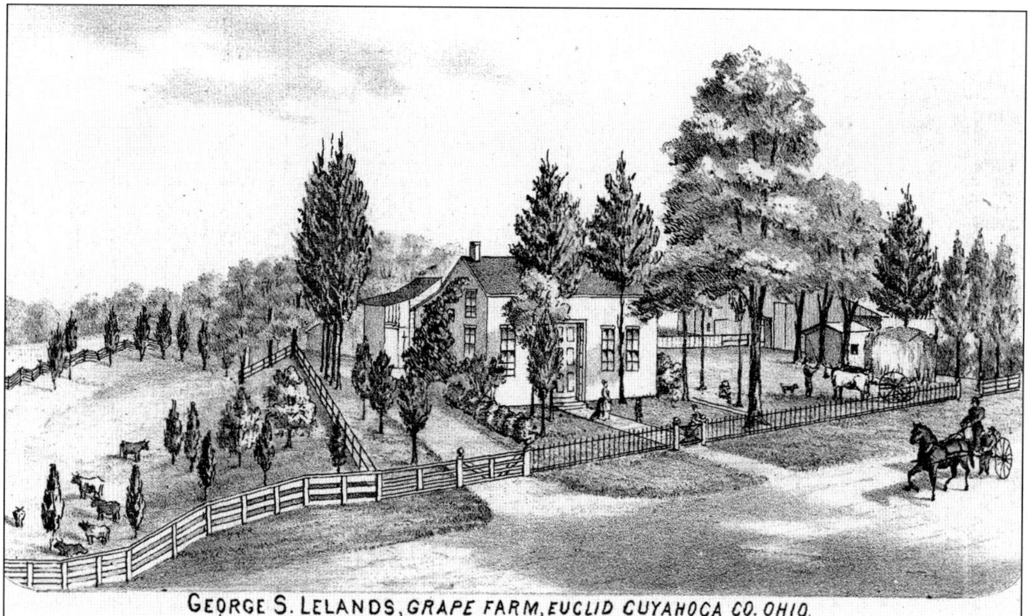

LELAND HOUSE. George Leland purchased one of the original Euclid contract square lots in its entirety. The 160-acre parcel, called a "quarter-section" in surveyor's parlance, was located on the northwest corner of Richmond and Highland Roads. (Lake, 1874.)

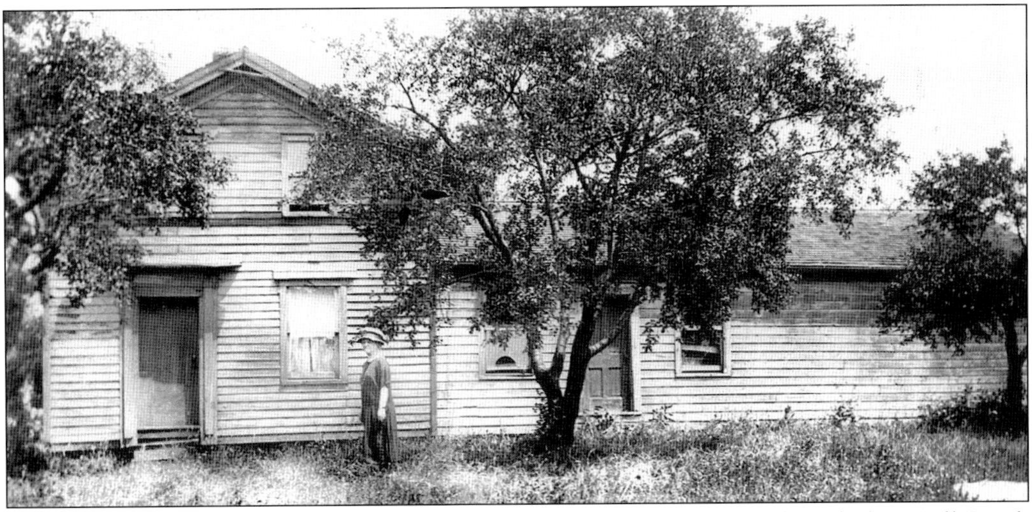

LaRue House. At the far southern end of the watershed, the LaRue family built this small Greek Revival–style house on North Woodland (current Fairmount) at Richmond. The crossroads became known as LaRues corners. This side view shows a "funeral door" on the upright and the kitchen ell on the right. (Jeffrey Morris.)

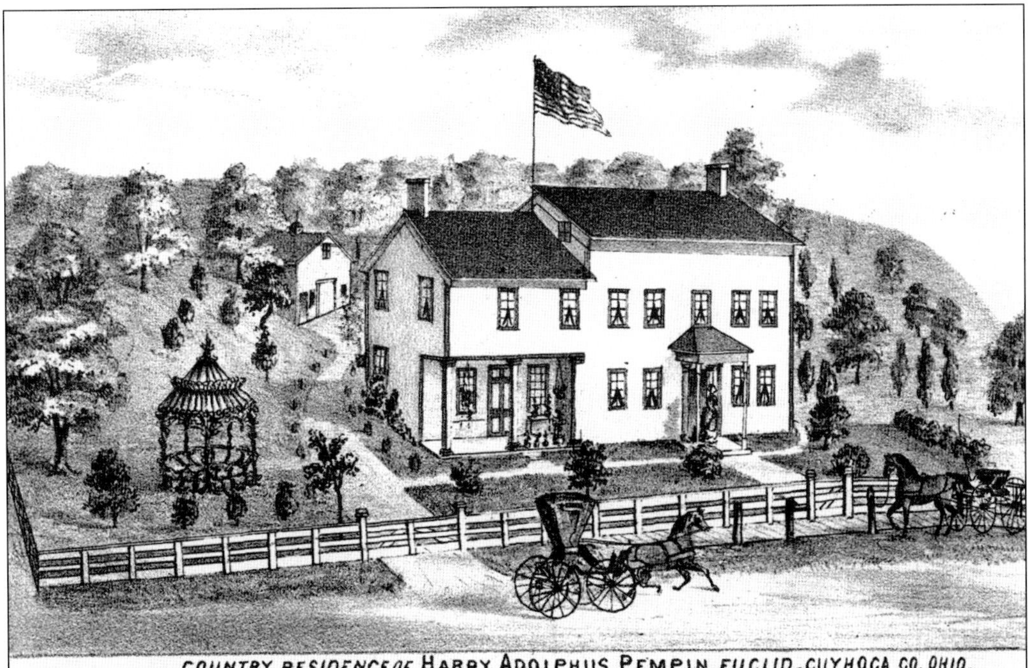

Pempin House. Harry Adolphus Pempin was a Connecticut immigrant to Euclid Creek village. He built this stylish winged Greek Revival–style house in the 1840s at current 21210 Euclid Avenue. The Pempins had extensive vegetable gardens for the retail trade. Once rail connection was made with Cleveland in 1852, the Pempins grew flowers for the Cleveland market. The house burned in the early 1880s. (Lake, 1874.)

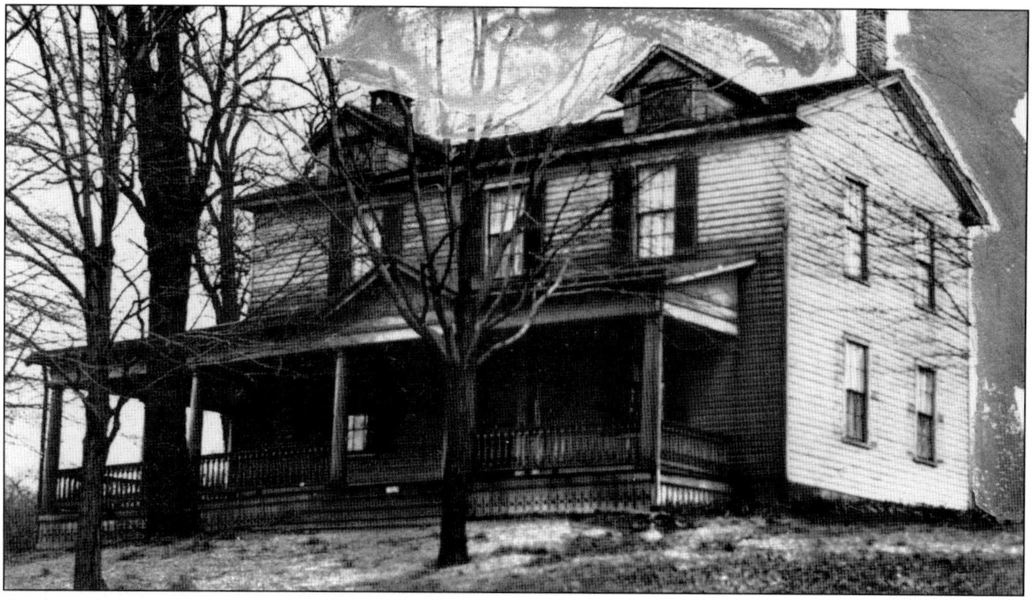

DILLE HOUSE. In 1835, the last year of his life, David Dille Jr. built this Colonial house—without the Victorian porch—on the Buffalo Road (current 19800 Euclid Avenue). The house's simplicity reflects Dille's origin in Quaker and Huguenot Pennsylvania. This unique surviving photograph was taken for a commemorative brochure entitled *Map and Guide of Cuyahoga County, 1796–1935, Historical and Other Points of Interest.* (CCA.)

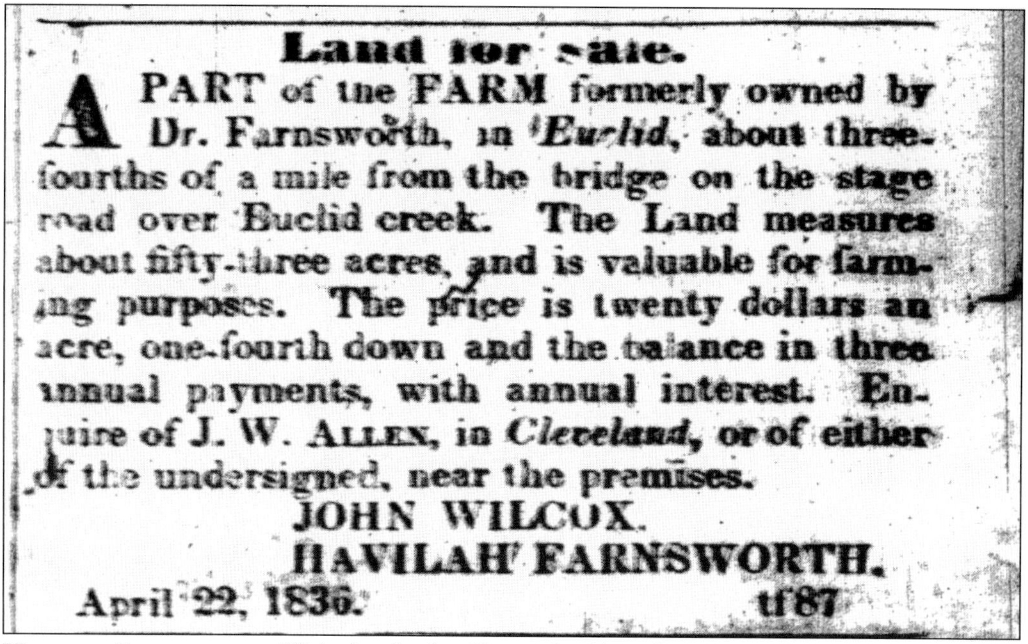

Land for sale.

A PART of the FARM formerly owned by Dr. Farnsworth, in *Euclid*, about three-fourths of a mile from the bridge on the stage road over Euclid creek. The Land measures about fifty-three acres, and is valuable for farming purposes. The price is twenty dollars an acre, one-fourth down and the balance in three annual payments, with annual interest. Enquire of J. W. ALLEN, in *Cleveland*, or of either of the undersigned, near the premises.

JOHN WILCOX.

HAVILAH FARNSWORTH.

April 22, 1836. tf87

HAVILAH FARNSWORTH. With the death of his wife, Abigail, in 1805, Connecticuter Havilah Farnsworth (1769–1834) and offspring Havilah Jr., Minerva, Francis, and Caroline came to Euclid. The notice refers to their home at the top of Chardon Hill. As the township's first physician, Farnsworth rode horseback to visit patients, often in distant locales. Havilah Jr. placed this ad two years after his father's death. (The *Herald*, April 22, 1836.)

TREAT BOATYARD. From 1838 to 1861, William Treat, Ruel House, Charles Moses, and crew built more than a dozen schooners, brigs, barks, and barges. The smaller schooners resembled the 165-ton *California*, shown on the ways at St. Catharines, Ontario, in 1849. While launchings were difficult in the small harbor, the lake's plain oak forest was a significant shipbuilding resource. (HCGL.)

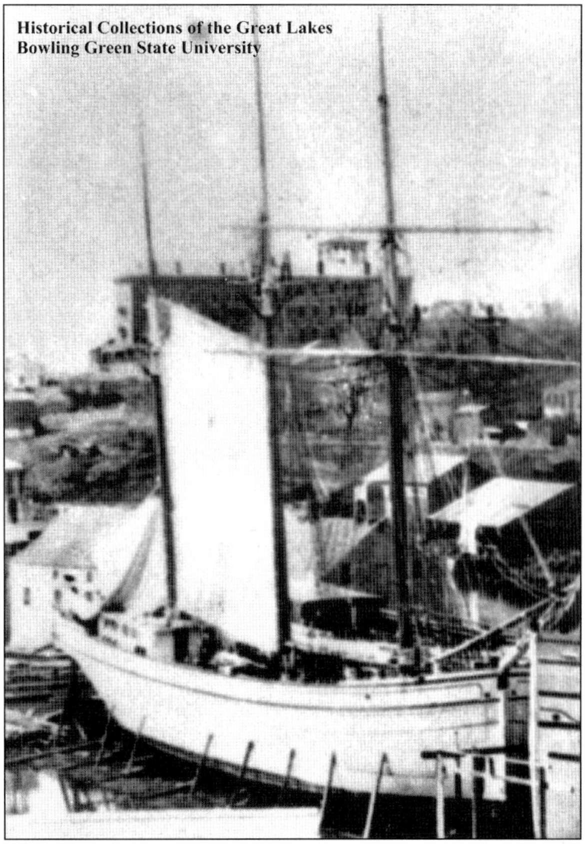

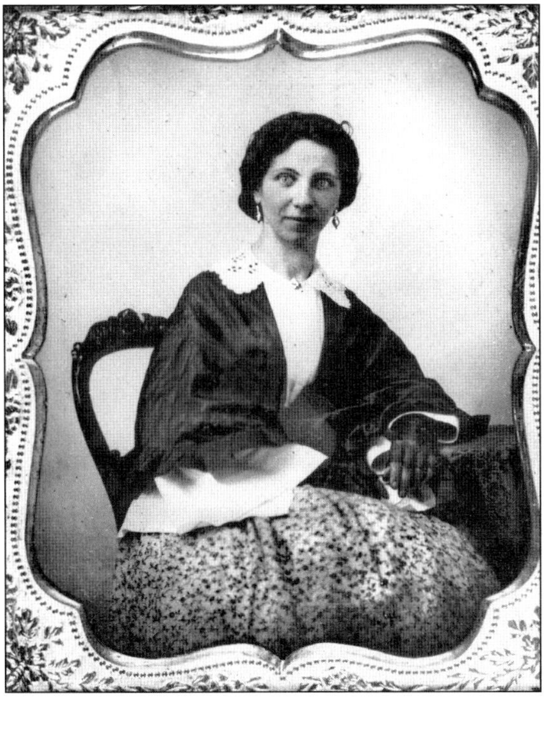

AGNES E. MARSILLIOT. After closing the Euclid Pottery, Leonard Marsilliot operated the two-masted schooner *Thomas Corwin* (Ohio governor, 1840–1842) out of Euclid Creek harbor. In 1857, Leonard renamed the ship *Agnes E. Marsilliot* after his new daughter-in-law but then sold it in 1859 to Canadian Mahlon Millard. On September 24, 1860, the *Marsilliot* was lost in a Lake Erie gale, along with a seaman and its captain, off Port Stanley, Ontario. (WRHS.)

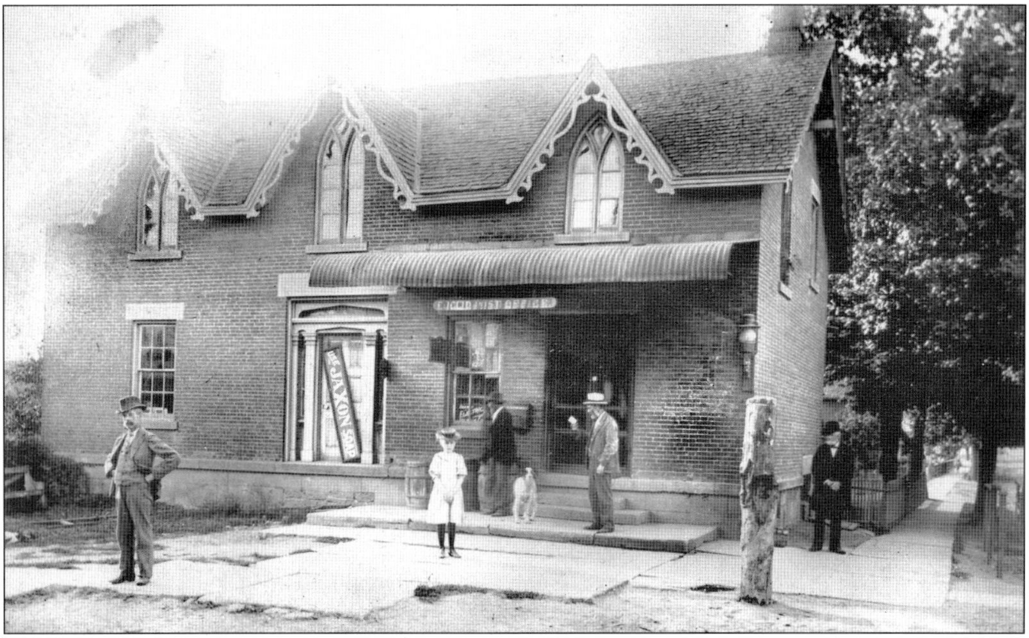

DILLE STORE. In 1849, the Dille family built this brick Gothic Revival residence on the northwest corner of Euclid and Chardon Roads. A dry goods store and post office stood behind in a wooden ell facing Chardon. Nelson Moses, Euclid's lumber entrepreneur, bought the facility in 1858. By the time this photograph was taken in the 1880s, the residence had been given over to store use. (WRHS.)

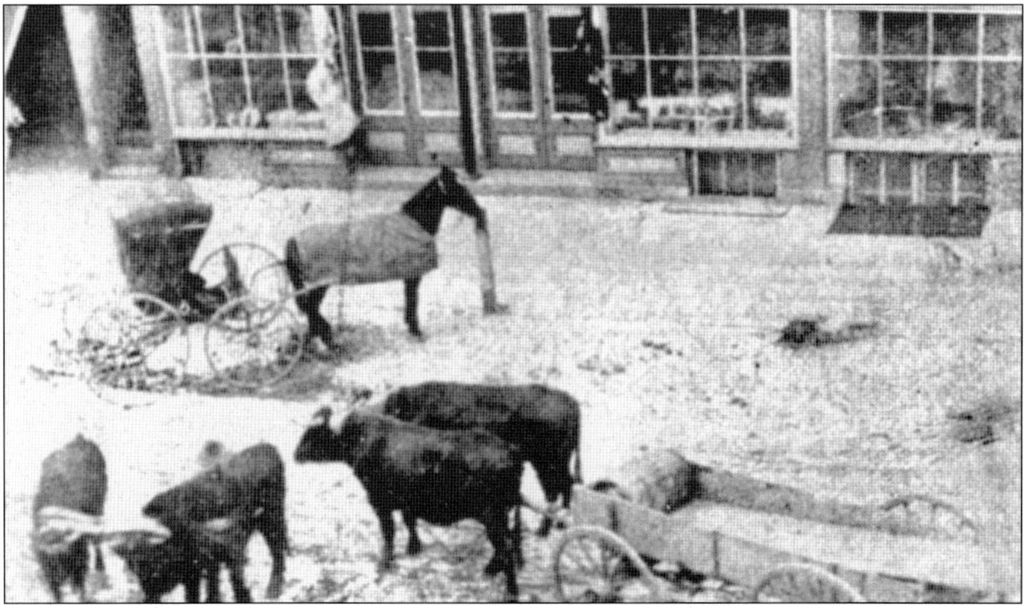

OXEN AND HORSE. This unique photograph captures the 1876 equivalent of today's 18-wheel tractor-trailer (the four-ox team and wagon) and a sport convertible (the one-horse, two-seat carriage). Animal power would dominate local transport until 1896, when the interurban rail line was laid along Euclid Avenue. The demise of draft animals came quickly after 1912, when automobiles became more than rich men's toys. (EHS.)

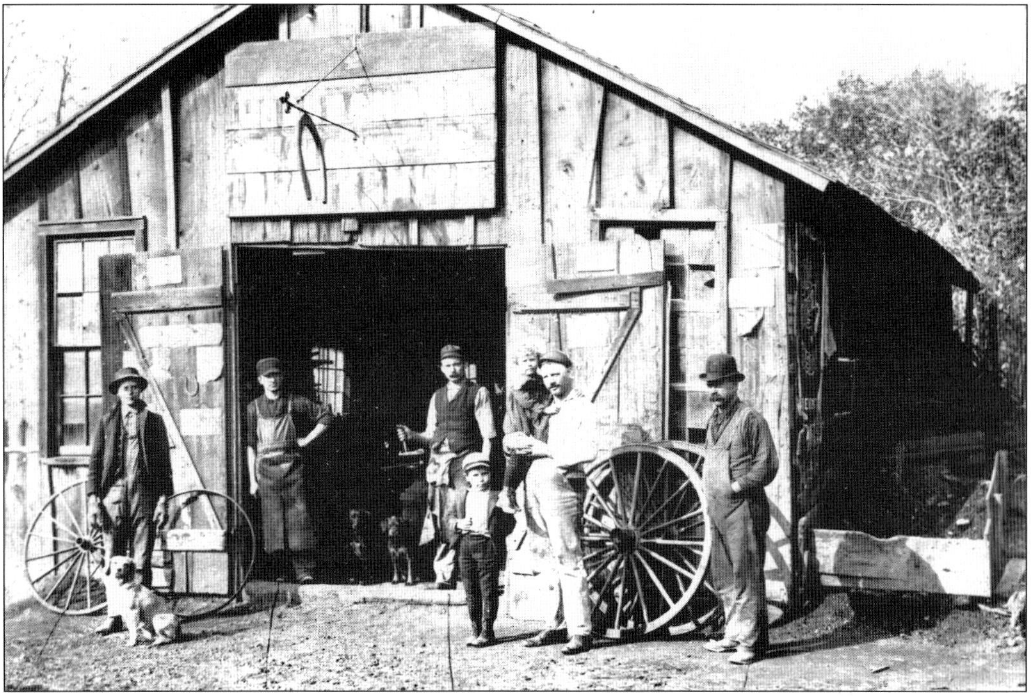

HERMLE SHOPS. In the early days, crossing Euclid Creek on the Buffalo-Detroit Road was difficult. Wagon cargo had to be unloaded and carried separately across the chasm. Sometimes the wagons themselves had to be partially dismantled. Blacksmiths and wheelwrights catered to this business. Among the best known were men of the Hermle family, who worked in all aspects of this trade across several generations. Two of the Hermle shops, for blacksmithing and carriage making, are shown here. (EHS.)

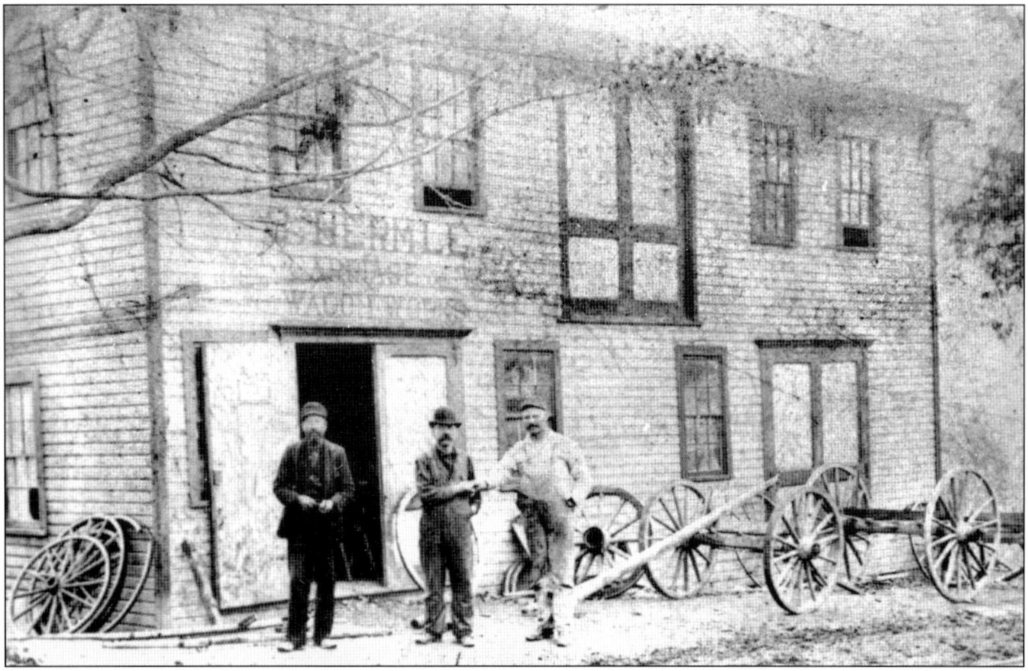

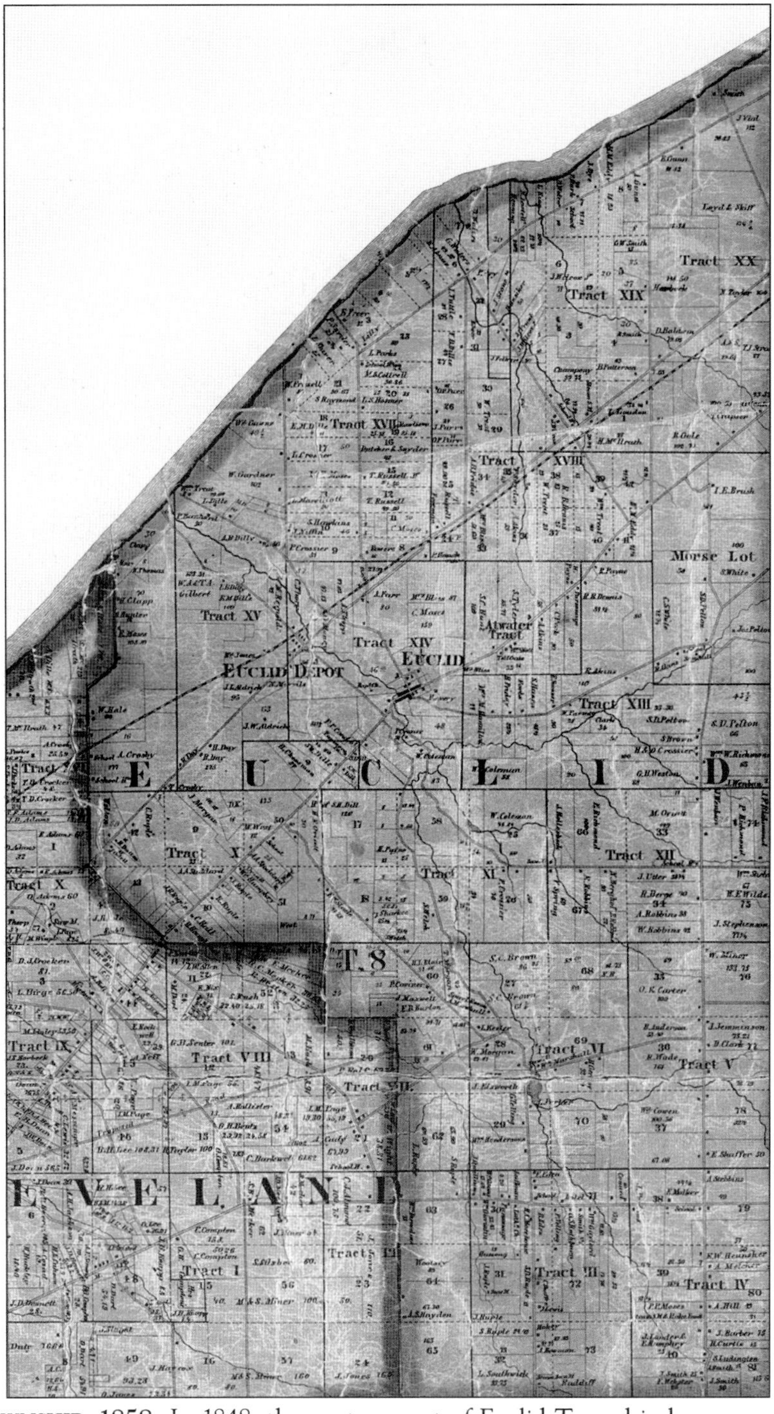

EUCLID TOWNSHIP, 1858. In 1848, the western part of Euclid Township became part of newly minted East Cleveland Township, as is shown on this only known original copy of George N. Hopkins & Company's 1858 map of Cuyahoga County. The 1858 map is prized for its accuracy in property lines and stream courses. Euclid Creek's east and west branches are detailed here, as are numerous small headwater runs. The true shading is pink on left and green on right. (MTHS.)

Three

Steaming Rails 1852–1895

In 1852, the Cleveland, Painesville and Ashtabula Railroad gave Cleveland strong links with Chicago and New York City. Immediately east of Cleveland, the railroad followed a fossil beach ridge, a landform that set the roadbed up a few feet on well-drained sandy soil. A Native American trail also followed this ridge. Early settlers appropriated this path and called it St. Clair Road, after the Northwest Territory's first governor, Arthur St. Clair.

Euclid Creek breached the beach ridge to form a small chasm about 200 feet wide and 40 feet deep. The CP&A built a very substantial bluestone bridge across the creek, wide enough to get horse-and-wagon traffic across in addition to the occasional train. St. Clair now came to rival the Buffalo Road as an east-west highway, and population began gravitating to this creek crossing. There was yet another factor that brought people to the CP&A crossing. Burning wood in small-capacity boilers, the early steam engines needed to recharge fuel and water every 10 miles or so. Lying nine miles east of Cleveland Depot, Euclid Creek was a natural stopping point. Euclid Depot was thus established in 1852, and it thrived. In 1865, the Lake Shore & Michigan Southern group bought the CP&A. The new owners renamed Euclid Depot as Nottingham Depot, and the surrounding village also took on the name. The name honored LS&MS supervisor Henry Nottingham.

During the 1850s, European immigrants began looking east of Cleveland to buy farmland or to work as farm laborers. Most were German and Irish with some Bohemians mixed in. Many were Roman Catholic. In 1860, the Cleveland Catholic Diocese established St. Paul as its first parish east of Cleveland. The church itself was set on the east bank of the creek, about halfway between Euclid Creek village and Euclid Depot. German immigrants tended to be knowledgeable and well-trained. For example, German vineyardist Louis F. Harms purchased prime land on Chardon Hill in 1864. By 1868, he was producing highly reputed Euclid wine.

After the Civil War, the desires of the well-off Clevelanders turned to leisure, and the train offered the means to get out of town. The earliest vacationers traveled to Camp Gilbert—the region's first shoreline resort—at the mouth of Euclid Creek. Camp Gilbert was the prototype country estate catering to leisure interests. It began a long line of leisure getaways that continued through the gentlemen's estates of the 1890s, the gambling clubs of the 1930s, and the golf clubs of today.

Of the several Euclid bluestone outcrops on the east side of Cleveland, Euclid Creek's saw the most intensive quarrying. The steam mechanisms that drove railroad locomotives also powered the drills, derricks, winches, and saws needed to extract and process the rock. By 1882, large amounts of bluestone were being exported directly by rail, along the Euclid Railroad.

House construction continued to use the Classical Revival temple upright flanked by one or two Palladian wings. The watershed even saw a few "connected" farmsteads that were so popular in western New England. The arrangement was alliteratively called "big house, little house, back house, barn." As seen in the Hager dwelling of 1853 (pages 39 and 121), the little house projects rearward from the big house as the kitchen ell with its own chimney. The back house is the shed type lean-to holding the kitchen entry porch. A garage has replaced the original barn but still stands connected with the back house.

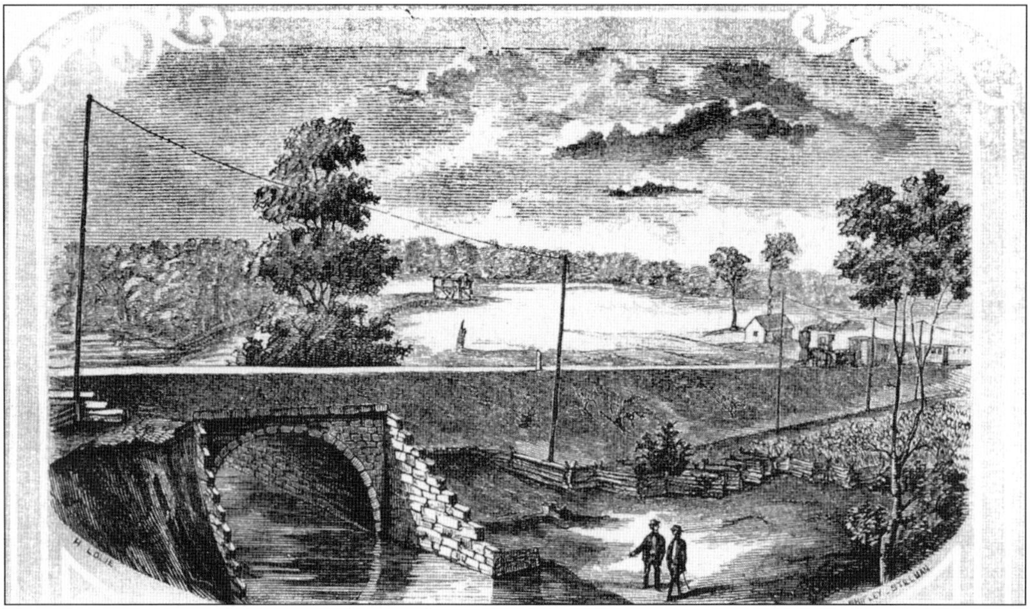

EUCLID DEPOT. The Euclid Creek train station sat on the creek's west bank, off to the right of this scene. Euclid's Moses family won lucrative contracts to supply oak rail ties and seasoned fuel wood. In 1870, the Lake Shore and Michigan Southern group acquired the CP&A and greatly expanded the operation. At this time, Euclid Depot was renamed Nottingham Station, after Henry Nottingham, company supervisor. (CCC&E Railroad Guide, 1854.)

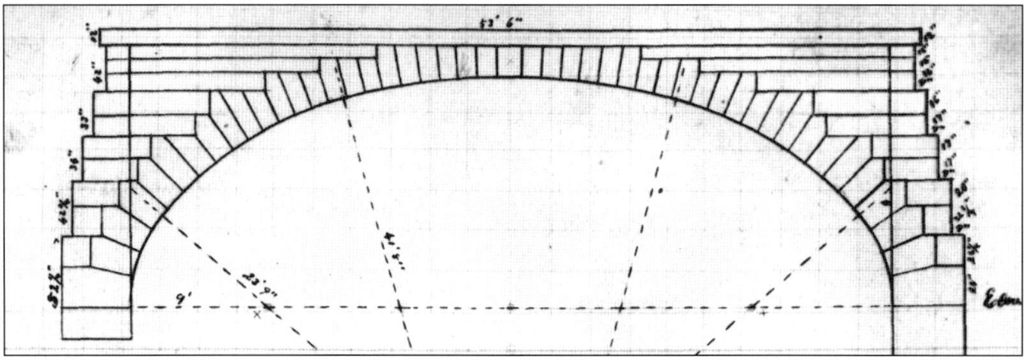

CP&A BRIDGE. The Cleveland, Painesville and Ashtabula Railroad bridged Euclid Creek with a handsome arch of Euclid bluestone. Cuyahoga County surveyor Isaac Newton Pillsbury drew the bridge in 1854. It is among a number of railroad construction drawings he made for tax-assessment purposes. (WRHS.)

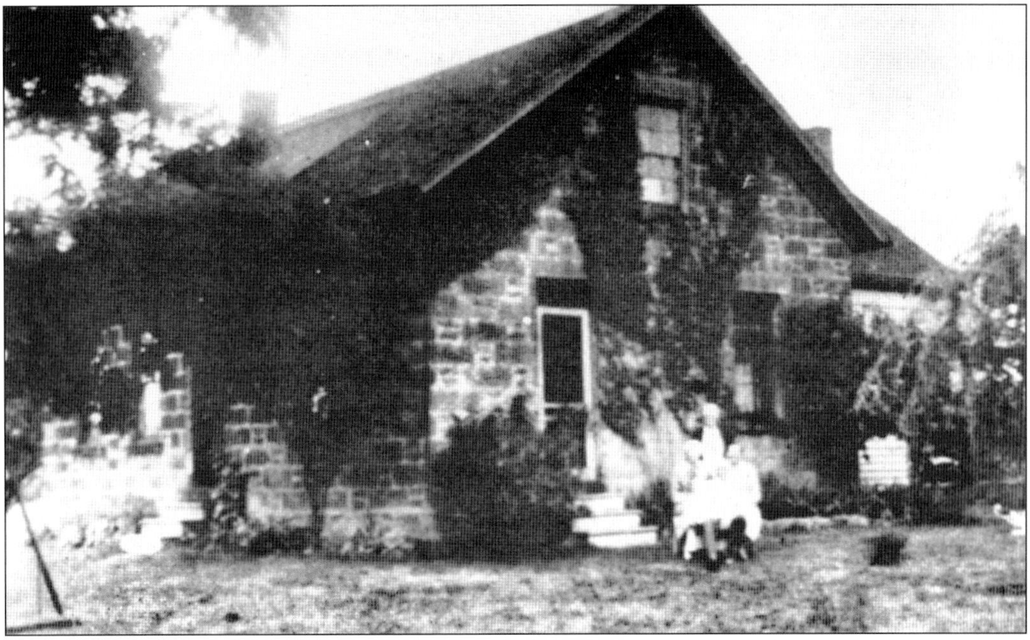

HAGER HOUSE. The John Hager family, settlers from eastern Pennsylvania, built their small house in 1853. The construction material, Berea sandstone, came from the Miner family quarry on Euclid Creek's east branch, a quarter-mile north of the site. The stonework is similar to that of the South Euclid stone school, built in 1865 (pages 50 and 121). (MTHS.)

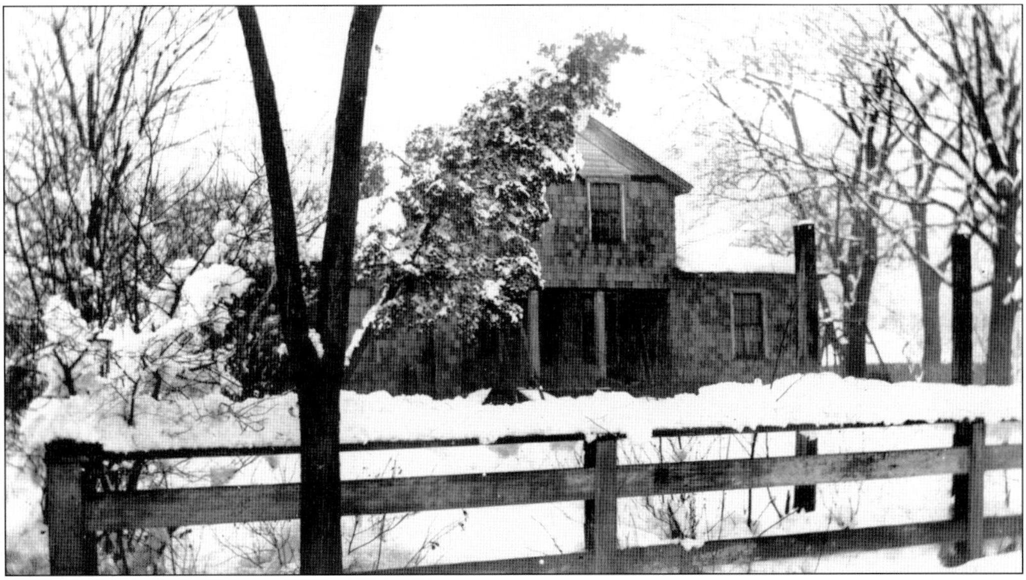

WELCH HOUSE. Around 1854, Connecticuter Sardius Welch built this double-winged house on current Glenridge Road. The photograph shows the original recessed entrance while shingles are being applied over the original siding and Classical Revival trim. During the 1870s, the Welch farm was the boyhood home of Alexander Hadden, renowned Cuyahoga County probate judge, law professor, and cofounder of Arter & Hadden, one of Cleveland's oldest law firms. The house was designated a City-of-Euclid Landmark in 2004 (page 125). (EHS.)

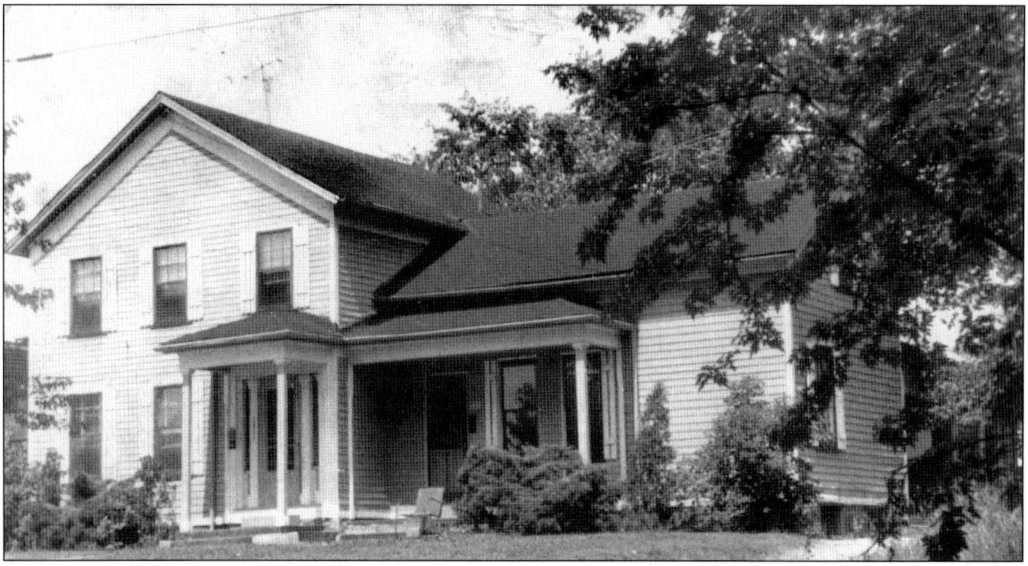

STRAWBRIDGE HOUSE. Around 1855, R. H. Strawbridge built this stylish house at current 1515 Chardon Road, just north of the Baptist parsonage. The design is a common abbreviation of the Palladian double-winged form. In the "upright-and-wing," just one wing flanks the temple unit. The upright-and-wing was the most common house form built in the Western Reserve between the 1830s and the 1870s. (CCA.)

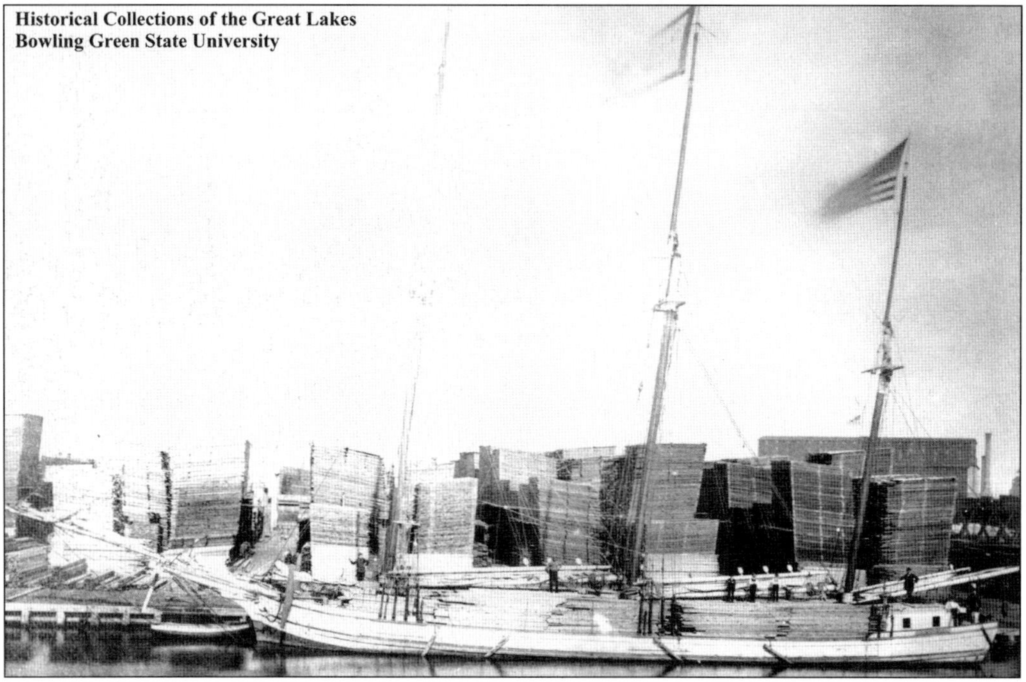

SCHOONER *ELLSWORTH*. Three-masted schooners were constructed at Euclid Creek from 1855 to 1861. The *Colonel Ellsworth* was launched on April 18, 1861, at 138 feet long, 26 feet wide, and 320 tons. It was tugged through the bar and quickly ran into a gale, nearly being wrecked within site of its shipyard. Pictured here is the *J&A Stronach* (built at Milwaukee in 1854), nearly identical in size with the *Ellsworth*, of which no photographs survive. (HCGL.)

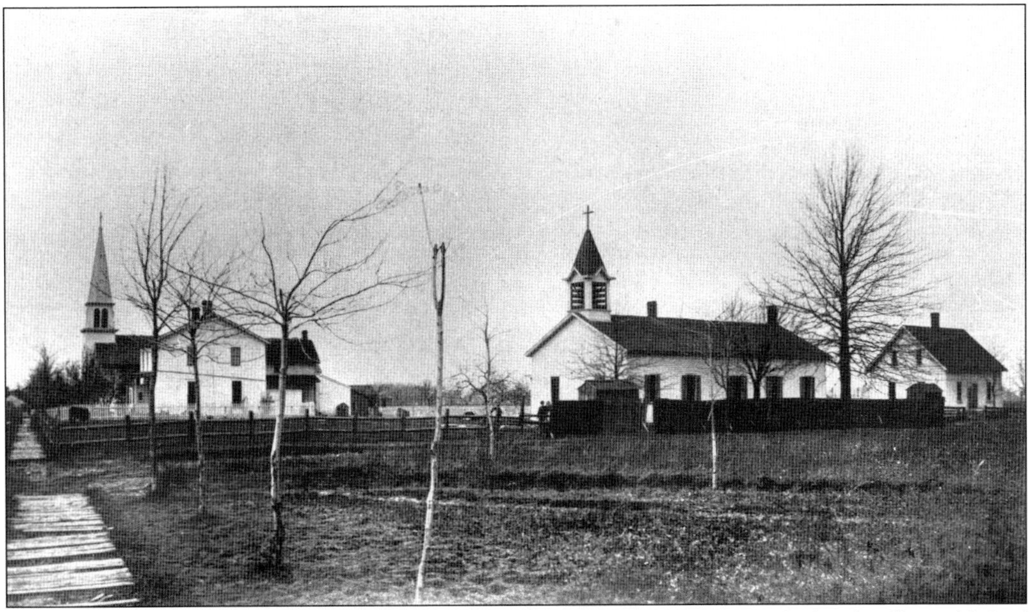

ST. PAUL. In 1860, Bishop Amadeus Rappe (Roman Catholic Diocese of Cleveland) established St. Paul as the first parish east of Cleveland. A church (second from the right) was built in 1861, and the religious school (far right) opened in 1867. The cemetery (far background) received its first burial in 1871. In 1875, a new church (far left) was dedicated with a 700-pound bell. (St. Paul Church.)

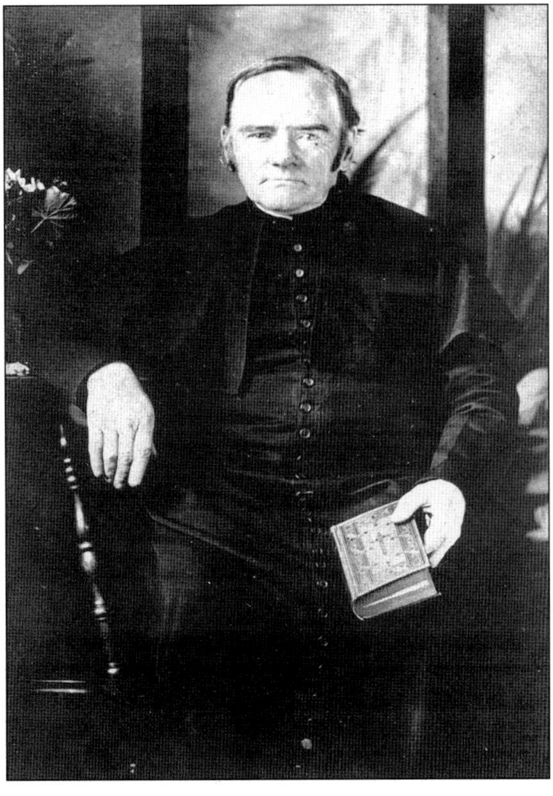

FATHER MARTIN. In 1865, Bishop Rappe assigned the parish to Fr. Anthony Martin, a 23-year-old Breton French immigrant. Father Martin energetically built the congregation and facilities until his untimely death in 1883. The original church bell and Father Martin's invaluable three-volume personal journal survive from the early years. (EHS.)

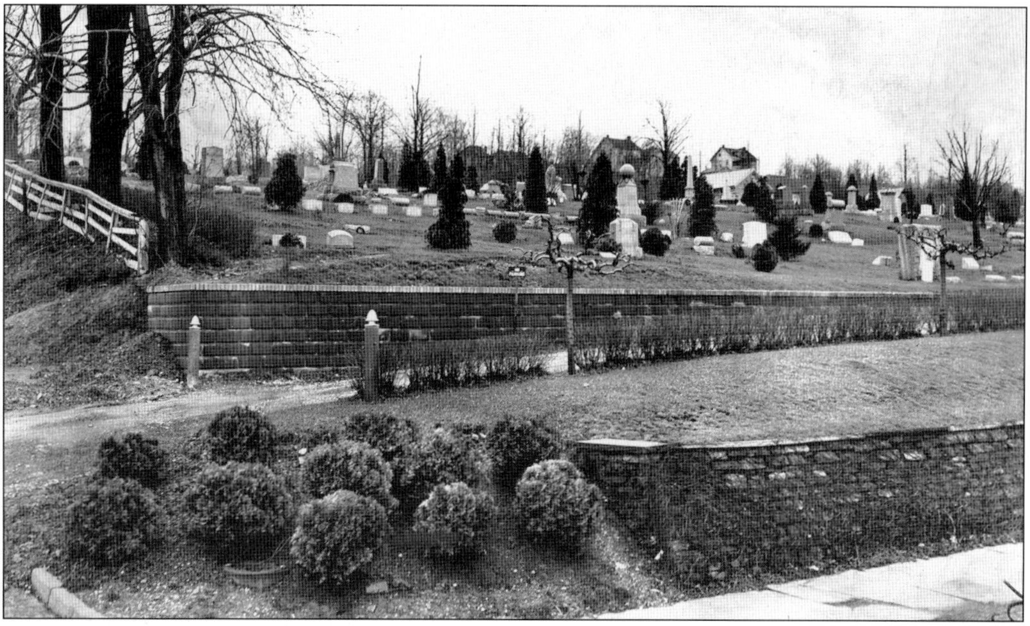

Euclid Cemetery. Opened in 1864, the township cemetery has 4,000 interments. Many were relocated here from older burial grounds (more than 80). There are members of most pioneer New England and early German families, including 60 individuals born before 1800. There are veterans of the Revolutionary War (5) and Civil War (23); 1908 Collinwood School fire victims (8); 1918 flu victims (more than 30); and "Potters Field" indigents (53). The *Cleveland Press* took these photographs in March 1939 for an article on a cemetery ownership dispute. The county auditor had auctioned the cemetery land title to a private individual for $120. Euclid mayor Kenneth Sims threatened to maintain possession with a police brigade. The auditor relented. Old Glenridge Road rises up the escarpment on the left. The Dille house lies in the far right background. (CSU.)

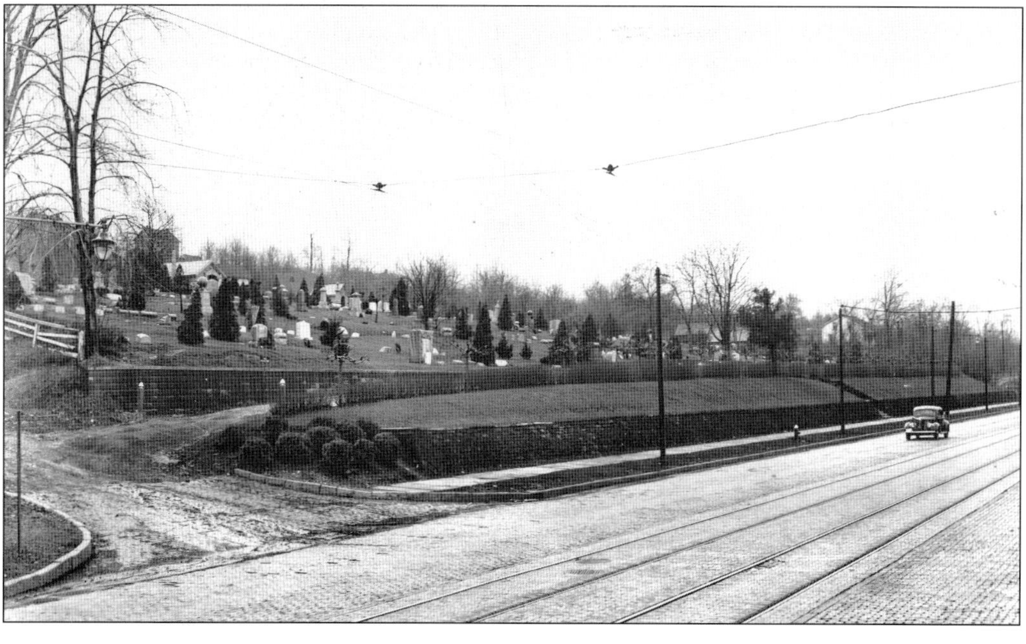

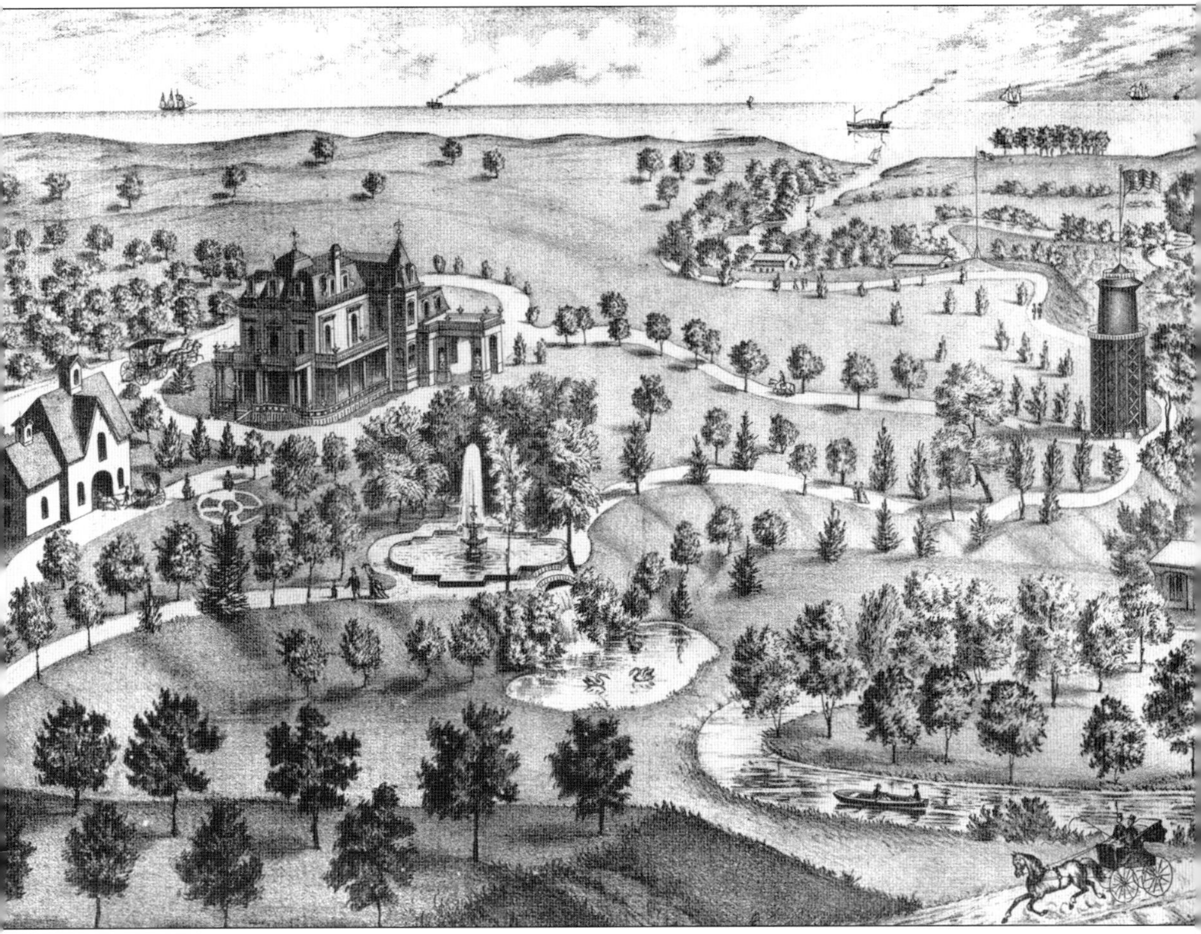

CAMP GILBERT. After Treat's shipyard closed in the mid-1860s, George and Sara Jewett Gilbert opened Camp Gilbert on the west bank of the estuary. The camp, the region's first lakeside resort, appealed to wealthy Clevelanders who arrived here from Nottingham Station, one mile upstream on the creek. Camp headquarters was a substantial brick, three-story house of Second Empire design. Tenting fields were provided around the property. Outbuildings included a clubhouse and fish shanty on the creek. Notable outings included the summer residence of the Snelligoster Club of Cleveland in 1871, and a target-shooting excursion for the Cleveland Grays in September 1873. The Ursuline Sisters of Cleveland bought the camp in 1874. (Lake, 1874.)

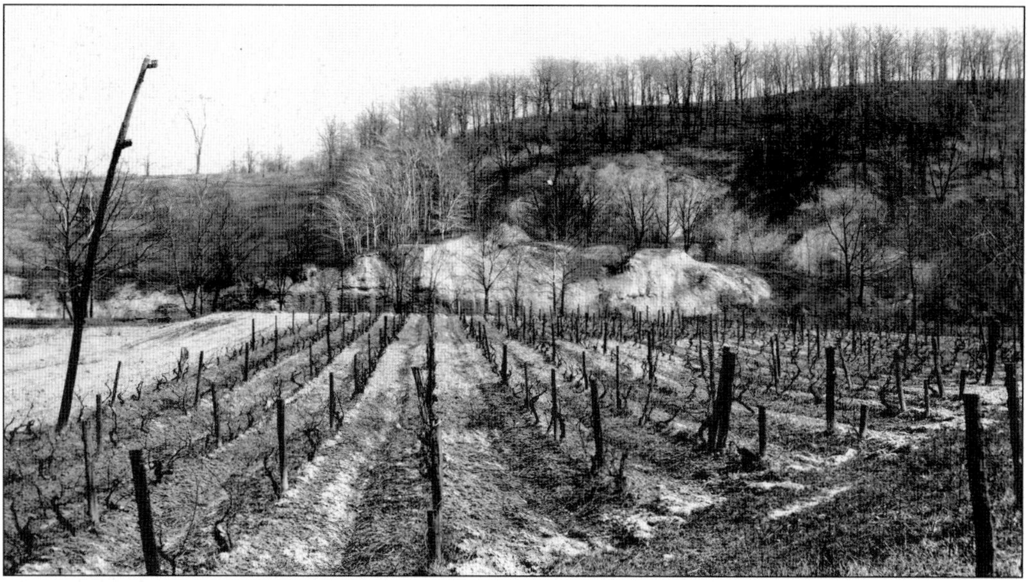

VINEYARDS. Vines and wine became major agricultural endeavors along the escarpment after the Civil War. German immigrant John J. Schuster and his English wife, Mary, planted this vineyard around 1870. It lay in the Euclid Creek floodplain just south of Euclid Avenue. The Schuster property neighbored that of Louis F. Harms. Professor Hyde took this photograph in 1923 to illustrate slumping soft earth on the far valley wall. (JEHC.)

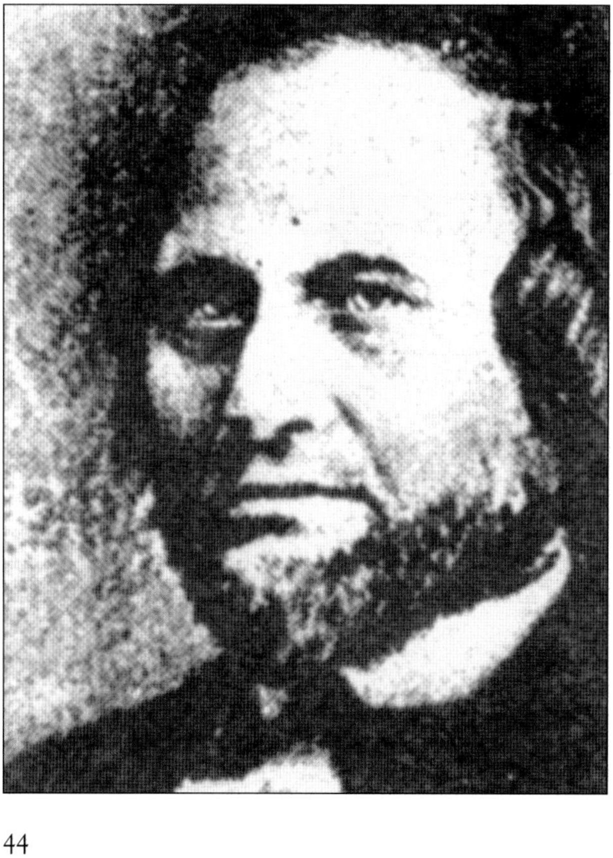

LOUIS F. HARMS. In 1850, German immigrant Louis F. Harms arrived to Sandusky with substantial training in vines and wine. He partnered with the Steuk family before starting on his own at Put-in-Bay and Kelley's Island. In 1864, Harms bought 40 acres on the Euclid Creek east branch gorge, and he began yet again. At the time of his death in 1888, Harms was considered one of Ohio's foremost authorities on vineyards and winemaking. (EHS.)

Harms Chalet. The Harms operation was the first, largest, and best known of six late-19th-century Euclid Township wineries. In 1876, the family built resort facilities and added retail sales. The public operation centered on this picturesque building that featured a rustic framed dining and tasting room on top of a massive bluestone cellar. The men served the wine while the women prepared meals and waited tables. (EHS.)

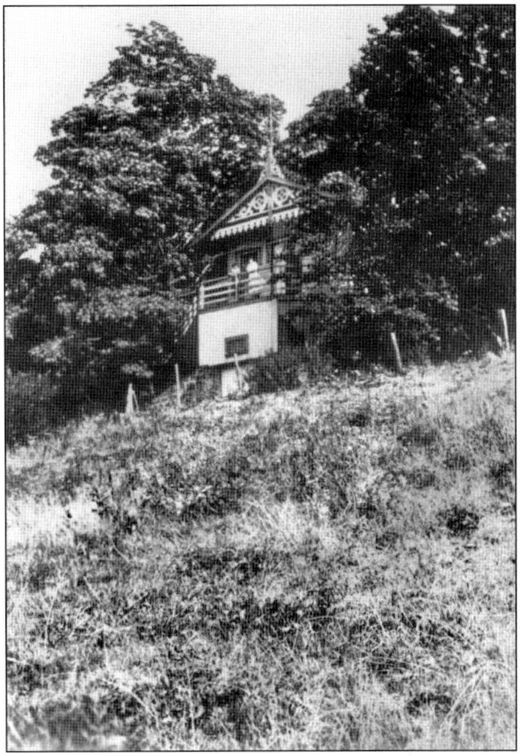

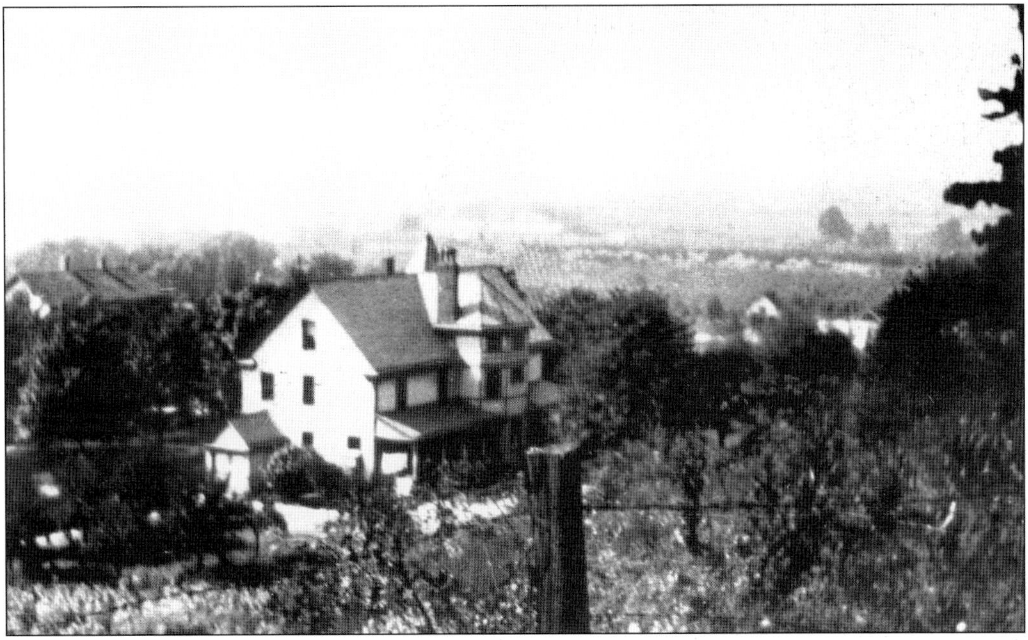

Harms Houses. Louis Harms's two younger sons, Carl and Richard, took over the winery during the late 1880s. They added this substantial turreted and towered Queen Anne–style house. Their father's house is at left. With national Prohibition looming in early 1920, the Harms brothers closed the operation and sold the land to the Sisters of the Good Shepherd, who converted the residences into a convent and school. (EHS.)

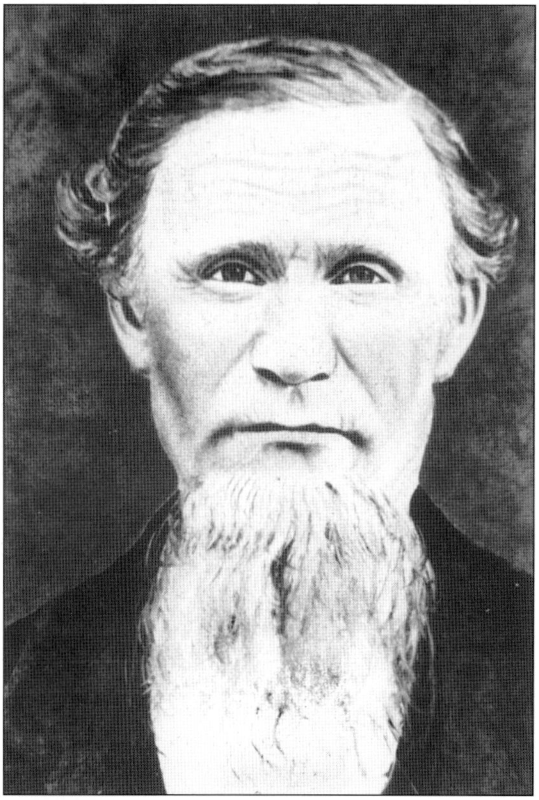

McFarland Family. Duncan and Margaret McFarland came to Euclid Township from Ireland in the 1860s. In 1867, Duncan opened a quarry on the east bank of Euclid Creek where Monticello now crosses. This was the first commercial stone quarry east of Cleveland. In 1870, his net worth was $20,000, making the family one of the wealthiest in the area. The two eldest McFarland sons, James and Thomas, took on quarrying at age 22 and 19, respectively. In 1871, they bought stone-laden land on the west bank. One of the McFarlands' four daughters married Robert Maxwell, a principal in a competing quarry business. In total, the McFarlands made good use of Euclid bluestone for 40 years. (SEHS.)

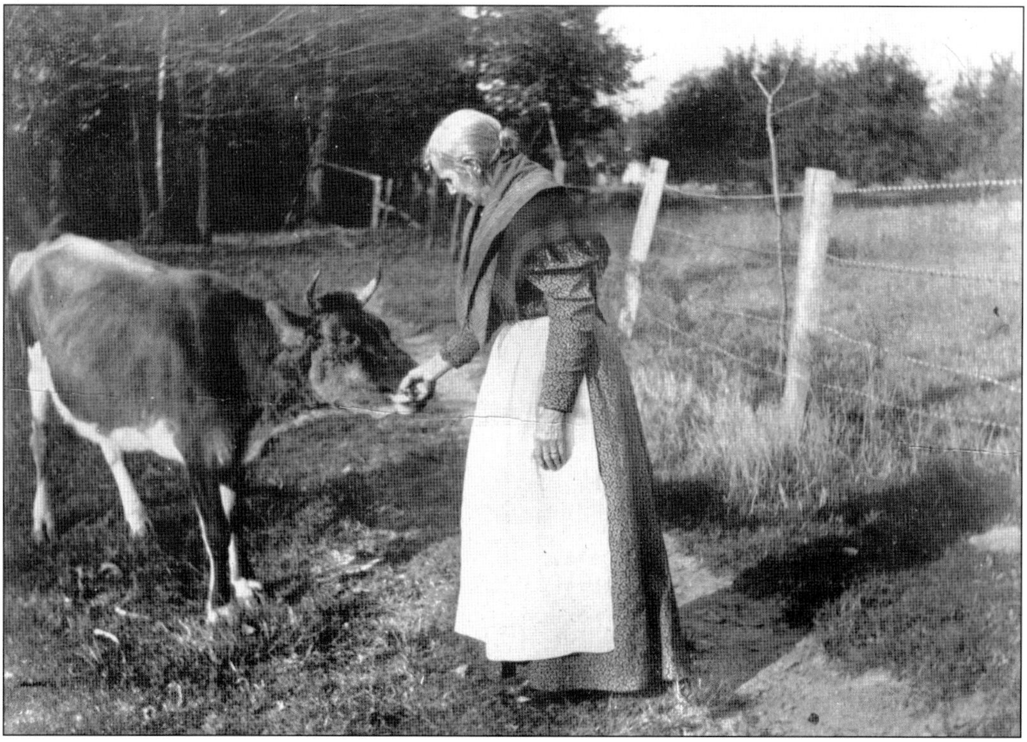

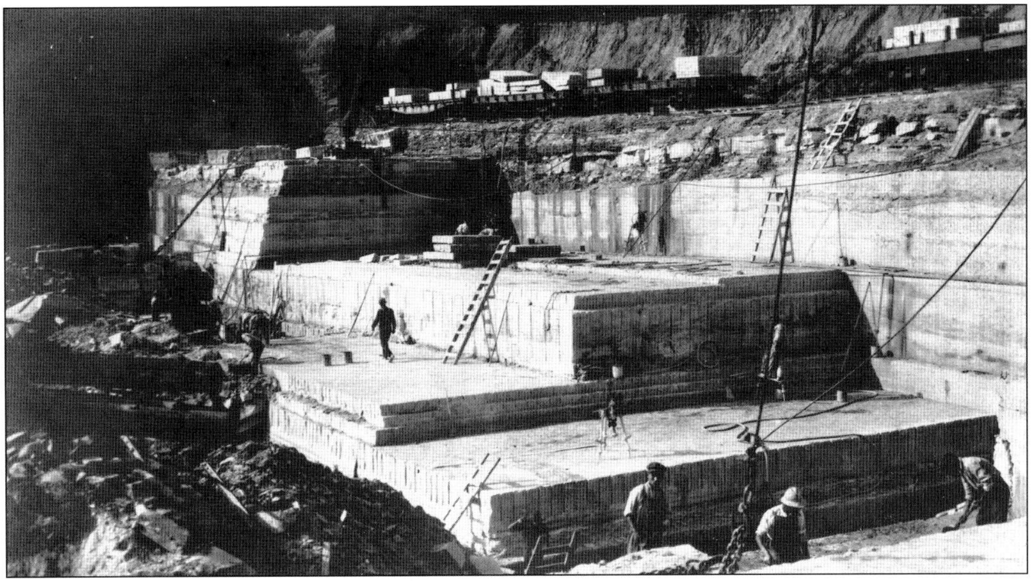

Bluestone Quarries. The stone business grew rapidly during the 1870s. McFarland's sons opened their own quarry on the west bank of Euclid Creek. In 1875, the brothers sold their quarry to the Forest City Stone Company, which also operated on Nine Mile Creek, a few hundred yards west. The photographs show the Forest City Euclid Creek operation at its peak during the late 1890s. Steam-powered saws made the major vertical cuts, while hand laborers split slabs horizontally by drilling lines of holes and driving in wedges. Commercial bluestone production focused on building foundation blocks, sills, steps, laundry tubs, and, above all, handsome sidewalk paving. (SEHS.)

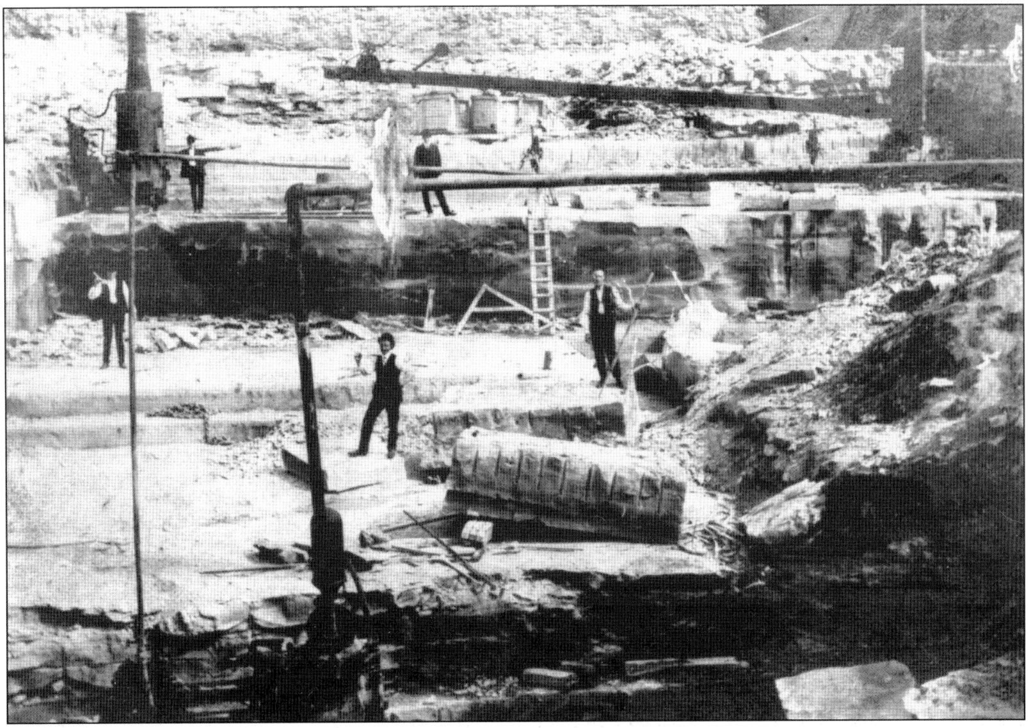

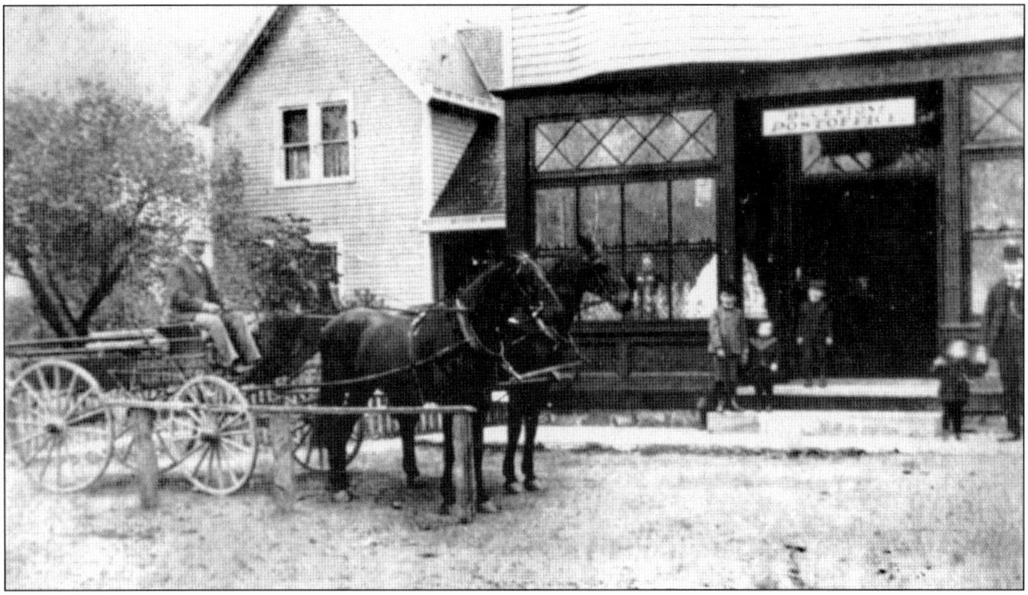

BLUESTONE VILLAGE. By 1880, milling and transport operations centered on the highland between Euclid and Nine Mile Creeks. This area grew a settlement of about 400 immigrant laborers from Sweden, Italy, Ireland, and Canada. Between 1880 and about 1915, this unincorporated village, called Bluestone, had a post office and general store, school, church, boardinghouses, bars, and Temperance Hall. The settlement declined with quarrying during the second decade of the 20th century. (SEHS.)

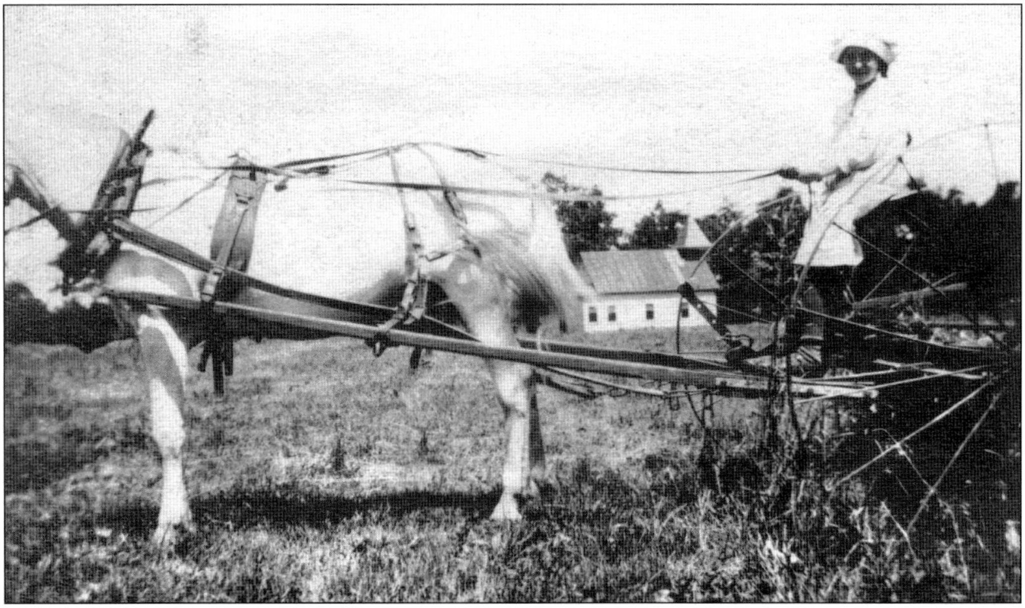

SWEDISH CHURCH. Immigrant Swedes arrived to Bluestone village during the 1880s. Most attended St. John's Lutheran Church on Mayfield Road. In 1898, the group petitioned to form their own church closer to Bluestone. This 1920s photograph shows the church in the background, on the south side of Anderson Road near Green. In the foreground, Margaret Leist, Duncan McFarland's granddaughter, poses on a mowing rig. (SEHS.)

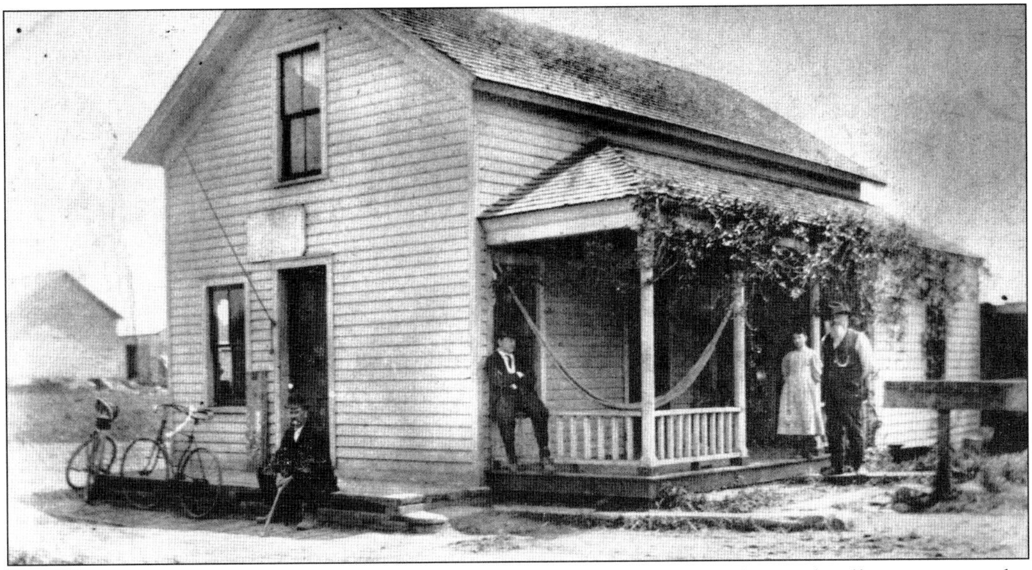

MAYFIELD TOLLGATE. Between 1878 and 1903, the Mayfield Plank Road tollgate sat on the southwest corner of Mayfield and Brainard Roads. Here, Brainard heads south just behind the tollhouse. Across Brainard lies the former Mayfield Academy building, which originally stood on the north side of Mayfield at Whitings Corners (now Lander). Longtime gatekeeper Gordon Abbey (1882–1902) passed on many stories and photographs through his granddaughter Belle Gary. (CPL.)

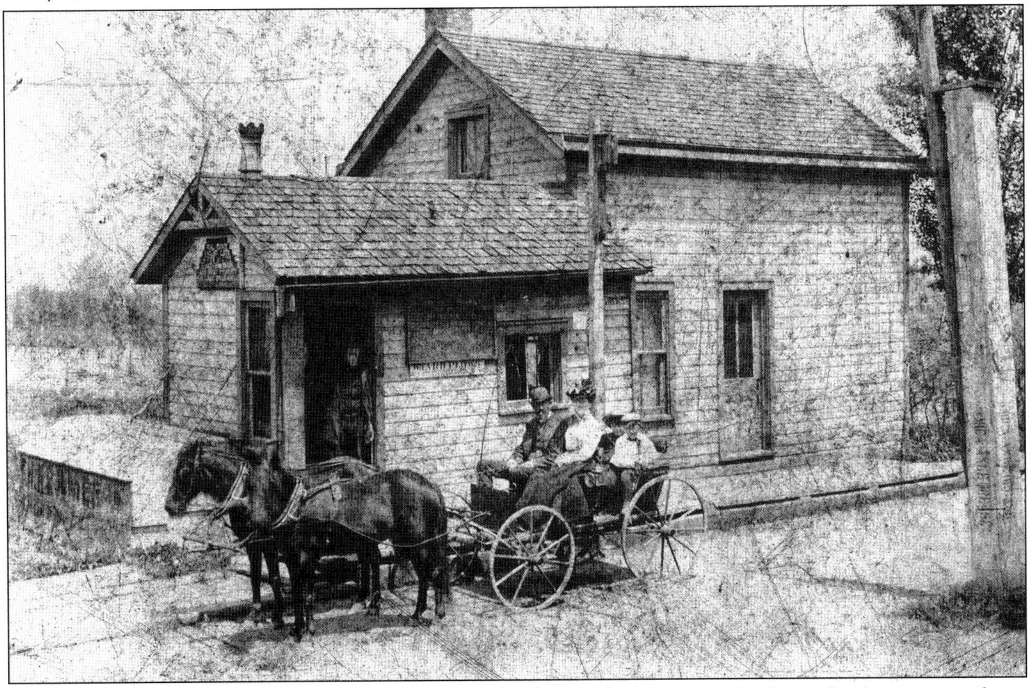

EUCLID TOLLGATE. In 1877, the Wickliffe Plank Road Company built its highway east from Euclid Creek village to the Lake County line along Euclid Avenue. This west tollhouse was built at 21221 Euclid Avenue. William Hazen was gatekeeper for many years. In later years, between 1890 and 1900, annual toll receipts averaged about $1,600, a good sum in those days. (EHS.)

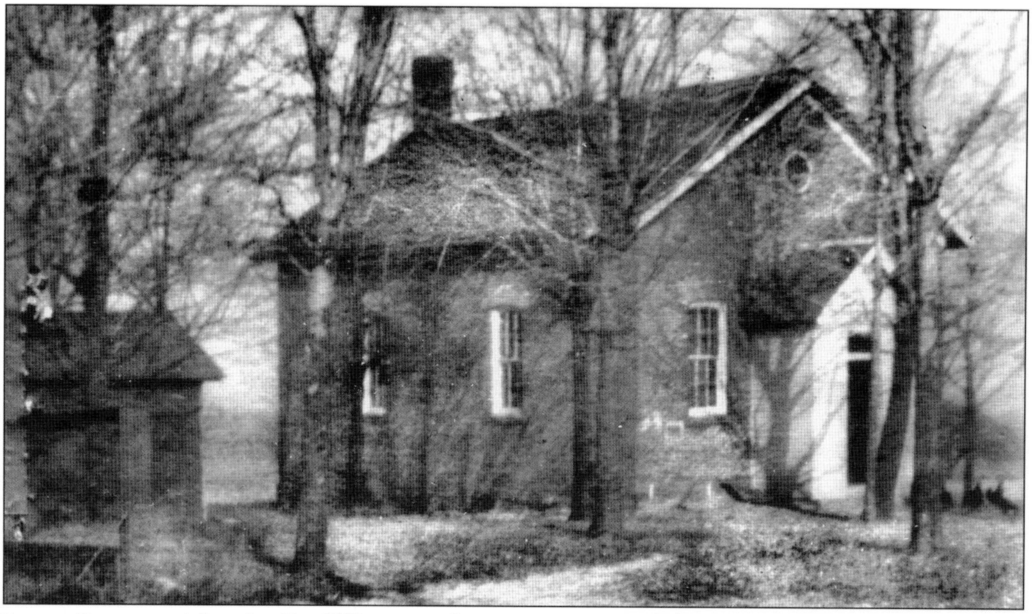

LEWIS SCHOOL. After the Civil War, township trustees around the watershed began replacing the old 1820s-era frame schoolhouses. The new ones still had one room but were made substantially of brick and stone. This one was built on the northwest corner of North Woodland (current Fairmount) and Richmond Roads in 1868. The schoolhouse had two informal names: Lewis (the landowner) and LaRue (the location). (Jeffrey Morris.)

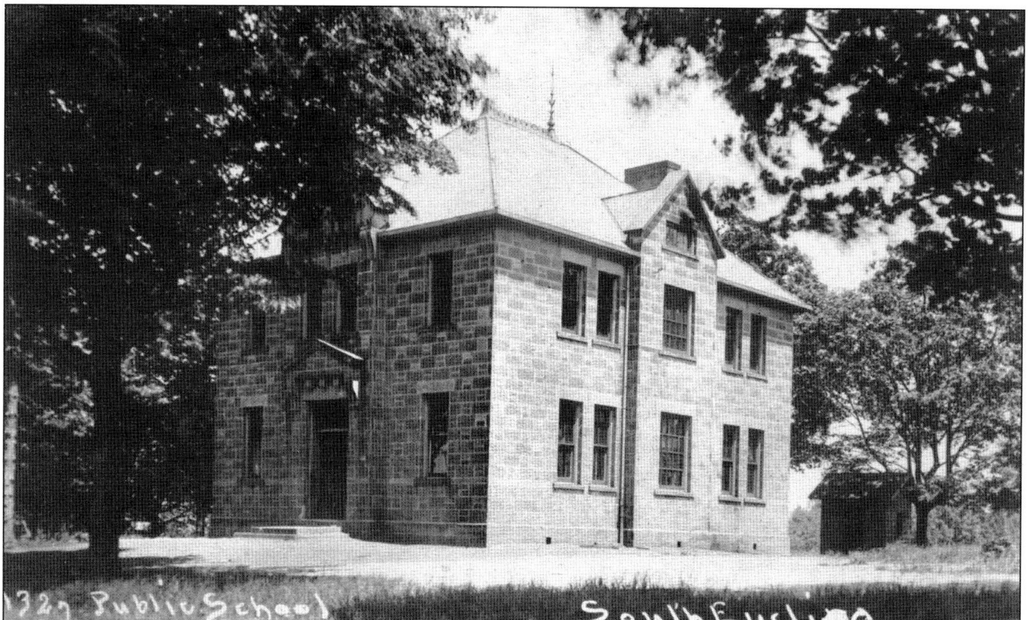

STONE SCHOOL. The Mayfield-Green crossroads has been a population center since the second decade of the 19th century. The northeast corner held schools continuously from the 1820s to 1957. In 1865, this eight-room Victorian edifice replaced a smaller brick schoolhouse built in 1845. The locally quarried sandstone gave rise to the common name for the District 7 School. The stone school was demolished for the South Euclid High School in 1912. (SEHS.)

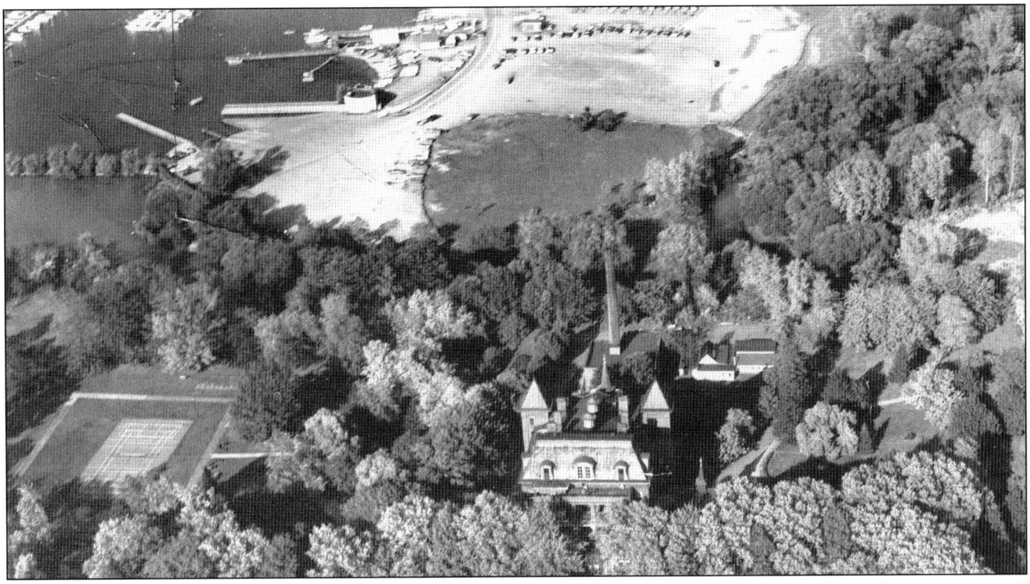

Villa Angela. In 1850, Bishop Rappe invited the French Order of Ursuline Sisters to staff Cleveland's parish schools. After working to great success for two decades, the Ursulines expanded eastward. In 1874, they bought the 55-acre Camp Gilbert for use as an educational campus. Villa Angela, a boarding academy for girls, opened in 1878. Charles Schweinfurth, Cleveland's most reputed architect of the period, designed the four-story school. (CPL.)

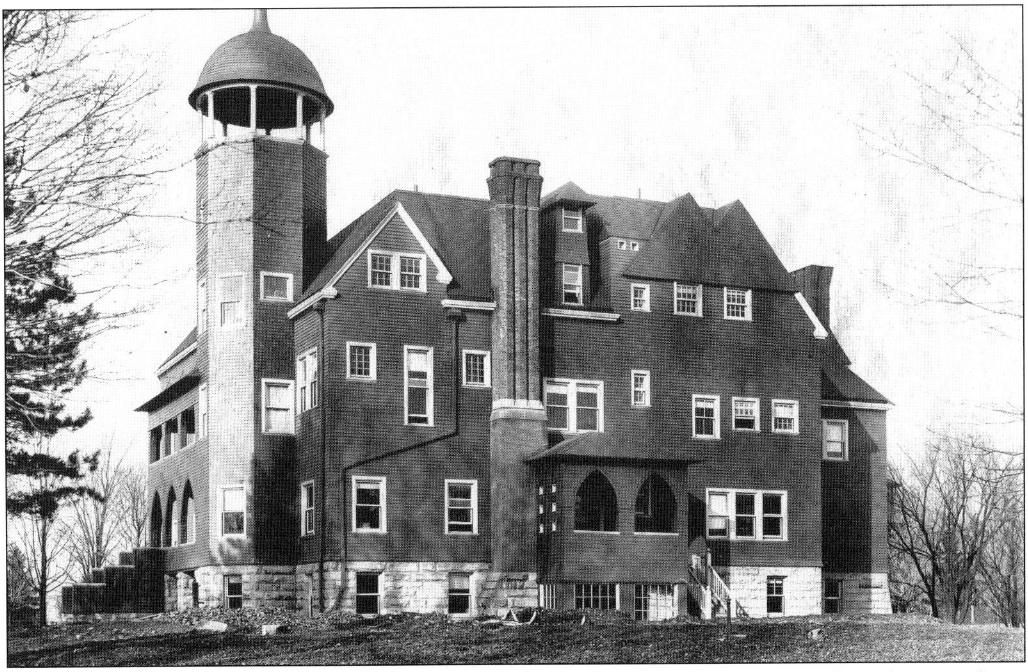

St. Joseph Seminary. In 1886, the Ursulines opened St. Joseph Seminary, a boarding academy for boys on the Villa Angela campus. This was the Ursuline's first school for boys. Charles Schweinfurth also designed this building, this time using a modified Gothic style in locally quarried stone. In 1941, the building became the Cleveland Ursuline novitiate center. It burned to the ground on February 4, 1946. (CPL.)

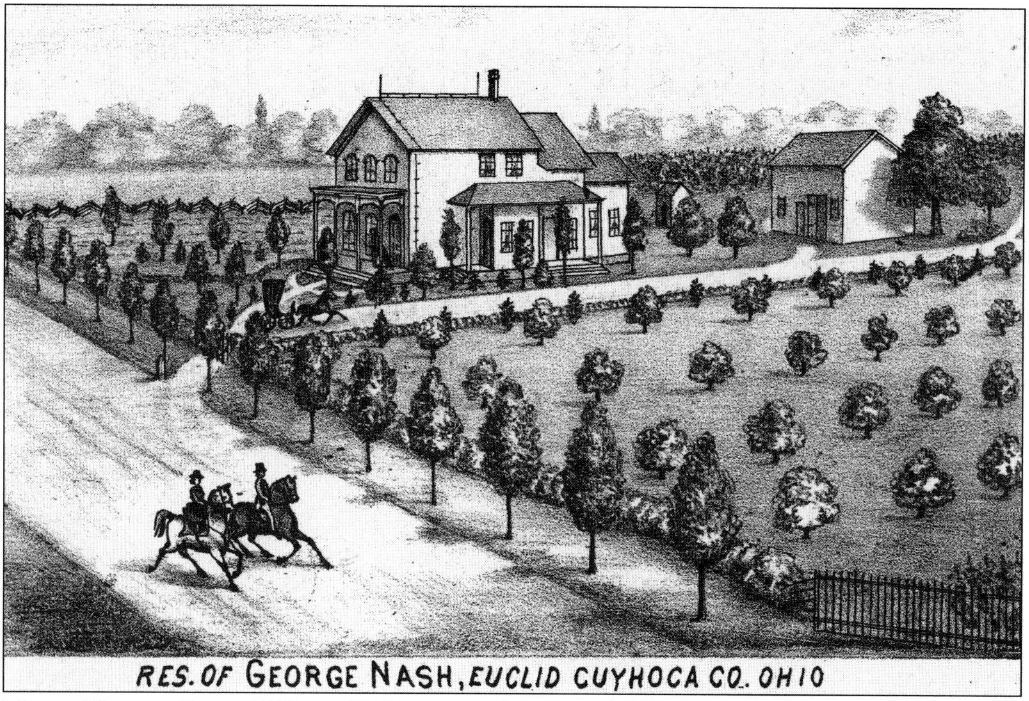

NASH HOUSE. From 1870 to 1910, vineyards covered the Highland Hill area of current Richmond Heights. The Alten, Harms, Nash, and Verbsky families all had vines on this well-drained exposure. George Nash built his house at the top of the hill, immediately west of the Harms vineyards. (Lake, 1874.)

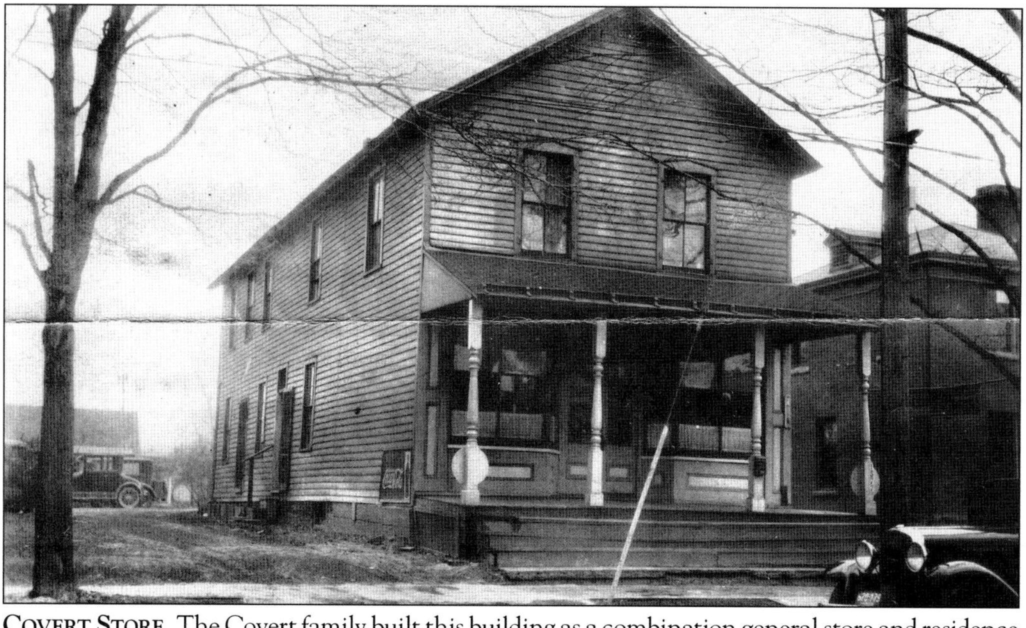

COVERT STORE. The Covert family built this building as a combination general store and residence at 1577 Chardon Road in the 1870s. The family began serving lunch around 1900. This photograph was taken in 1929. The building still stands as Edwards Plumbing and Heating. (CPL.)

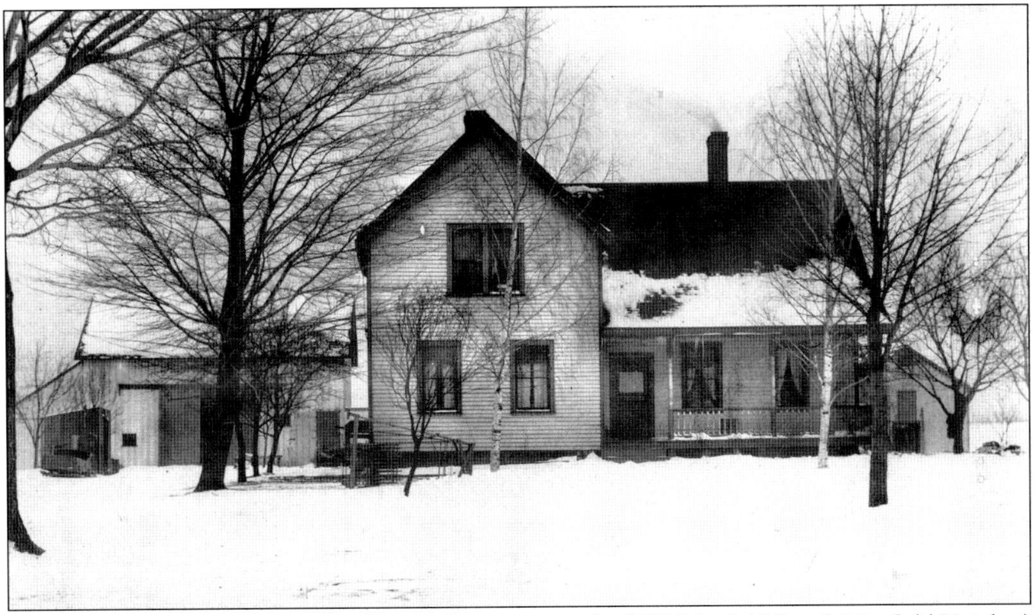

HAUSCHILD HOUSE. Built around 1870, this structure (at 5817 Mayfield Road, Mayfield Heights) represents the final form of the Western Reserve farmhouse. A single wing has been raised as high as the upright and now holds the formal front entrance. The Ernest A. Hauschild family bought the farm in the late 1880s and sold its produce on Mayfield Road through the Great Depression. (MTHS.)

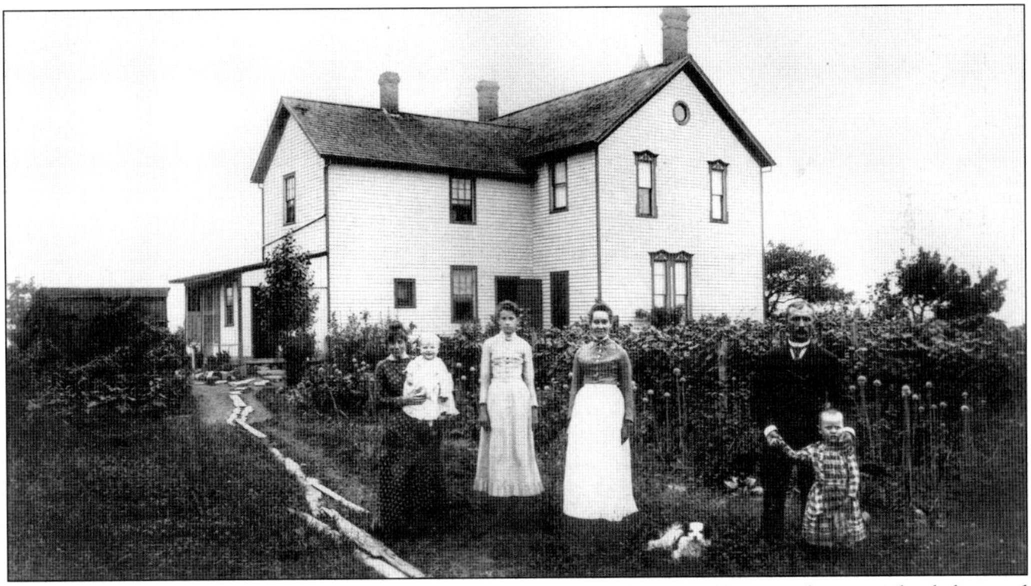

PEMPIN HOUSE. This was the replacement for the Harry Artemus Pempin house, which burned in the early 1880s. Harry's son Horace built the house at 21271 Chardon Road. Part of the Pempin gardens are visible beside and behind the house. By the 1890s, when this photograph was taken, the Pempins were supplying all manner of garden produce to the major Cleveland market centers. (WRHS.)

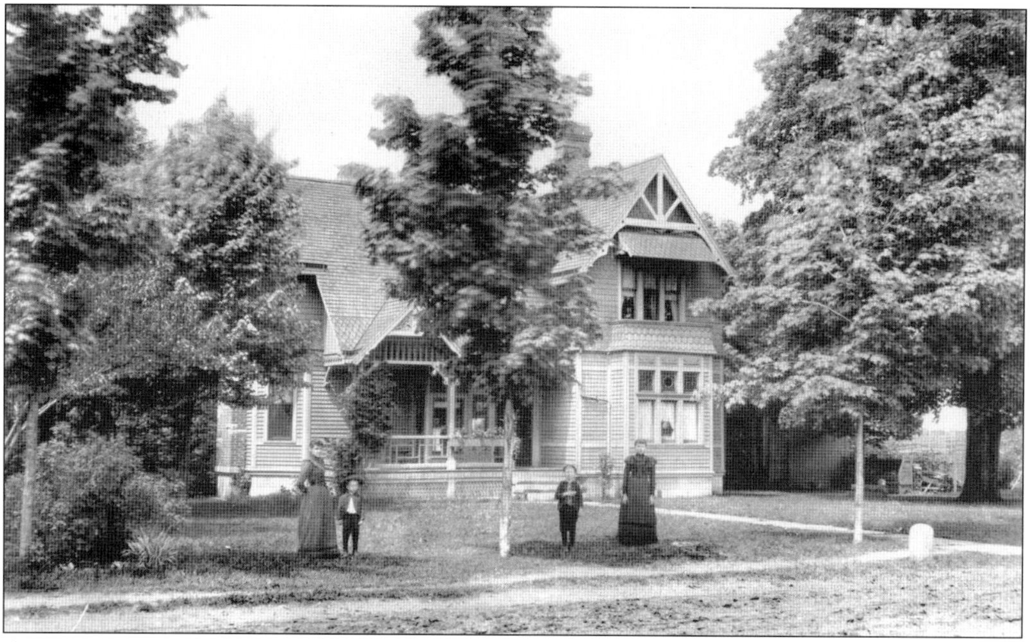

Owners' Row. Anderson Road east of Euclid Creek held the dwellings of a number of principals in the Bluestone quarry business. Shown here are the houses of the McFarland (top) and Maxwell (bottom) families, both owners of individual bluestone operations. Both houses are typical of the early 1880s and represent the urban Victorian evolution of the Western Reserve house into its townhouse form. On each, the wing has been shortened and integrated with the narrow upright using a colonnaded porch. Ornamentation has become important to the design of the house. (SEHS.)

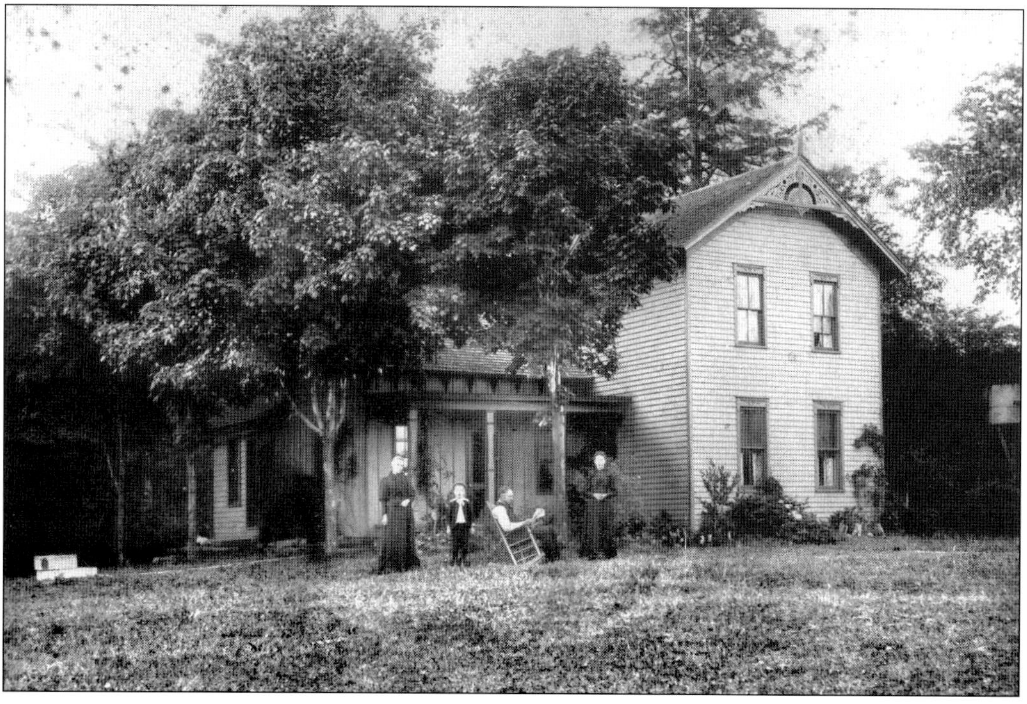

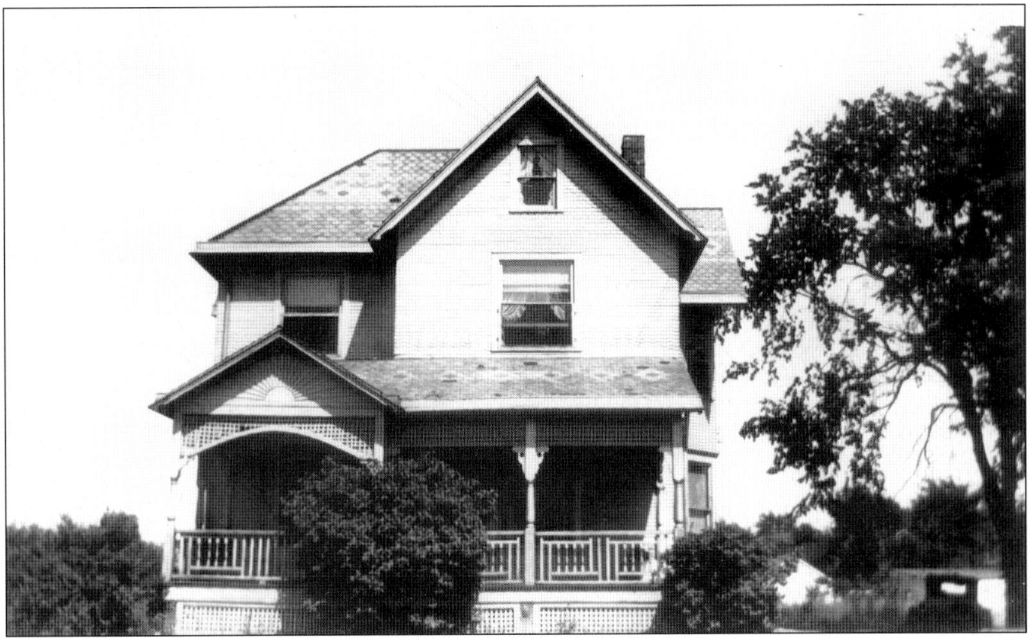

Bennett House. Alfred R. Bennett and Hattie Thorp, members of two prominent 19th-century Mayfield Township families, got married and built this house in 1893. It still stands near the northeast corner of Mayfield and Lander (1481 Lander Road). Jewish Family Services Association of Cleveland bought the house in 1989. It now operates as Lander House, a group home for developmentally disabled local residents. (MTHS.)

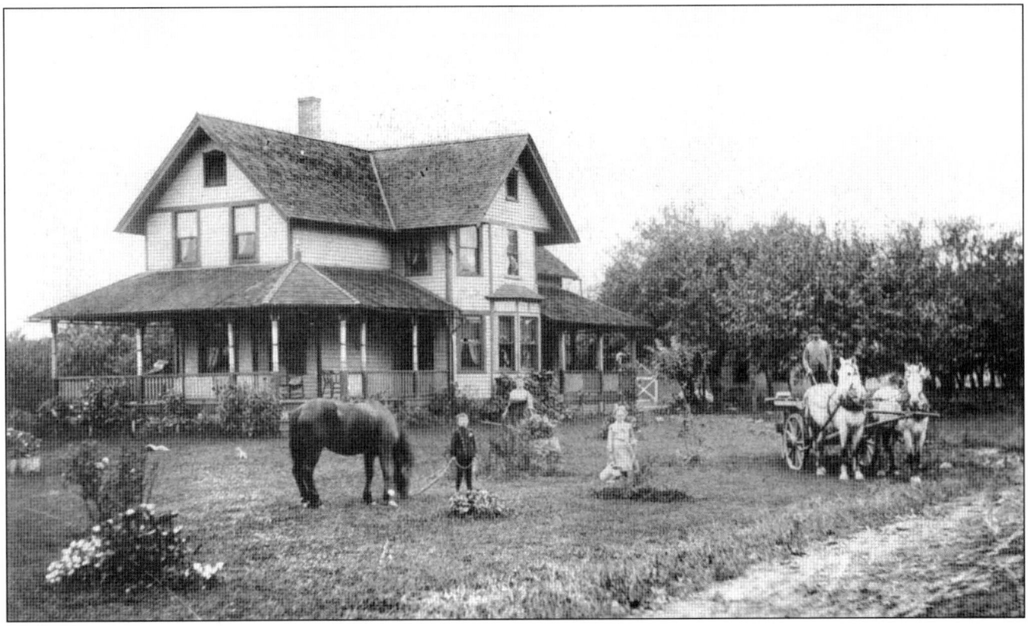

Linnert House. The camera looks past the southeast corner of Mayfield and Lander around 1900. Lander Road is in the foreground. The Linnert family built this large townhouse-style farmhouse in 1894. The old Western Reserve wing has retreated back to become smaller, now essentially a two-story front entry hall. (MTHS.)

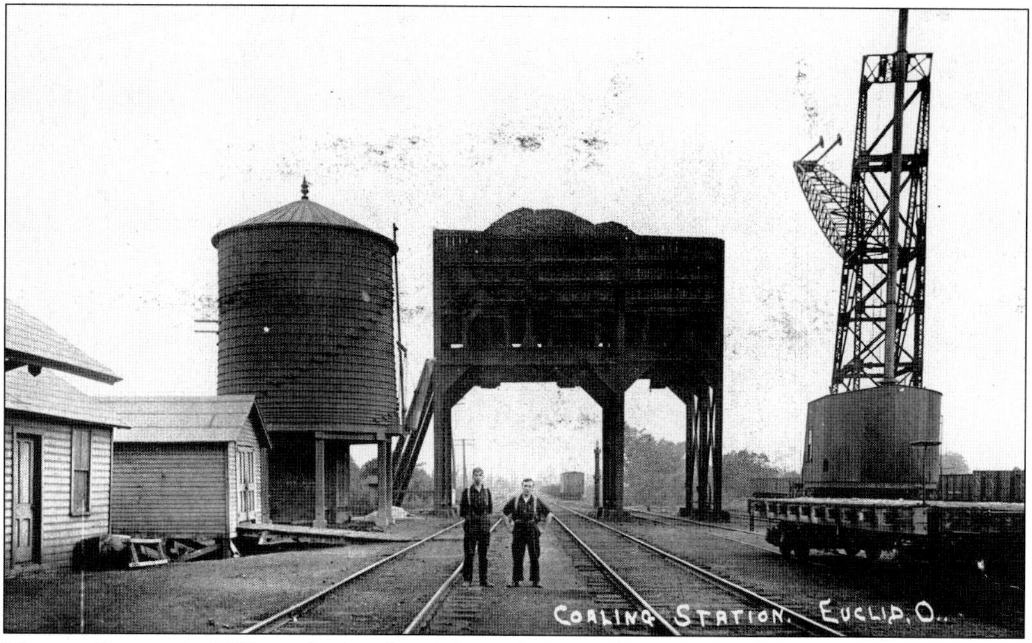

NICKEL PLATE. In 1881, at the height of Great Lakes industrial growth, the Norfolk Southern and St. Louis Railroad opened along Lake Erie's south shore. The "Nickel Plate" track ran parallel to the 1852 LS&MS line. Once again, Euclid Creek became an important stopping point. This 1908 photograph looks west from Chardon Road to view the coaling and watering apparatus at Euclid Station. (EHS.)

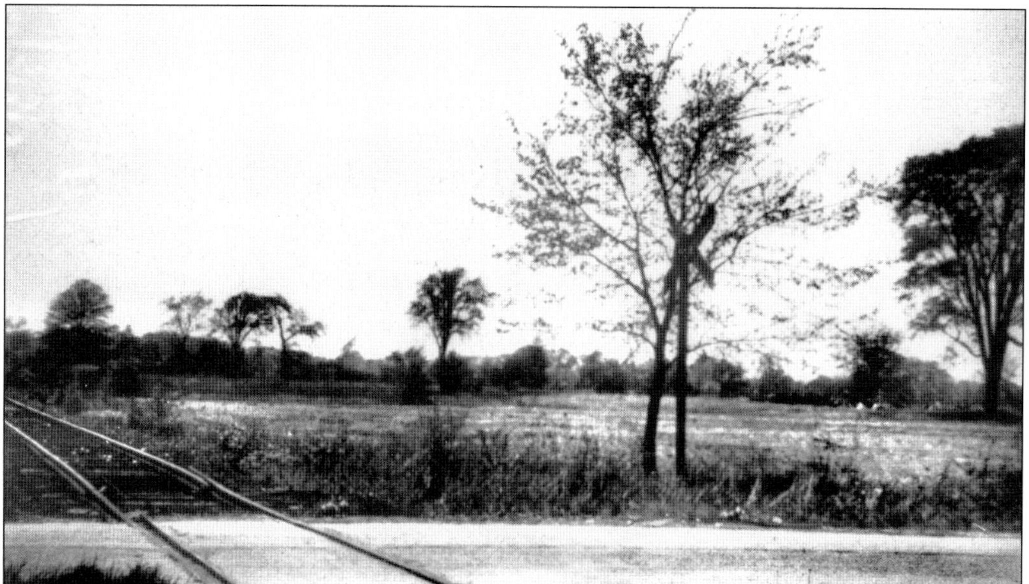

EUCLID RAILROAD. In 1882, the Euclid Railroad was incorporated as a small Nickel Plate branch line to serve the bluestone quarries at Green and current Monticello Roads. The Euclid Railroad was distinguished by its mountainous grade. The tracks rose nearly 300 feet in the one-mile climb to South Euclid along a branch of Dille Creek. The photograph shows the track crossing Glenridge Road on top of the plateau. (SEHS.)

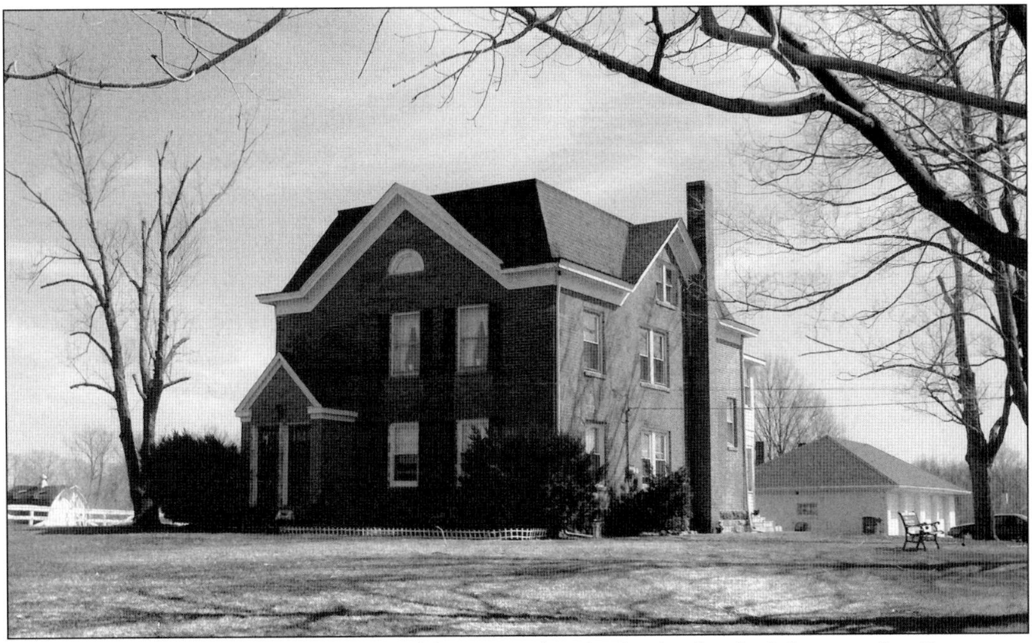

Schram School. In 1899, Willoughby Township built the brick Schram schoolhouse on Chardon Road east of Rockefeller. It appeared very much like Euclid Township's Beechnut schoolhouse at Peltons Corners. After the school closed in the 1920s, an individual bought it, demolished it down to the local stone foundation, and rebuilt it as this substantial house. The two-door entry represents the structure's recent conversion into a duplex. (Roy Larick.)

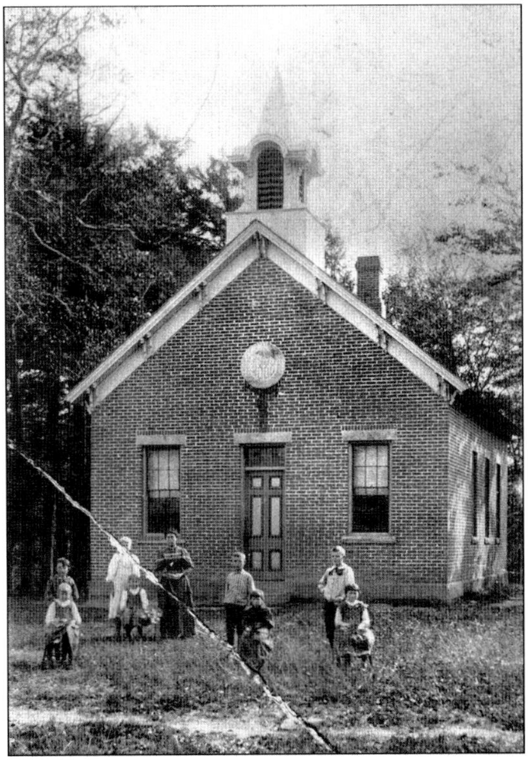

Beechnut School. Euclid Township School District 8 was centered at Peltons Corners above Euclid Creek's east branch. A frame schoolhouse was built in 1873, at current 26906 Chardon Road, and then moved to 25800 Chardon. In 1888, this handsome brick schoolhouse was erected in its place. The colloquial name, Beechnut, derives from the beech trees that still thrive here. The building is currently one component of a residence. (EHS.)

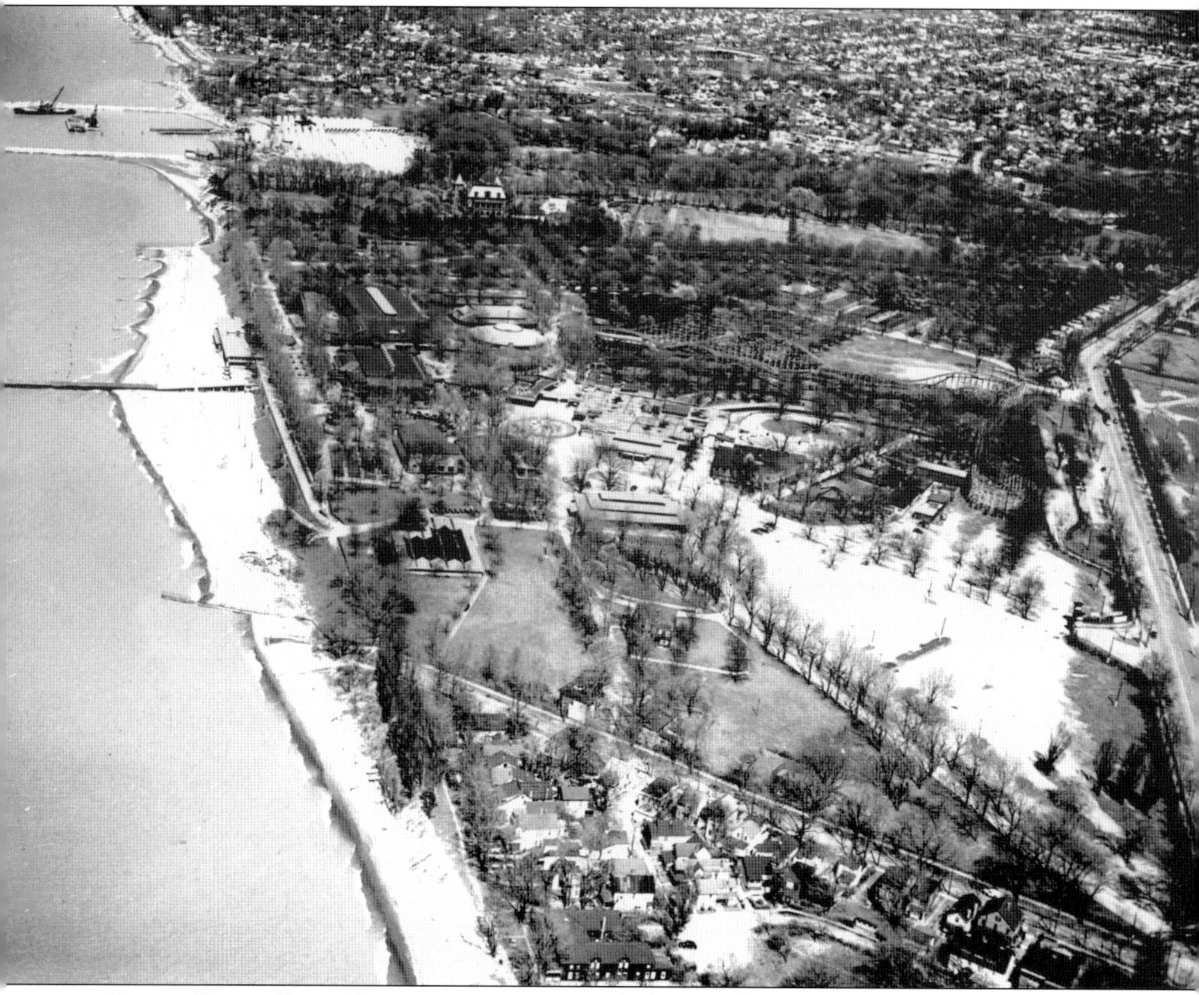

EUCLID BEACH PARK. Electricity came spectacularly to Euclid Creek in 1895, when a Cleveland business syndicate opened the 64-acre Euclid Beach Park just east of Villa Angela. Euclid Beach was the second electrified amusement park in the United States (the first opened in 1894 in Chicago). In this pre-trolley era, two 98-foot steam ferries were the principal means of entry from downtown Cleveland. This April 1949 photograph shows the park emerging from the winter to have another high-attendance season. The Euclid Creek mouth lies just this side of the Wildwood Park break wall. (CPL.)

Four

Electric Rails
1895–1918

Electricity was the stuff of progress during the 1890s and early 1900s. In this brief period, electric power came to transportation, the workplace, commercial amusement parks, and finally to the homestead. Electrification was one of the more important technological advances in American history, and it greatly moved life on Euclid Creek. The famed Euclid Beach amusement park—the second electric park in the nation—is a perfect icon for the period.

Nevertheless, electricity changed life in more earthly ways. In particular, the electrification of rail travel—which introduced the interurban railroads—made the watershed accessible to outsiders in a way not seen before or since. Electric trains also took local farm produce quickly to larger markets. It is in this period that suburbanization and agriculture clashed head-to-head. Euclid Creek at once saw trendy if rough-hewn residential subdivisions compete with ever more productive farmers.

Yet another electrification development left a strikingly visible impact on the watershed: the country estates of wealthy Cleveland industrialists and professionals. Depending on how one defines an estate, the watershed saw between one and two dozen built between 1895 and 1928. The builders were notable in their desire to be country gentlemen and in their means to accomplish the task. Some, seemingly inspired by Thomas Jefferson himself, took active roles in constructing and operating their houses and gardens. Henry S. Pickands on Chardon Hill fits this mold. Others, like the Fords and the Grassellis, traveled or worked away quite often and had what might be described as large suburban houses on back roads. Estate house architecture went to two extremes. Most, such as the Arter and Bolton houses, were based on formal "historical revival" styles. Others, such as the Ford and Grasselli houses, incorporated the more relaxed character of the bungalow style emanating from California.

Electrification also brought manufacturing and a burgeoning middle class to Euclid Creek. Quarrying, with its commercial origins in the steam era, peaked with the late-19th-century demand for traditional building materials. With a large immigrant labor force and with electric tools to replace the cumbersome steam-driven machines, quarrying productivity climaxed around 1900.

With a growing middle class, the watershed hamlets saw a greatly increased demand for public services. Nottingham, Euclid, Richmond Heights, South Euclid, Lyndhurst, and Mayfield Heights incorporated in this period to be able to let out legal construction contracts. Finally, newfound local wealth brought opportunities for rebuilding churches, schools, and other finer establishments. By 1910, watershed became the realm of exclusive private estates, middle-class resorts, and incipient suburbs.

In the steam era, the Ursuline Sisters built Villa Angela on Camp Gilbert, thereby setting a precedent for transforming Euclid Creek's leisure estates into streamside beneficent institutions. Electrification produced a number of estates similarly transformed during the coming automobile era. But one electric home made the transition very quickly. Just before 1900, Cleveland lawyer Jacob Nowak built a 10-acre streamside estate on Green Road, just south of Mayfield. Unfortunately, Nowak died prematurely in 1903, leaving his holding in peril. A year later, the Rainbow Circle of King's Daughters, a Cleveland society service organization, suffered a devastating fire in their Rainbow Cottage for Convalescent Children on Richmond Road. The Rainbow-Nowak match was perfect, and so the King's Daughters continued the Ursuline precedent.

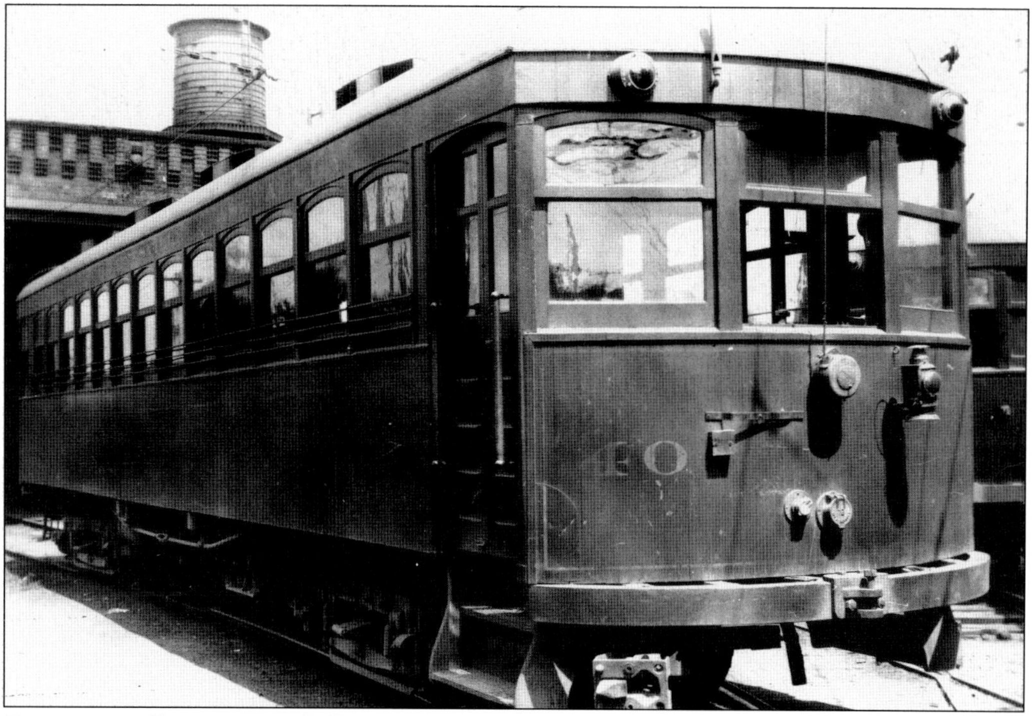

CLEVELAND, PAINESVILLE & EASTERN. In 1896, Everett and Moore laid the CP&E Railway along Euclid Avenue. In 1898, the CP&E opened its Shore Line along the Euclid Township lakefront. The Shore Line descended to the lake via Gardner Road (East 185th Street) at Nottingham Village and then remounted inland along Vine Street to Willoughby. Here a CP&E car emerges from the Nottingham barns. (EHS.)

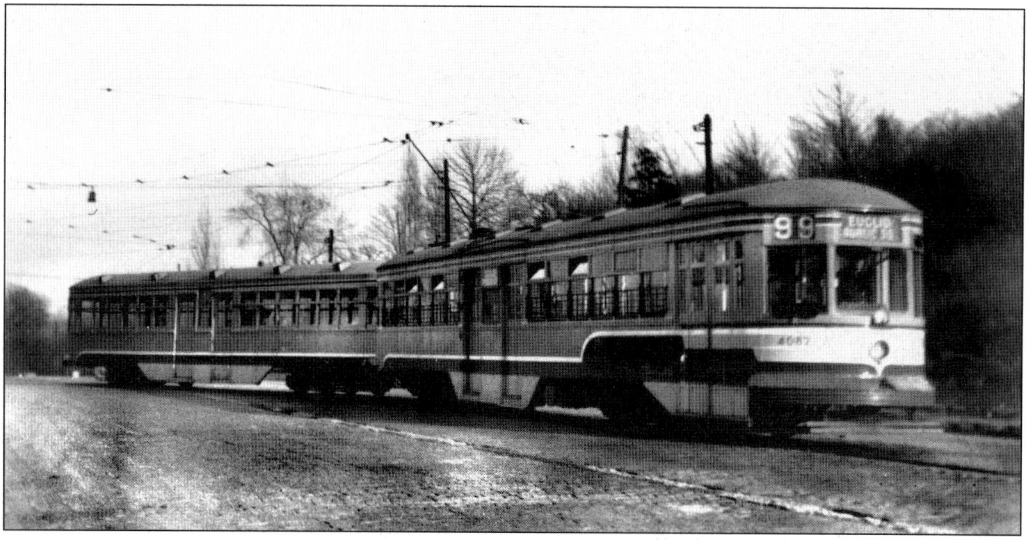

CLEVELAND RAILWAY. With the formation of the Cleveland Electric Railway Company in 1903, Euclid Avenue trolley service expanded eastward to Euclid Creek village. In 1910, the Cleveland Railway Company took over, and in 1942, the Cleveland Transit System assumed control. The Euclid Avenue Line (No. 99) was shut down in 1948. On December 19, 1939, a Cleveland Railway car and trailer negotiate the line-end turnaround at East 212th Street. (EHS.)

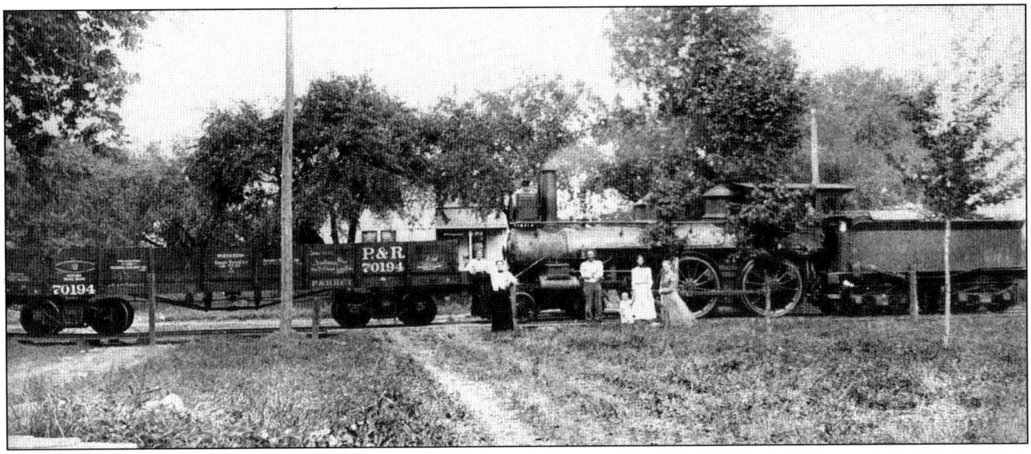

CLEVELAND AND EASTERN. The Cleveland and Eastern Railway was incorporated in 1898 to run between downtown Cleveland and Burton. In this August 4, 1899, photograph, members of the Gates and Thorp families pose in front of a steam-powered work train on Mayfield Road in current Mayfield Heights. (MTHS.)

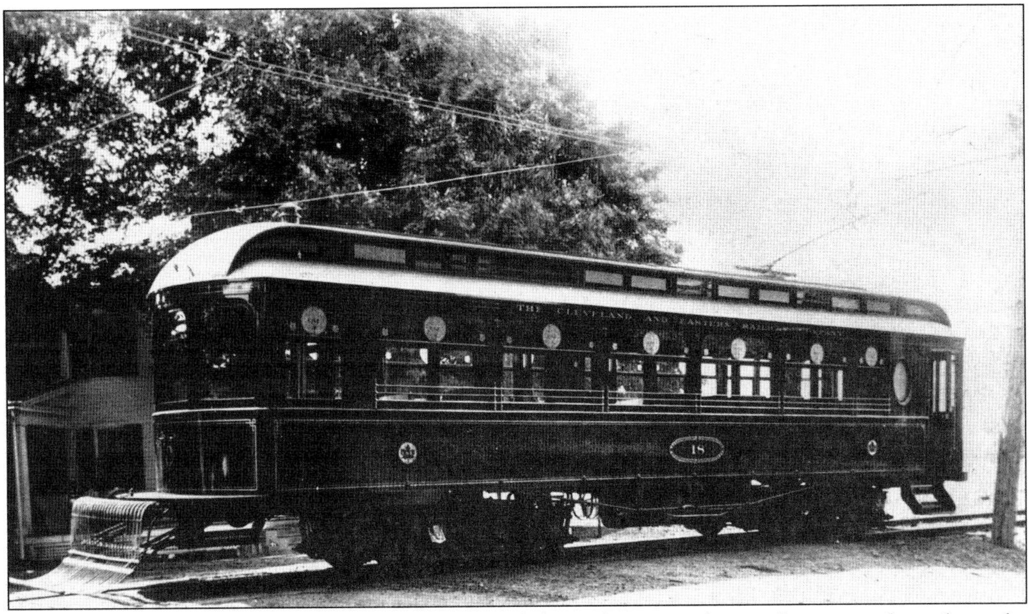

C&E CAR. More cheaply and flexibly operated than the steam lines, the interurbans brought the middle class to Euclid Creek and the Euclid beaches. Here, a C&E car, with its distinctive maple leaf logo, crosses Green Road on its Mayfield Road track. (CPL.)

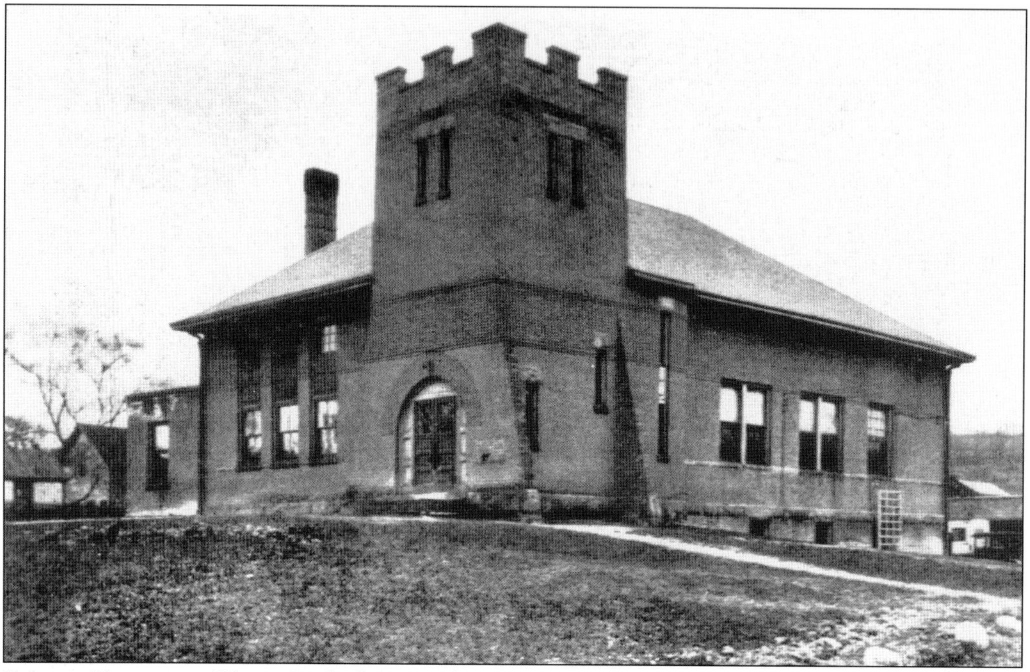

EUCLID TOWNSHIP HALL. In flush 1894, the township mounted a Romanesque-style municipal campus on North Street, just east of Chardon Road. This was one of five buildings built of local brick and bluestone. The township sold it to new Euclid Village in 1903 and moved offices to South Euclid. Shown here is the Euclid Village Hall after a major fire in 1923. The building burned completely in 1929. (EHS.)

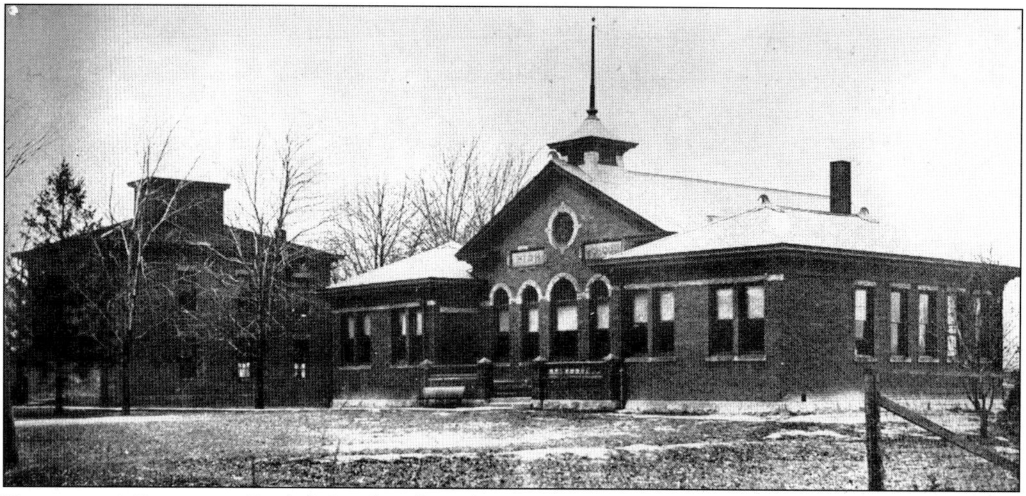

DISTRICT 1 SCHOOLS. Euclid Creek village became Euclid Township School District 1 in 1848. The township high school (right) and new District 1 grammar school (left) arose simultaneously in 1894. Sold to private interests in 1913, both were divided up into apartments. A 1929 tornado demolished the grammar school, but it was soon rebuilt as a duplex residence. The City of Euclid now owns both buildings. (EHS.)

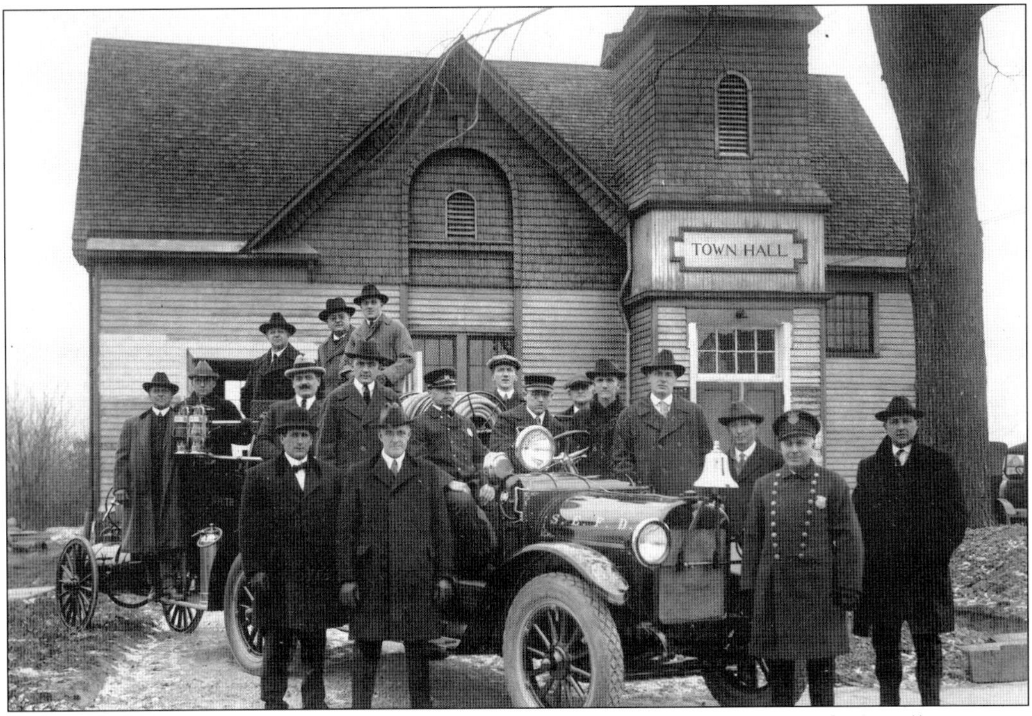

South Euclid Town Hall. By the mid-1890s, Euclid Township's far-flung villages were beginning to fragment. The trustees responded in 1899 by building an auxiliary town hall on Green Road in South Euclid. When the trustees sold the North Street hall to Euclid Village in 1903, Green Road became the unique administrative space. When South Euclid Village incorporated in 1917, this became the village hall as well. (SEHS.)

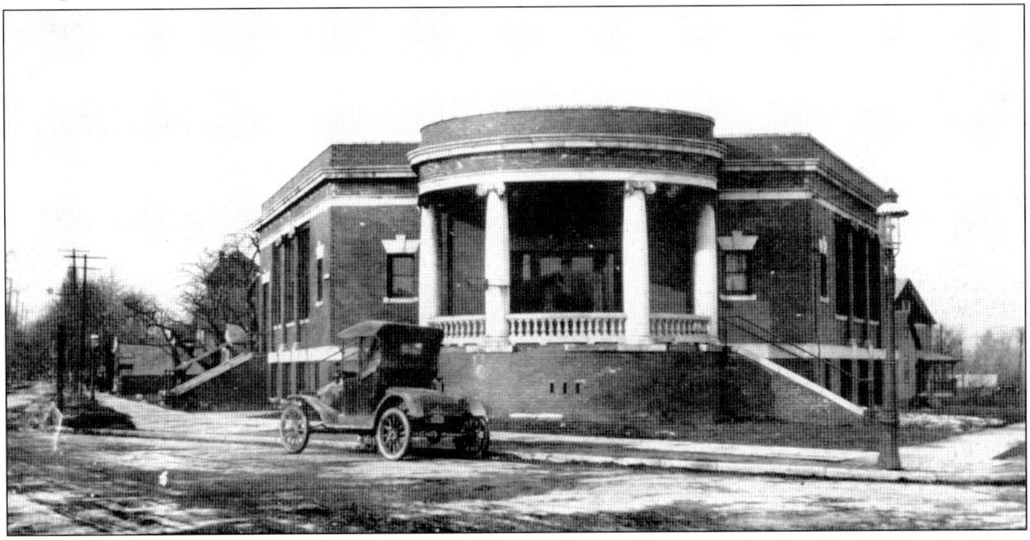

Nottingham Village Hall. By the 1870s, Nottingham village was rivaling Euclid Creek village as a commercial and residential center. Residents tried to incorporate the village in 1877, but success came only in 1899. Nottingham remained chartered until 1917, when Cleveland annexed it. Looking due north in 1917, we see the 1910 village hall on the north point of the Neff-Gardner (East 185th Street) intersection. This handsome building stood until 1961. (NHS.)

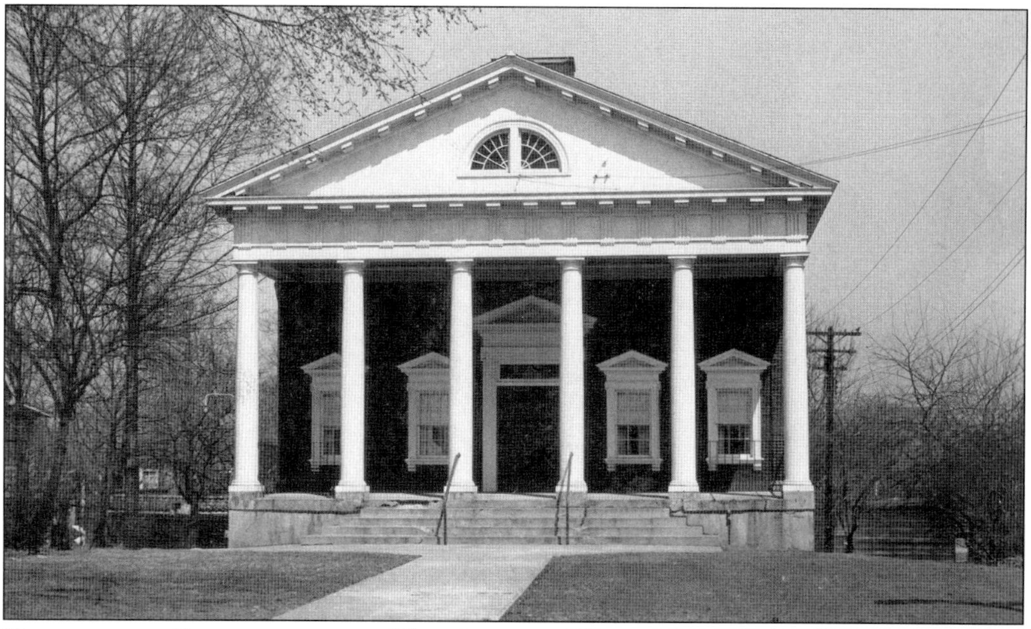

NOTTINGHAM CONGREGATIONAL. This charming Classical Revival church stood east of old Nottingham Road, directly on the west bank of Euclid Creek. The bluestone basement was mounted in 1910, and the superstructure required several more years to complete. The final service was held in September 1960. Shortly thereafter, the church was demolished for the Lakeland Freeway. (CSU.)

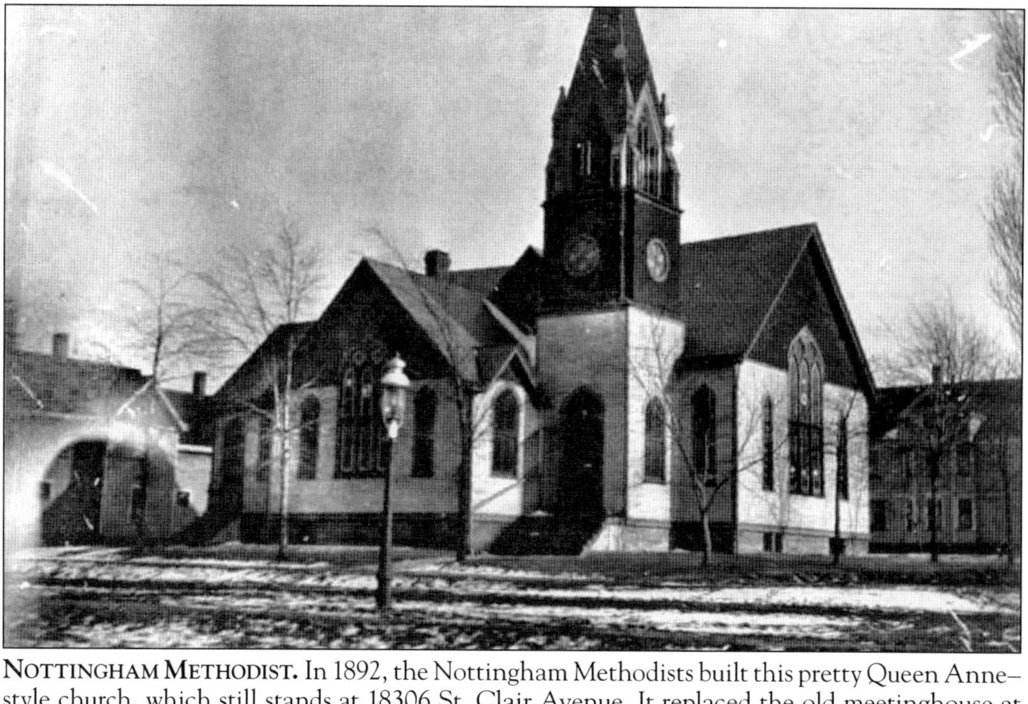

NOTTINGHAM METHODIST. In 1892, the Nottingham Methodists built this pretty Queen Anne–style church, which still stands at 18306 St. Clair Avenue. It replaced the old meetinghouse at 18391 St. Clair. The new church was built on the Akron Plan, in which the adjoining sanctuary and parlor could be linked or separated with a set of movable panels. (NHS.)

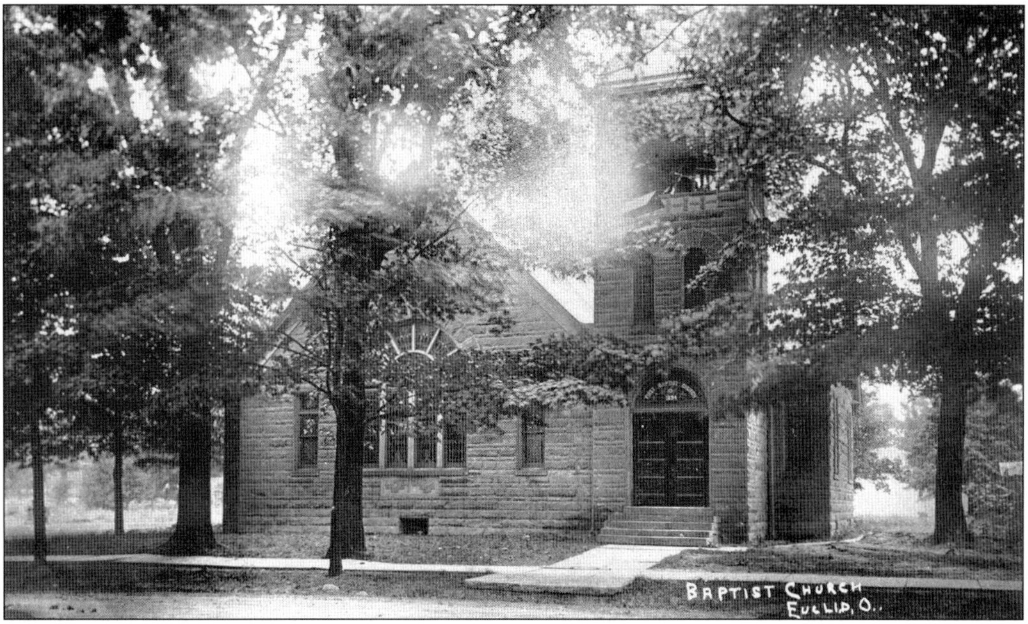

FIRST BAPTIST. The Euclid Baptist Society was established in 1820 as the first church in the watershed and one of the first Baptist groups in all of Ohio. They built a Puritan-style square-plan meetinghouse in 1821, and replaced it with a Colonial-style brick edifice in 1835. In 1894, the society built this pretty First Baptist Church of Euclid bluestone, but replaced it with a modernist structure in the 1950s. (EHS.)

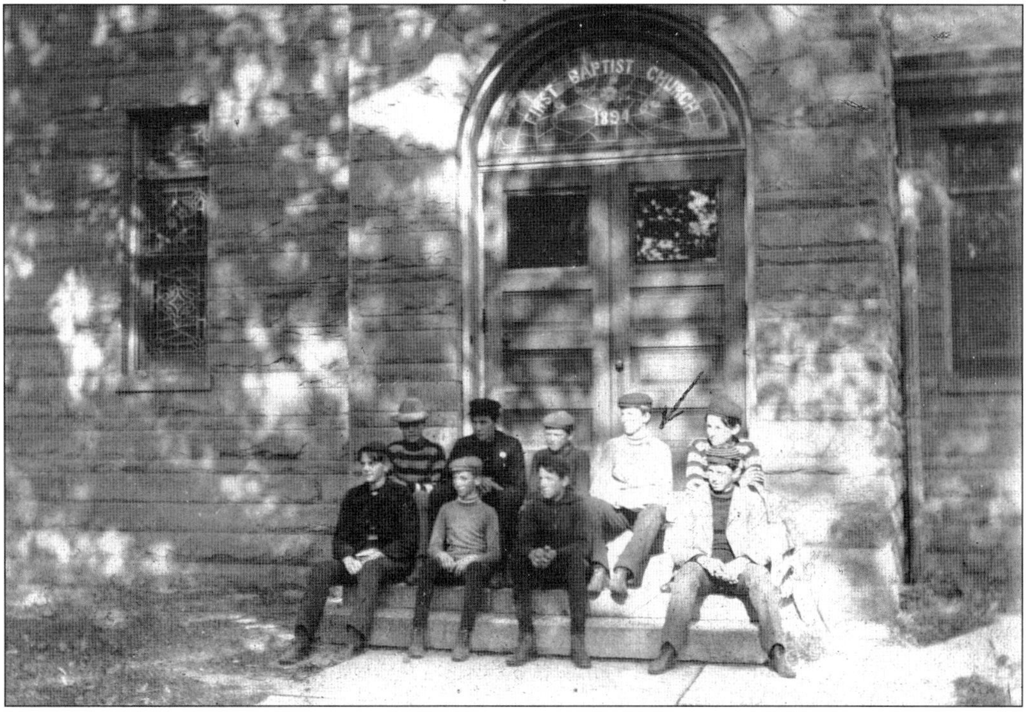

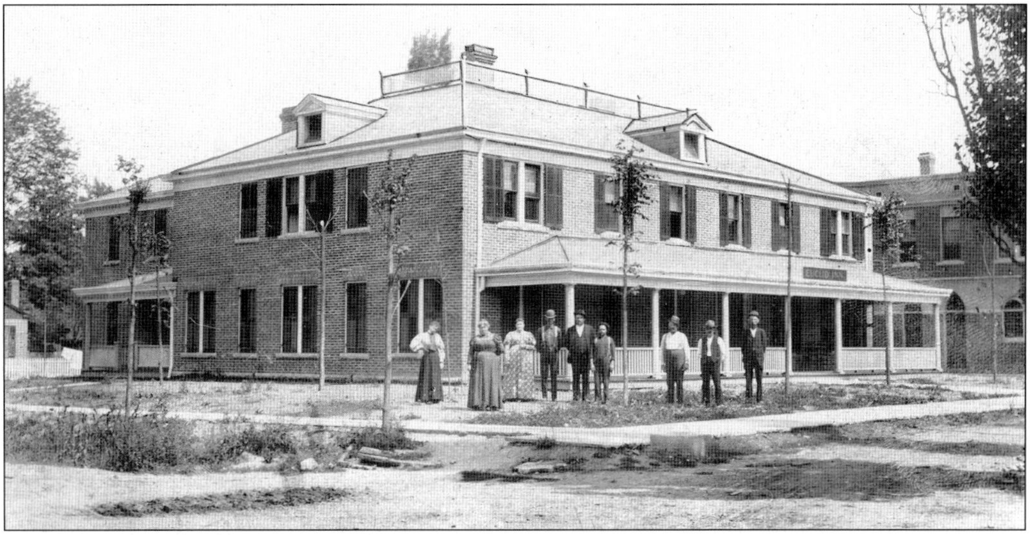

EUCLID INN. This brick, Colonial Revival–style hotel replaced the old frame Euclid House in 1896, just as the CP&E main line was opening. Business declined during the 1920s as the village suburbanized and as automobile travel bypassed local hotels. During the 1930s, storefronts sprouted on the front and side yards to bury the hotel. Demolition came in 1967. (EHS.)

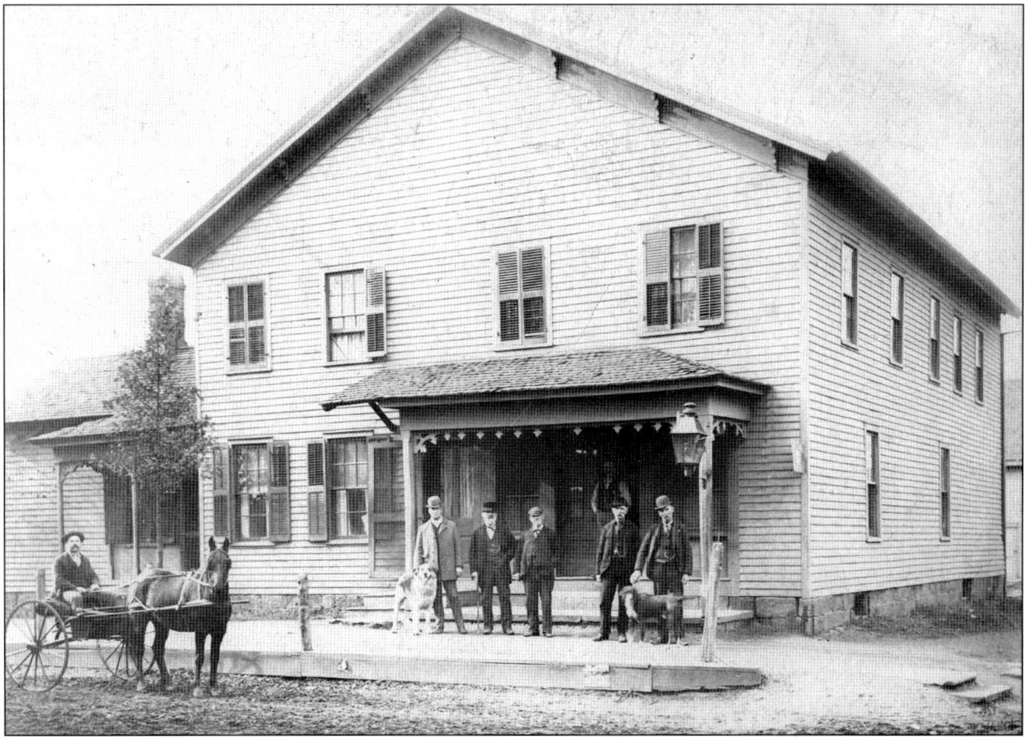

LOGAN HOUSE. Nottingham village held several hotels in its heyday. The Logan saloon was the big draw when this photograph was taken in 1897. The view looks north from the middle of St. Clair Avenue. Old Nottingham Road heads north along the right side of the building. The Voorhees family owned and operated the Logan House in its later years. Cleland Voorhees stands on the porch. (EHS.)

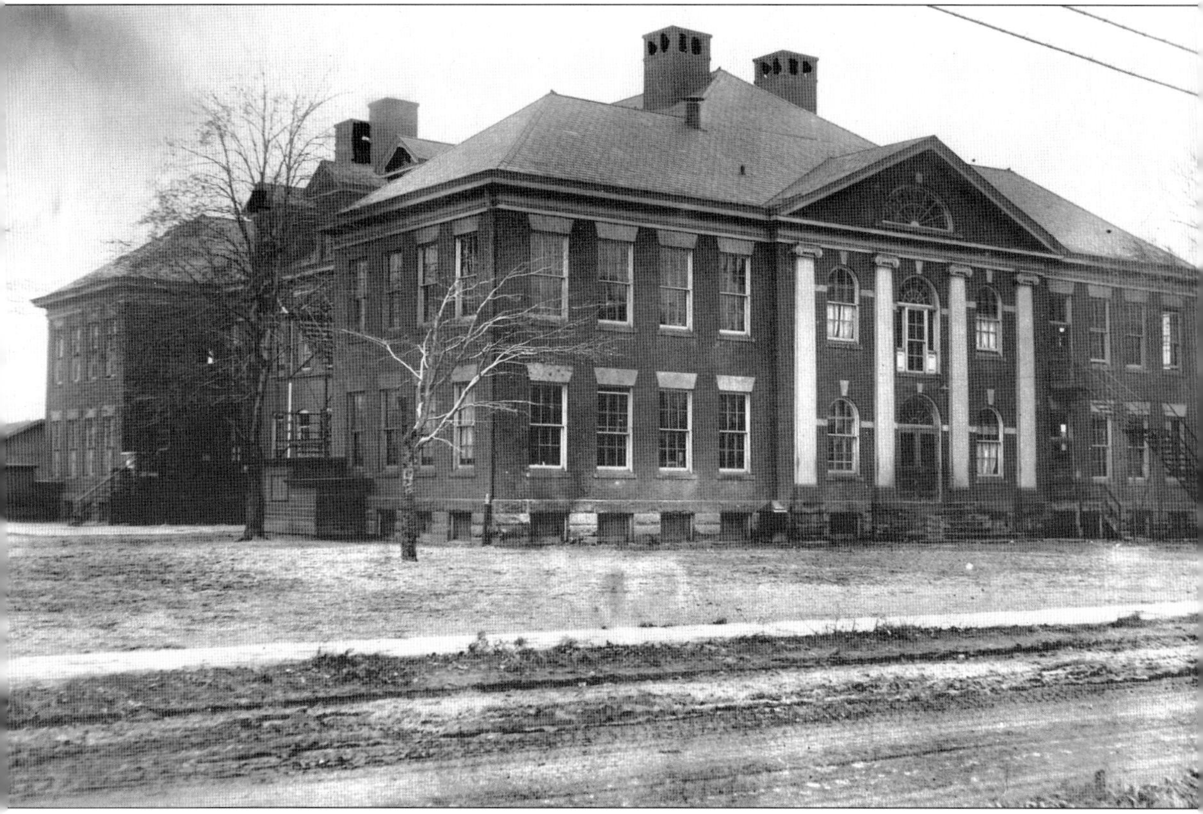

NOTTINGHAM SCHOOL. The Euclid Township trustees built a four-room school on Nottingham Road in 1880. With additions in 1900 and 1907, the building topped out at the 16 rooms shown in this 50th-anniversary photograph (1957). The school closed in 1961, when Lakeland Freeway work wiped out its neighborhood. The building was demolished in 1962. (NHS.)

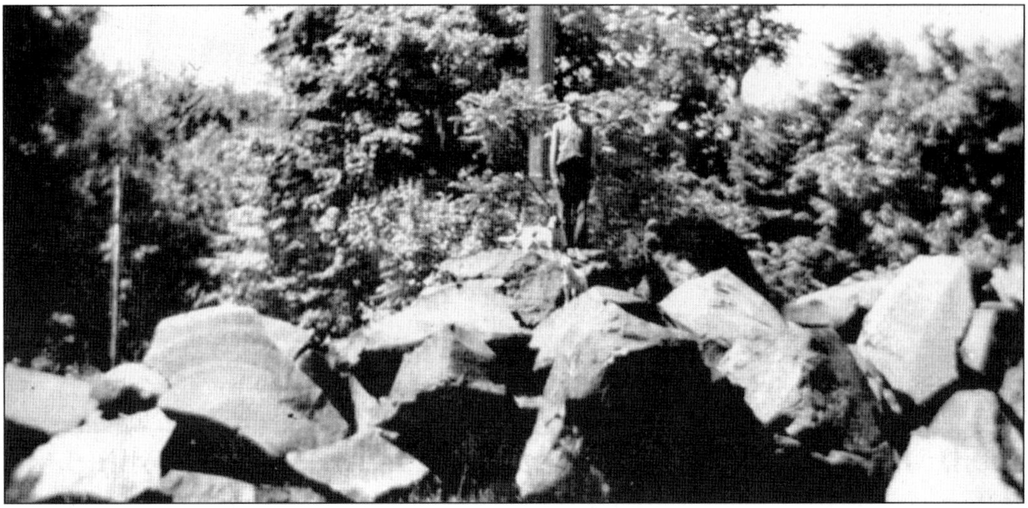

Red Sandstone. The Berea sandstone outcrops in the area of Richmond Road about halfway between Highland and Wilson Mills Roads. The rock in this outcrop has a distinctive reddish shade. The Samuel Robbins family settled here during the second decade of the 18th century and quarried the outcrop intermittently through the years. Staple Stevenson bought some quarry land around 1900 and made it into the small commercial operation shown here. (*Golden Anniversary.*)

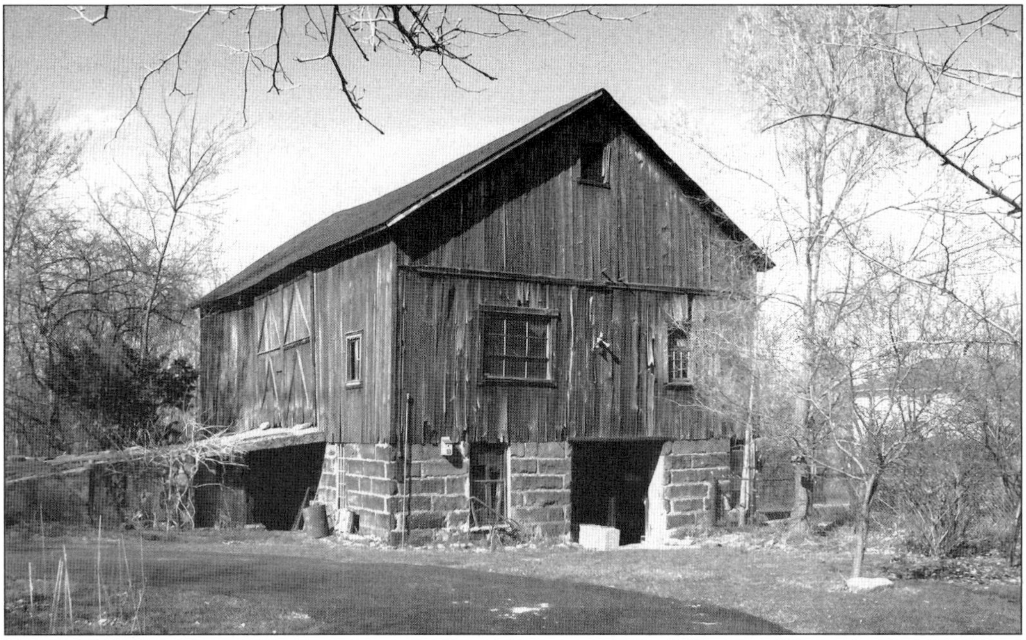

Stevenson Barn. Staple Stevenson built this barn in the early 1900s just east of Richmond Road (opposite current Gleeten Road). The ground-floor walls are built up of massive red sandstone blocks quarried less than a quarter-mile to the south. A similar barn still stands on Tribisky Road, just south of Highland. (Roy Larick.)

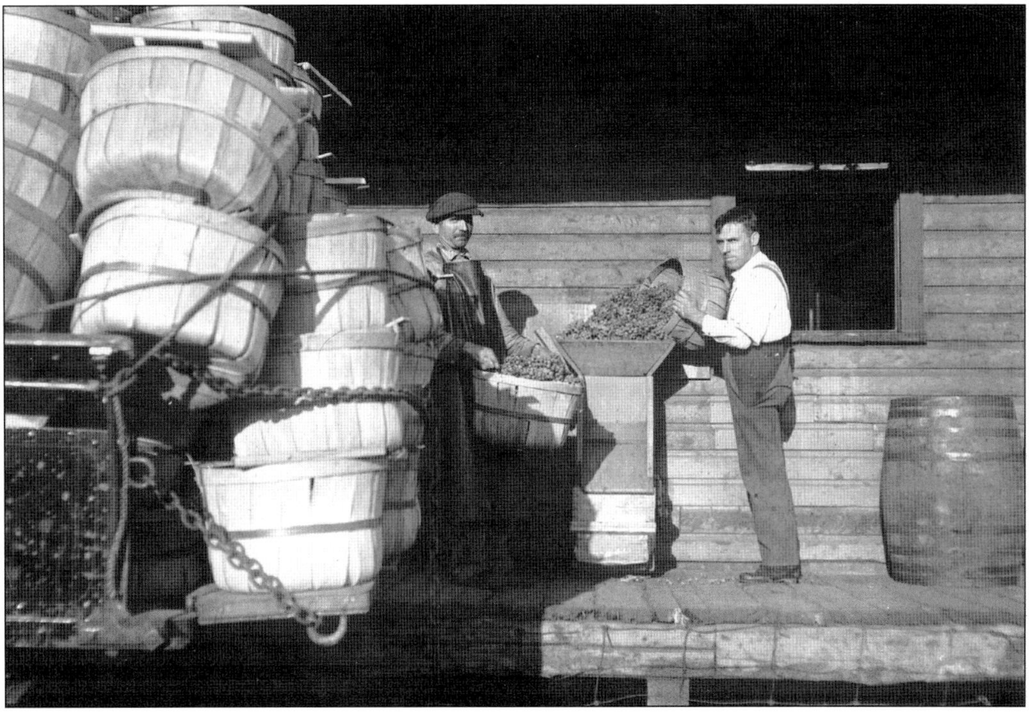

SCHUSTER WINE COMPANY. In 1885, the German immigrant Schuster family began making wine from their Euclid Creek vineyards. Edward Schuster was the principal; he maintained residences at Peltons corners at East 18th and Superior Avenue, where the actual winery was located. Schuster specialized in Catawba wines, the grapes for which are seen in these photographs. (CSU.)

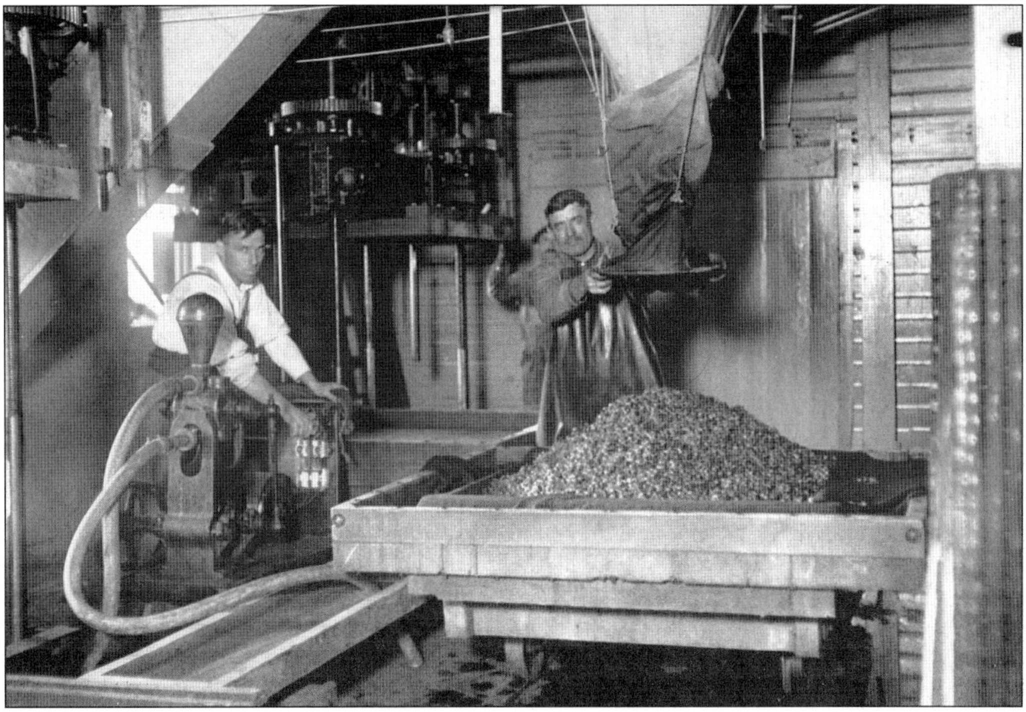

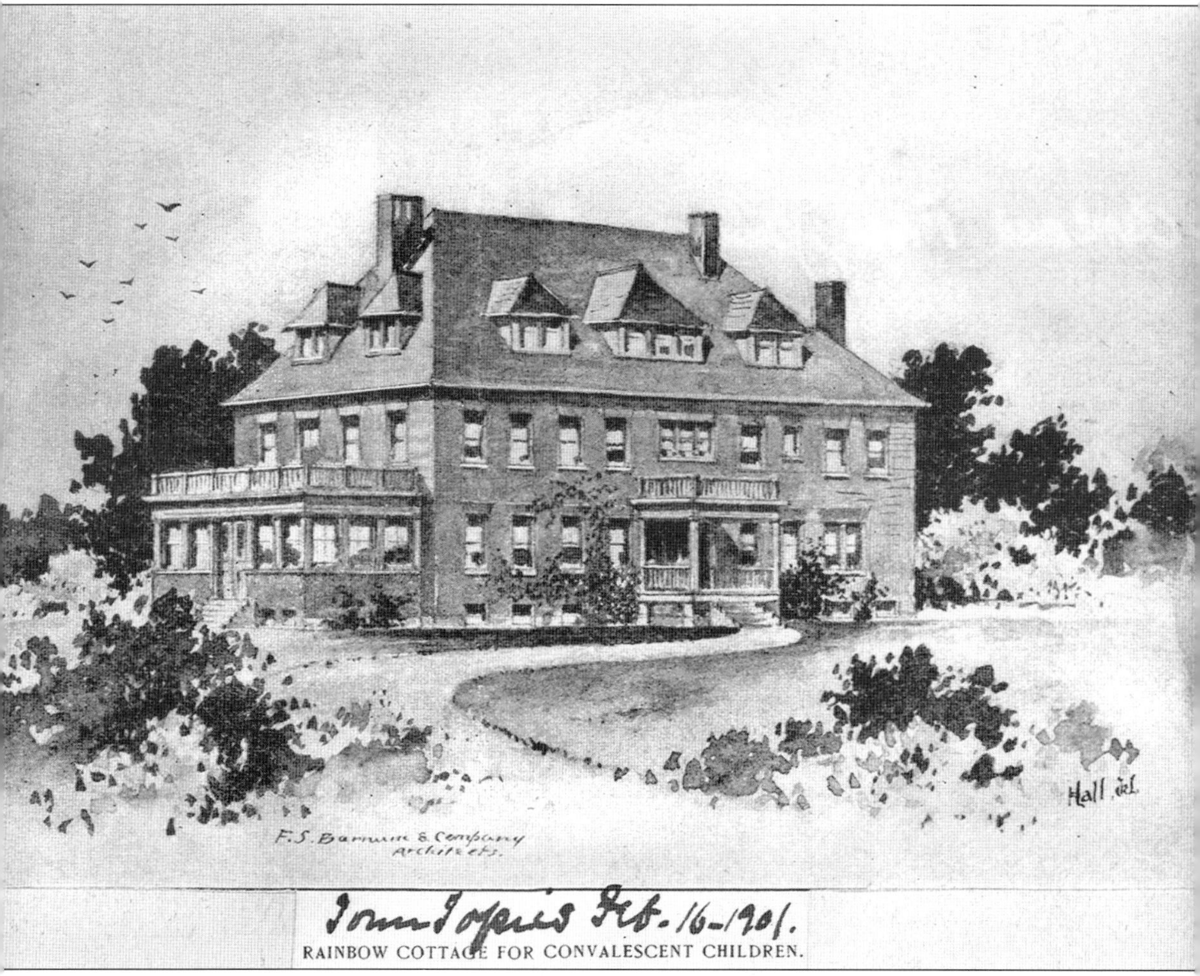

RAINBOW COTTAGE. In 1891, the Rainbow Cottage for Convalescent Children was opened at East 105th and Lakeside. In 1900, the William L. Harkness family gave $25,000 to build on a 10-acre Richmond Road parcel north of Mayfield. Cleveland architect Frank S. Barnum designed a three-story brick, bungalow-inspired facility. Alas, upon being closed for the winter on October 31, 1904, the second Rainbow Cottage burned to the ground. (UHA.)

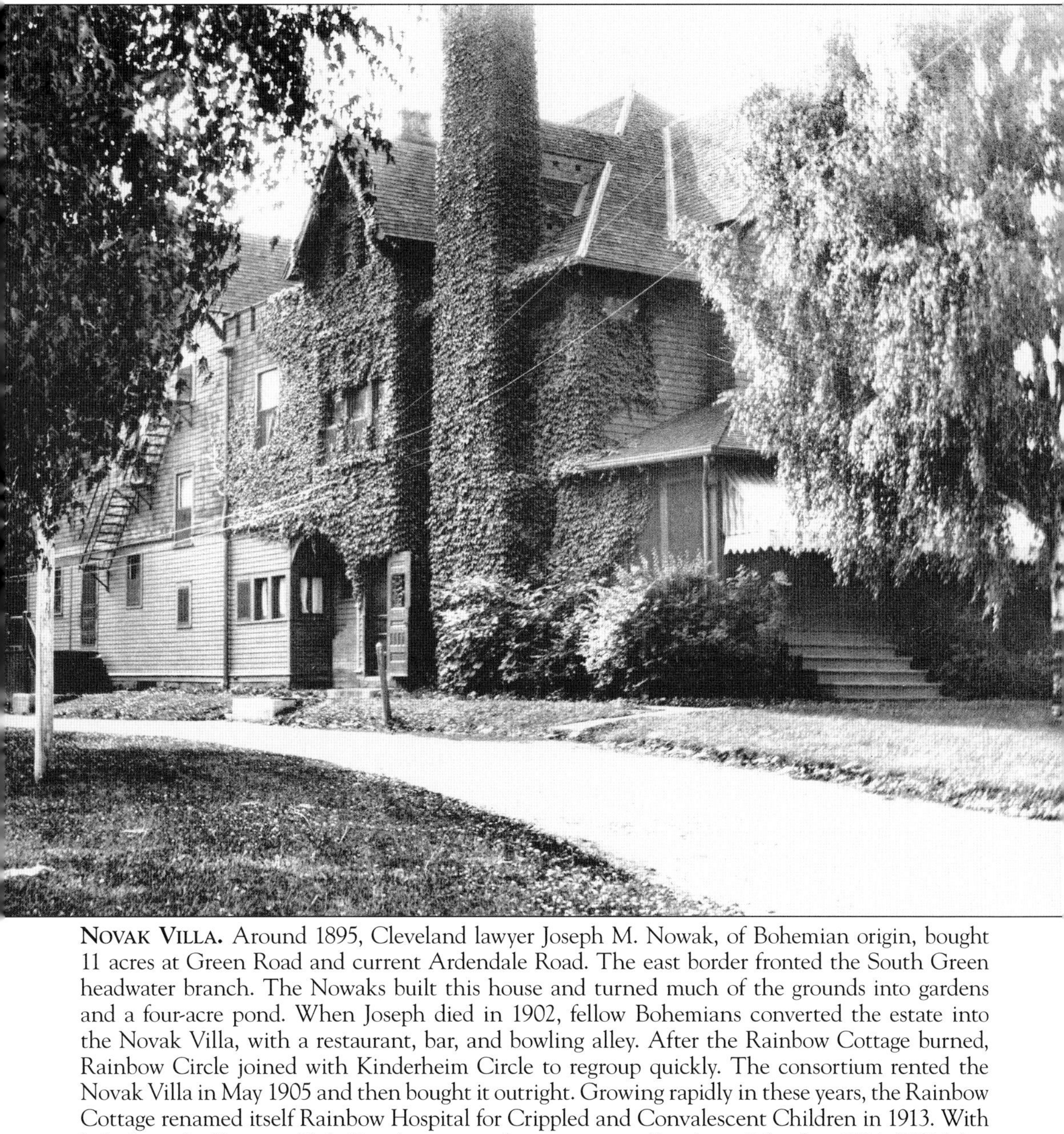

NOVAK VILLA. Around 1895, Cleveland lawyer Joseph M. Nowak, of Bohemian origin, bought 11 acres at Green Road and current Ardendale Road. The east border fronted the South Green headwater branch. The Nowaks built this house and turned much of the grounds into gardens and a four-acre pond. When Joseph died in 1902, fellow Bohemians converted the estate into the Novak Villa, with a restaurant, bar, and bowling alley. After the Rainbow Cottage burned, Rainbow Circle joined with Kinderheim Circle to regroup quickly. The consortium rented the Novak Villa in May 1905 and then bought it outright. Growing rapidly in these years, the Rainbow Cottage renamed itself Rainbow Hospital for Crippled and Convalescent Children in 1913. With help from the Kiwanis Club, Rainbow opened its innovative Bingham School in 1924. (UHA.)

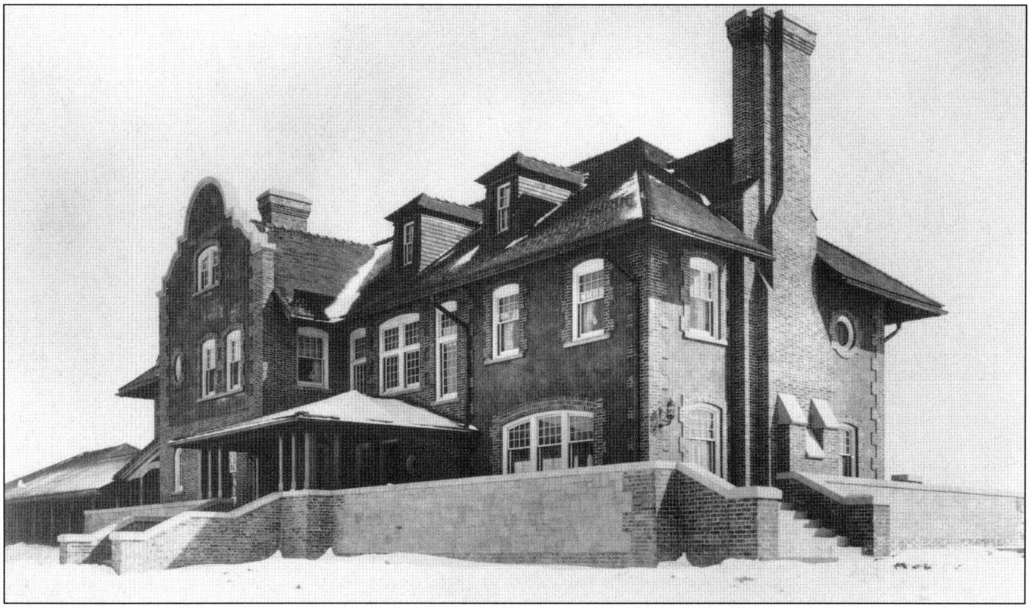

Chestnut Hills. Henry Pickands inherited the wealth and work of Pickands-Mather, pioneers in Lakes shipping and mining. Eschewing the urban lifestyle, Pickands bought 25 acres on top of Chardon Hill in 1902. He loved and disparaged his municipal surroundings and had the resources to effect change. Pickands was elected Euclid Village's first mayor in 1903, and he self-funded many basic improvements. He built his baronial Flemish-style house in 1905. (EHS.)

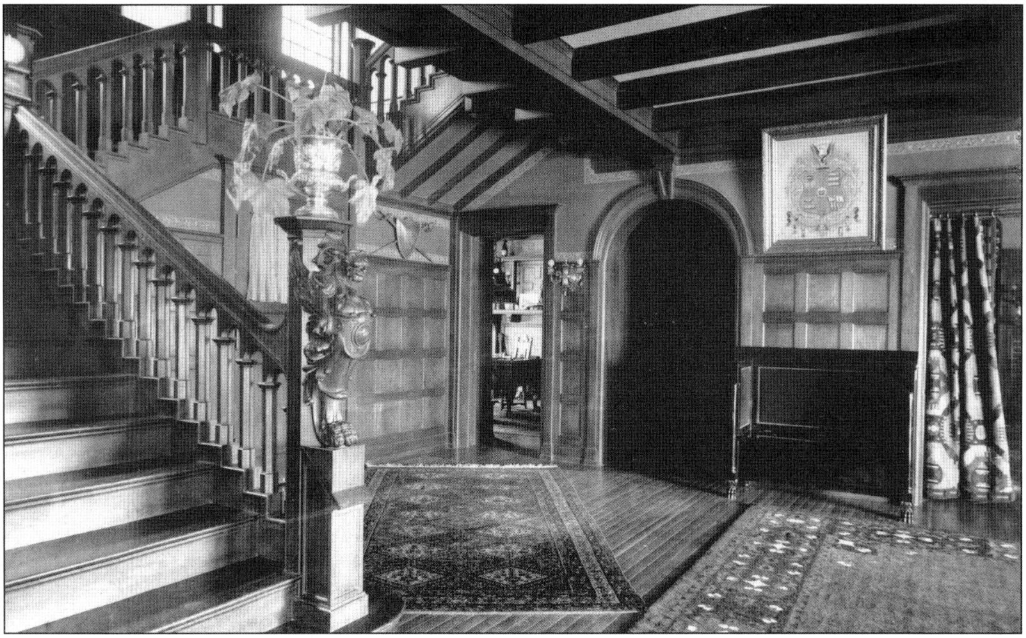

Chestnut Hills. Pickands hired engineer Whitford Jones to develop electrical generation and water systems fueled by locally tapped natural gas. Estate-grown produce went to large freezers and refrigerators. Kitchen and laundry appliances were fully electrified. The house had a complete security system, including room call bells and a burglar alarm. The grounds held northeast Ohio's first concrete in-ground swimming pool—all by 1910. (EHS.)

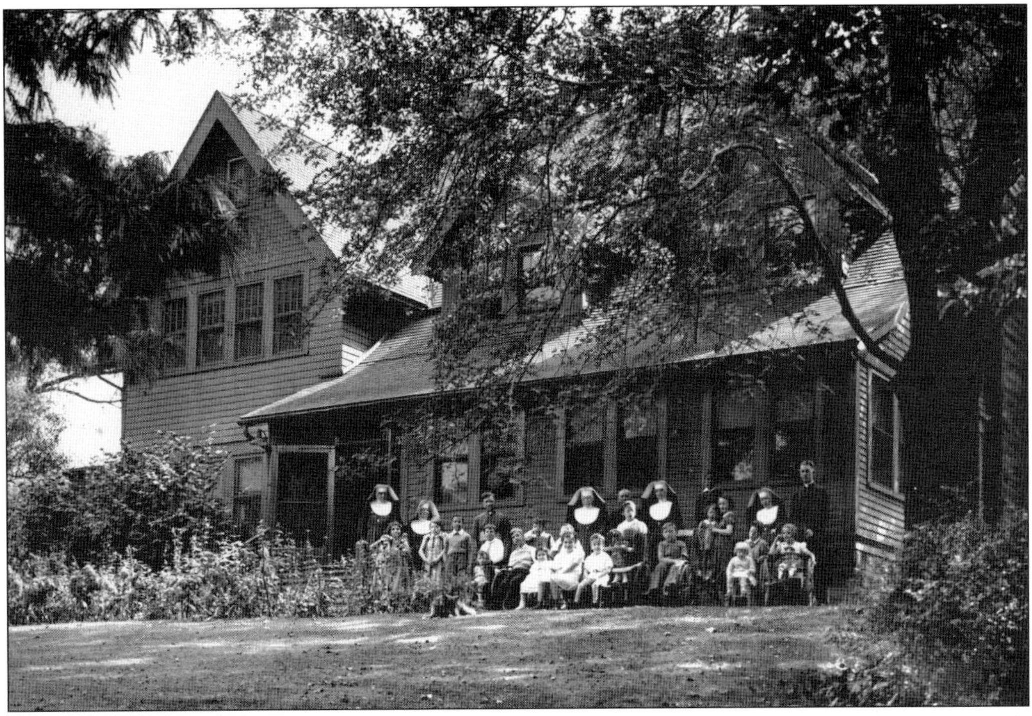

WEDDELL-GRASSELLI HOUSE. The Grasselli family began manufacturing chemicals in Italy during the 1440s. Caesar A. Grasselli built Grasselli Chemicals into a $30 million Cleveland giant. In 1904, Caesar and his wife, Johanna Ireland, bought the N. S. Weddell summer house above Euclid Avenue in Euclid. In 1922, honoring his deceased wife, Caesar refurbished the house and gave it to the Cleveland Catholic Diocese as "Rose-Mary, the Johanna Grasselli Home for Crippled Children." (RMC.)

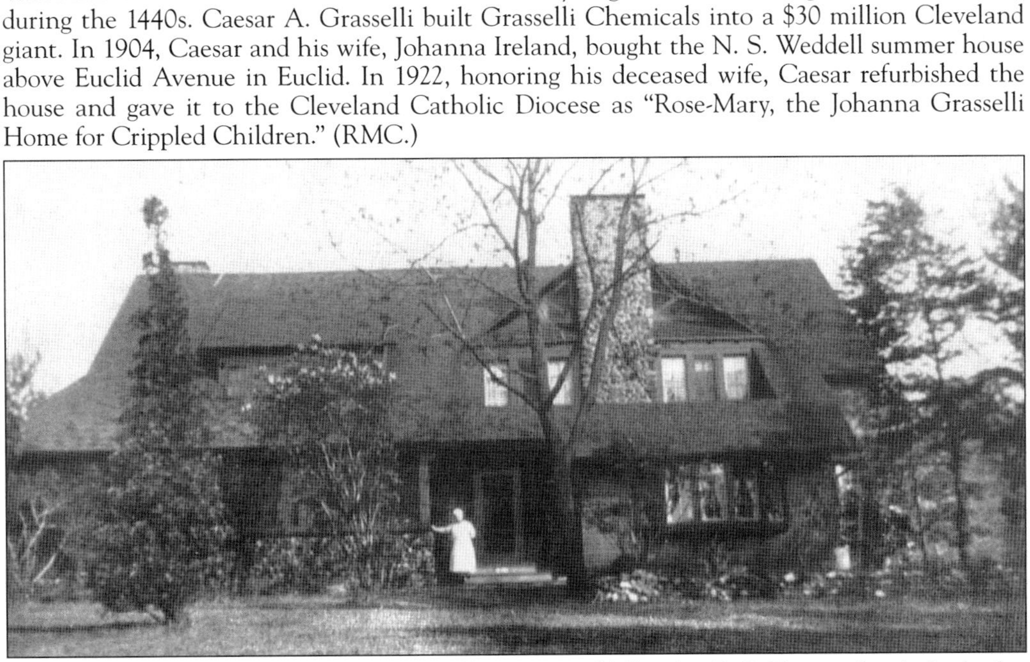

FENTON-DELANEY HOUSE. Like the neighboring Weddells, the E. P. Fenton family built this summer bungalow on the Portage escarpment in 1896, with the opening of the CP&E rail line. The chimney and front façade were made of granite erratics, cobblestones pushed south by glacial ice from the far north. In 1943, the resident Delaney family gave the estate to Rose-Mary, which then expanded its mission to include those with developmental disabilities. (RMC.)

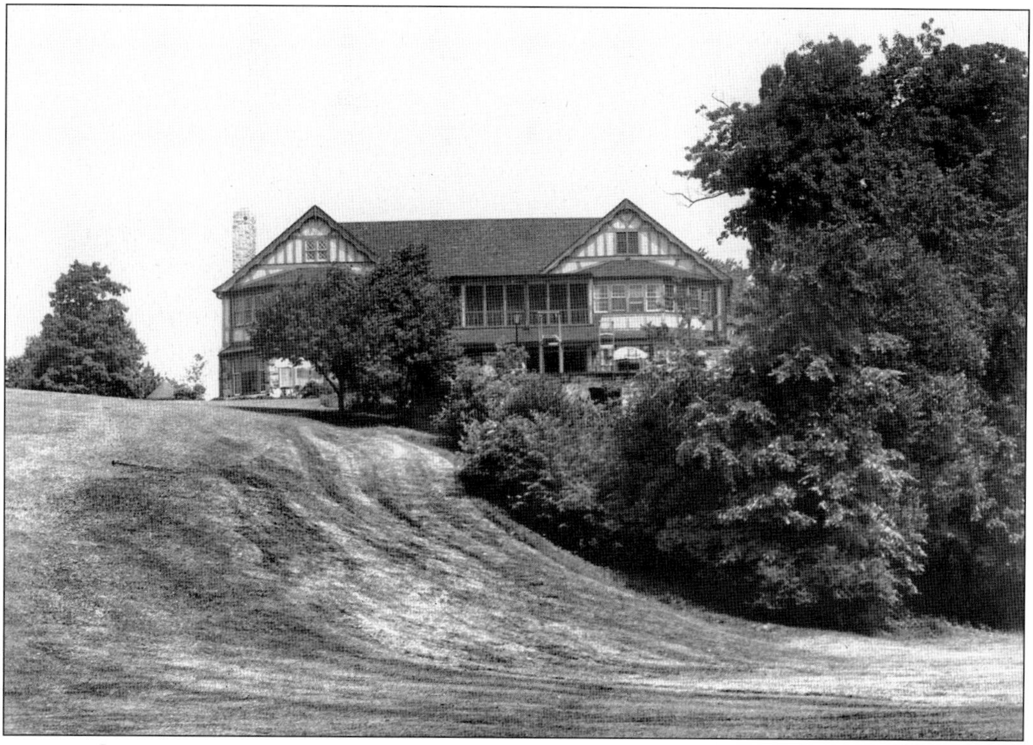

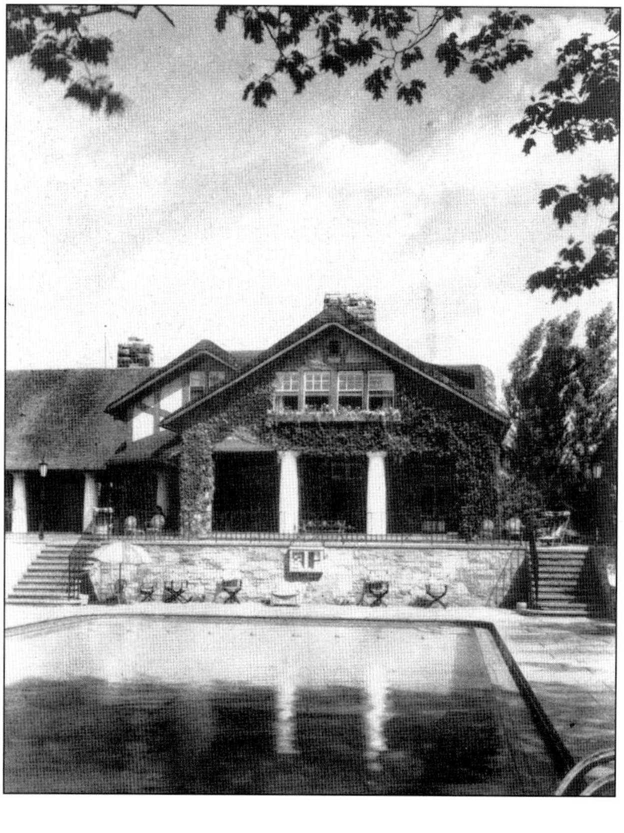

MAYFIELD COUNTRY CLUB. Organized in 1909 with more than 210 acres, Mayfield is the oldest and largest country club in the watershed. It grew out of the Euclid Club near the intersection of Cedar and Fairmount. W. H. "Bertie" Way selected the Euclid Township site straddling two headwater streams and then designed the golf course around them. Architect Frank B. Meade penned the clubhouse, which opened in 1911. The facility was damaged by fire and repaired in 1914 and then burned definitively in 1948. (CPL, CSU.)

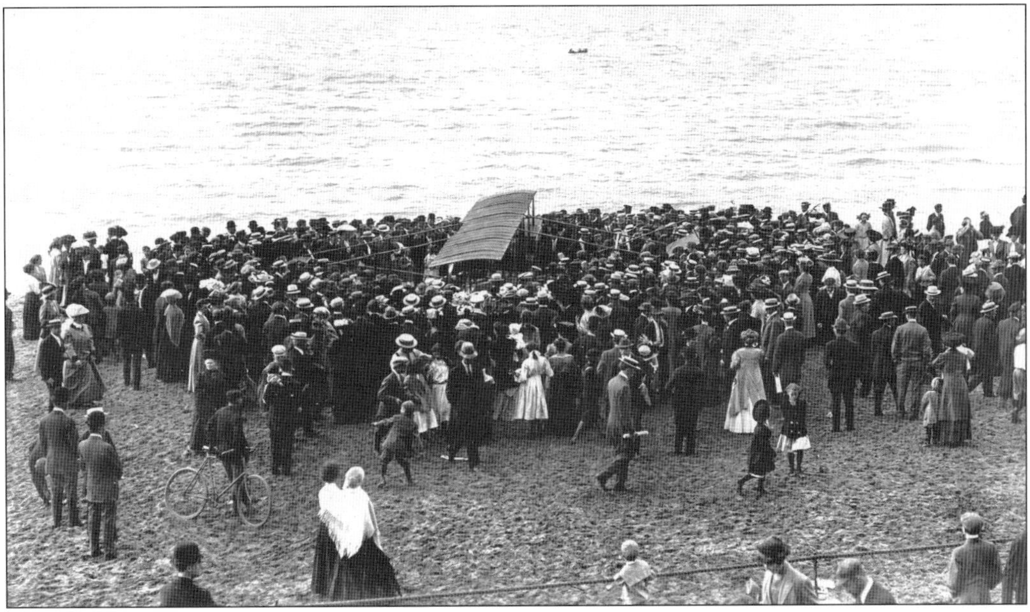

GLENN H. CURTISS. Seven years after the Wright brothers flew at Kitty Hawk, Cleveland's Glenn H. Curtiss set the record for over-water flight. On September 1, 1910, Curtiss took off from Euclid Beach and flew over Lake Erie for 60 miles to Cedar Point. He collected a $5,000 prize from the Cleveland Press. Curtiss went on to join with the Wright brothers to produce Curtiss-Wright aircraft. (CPL.)

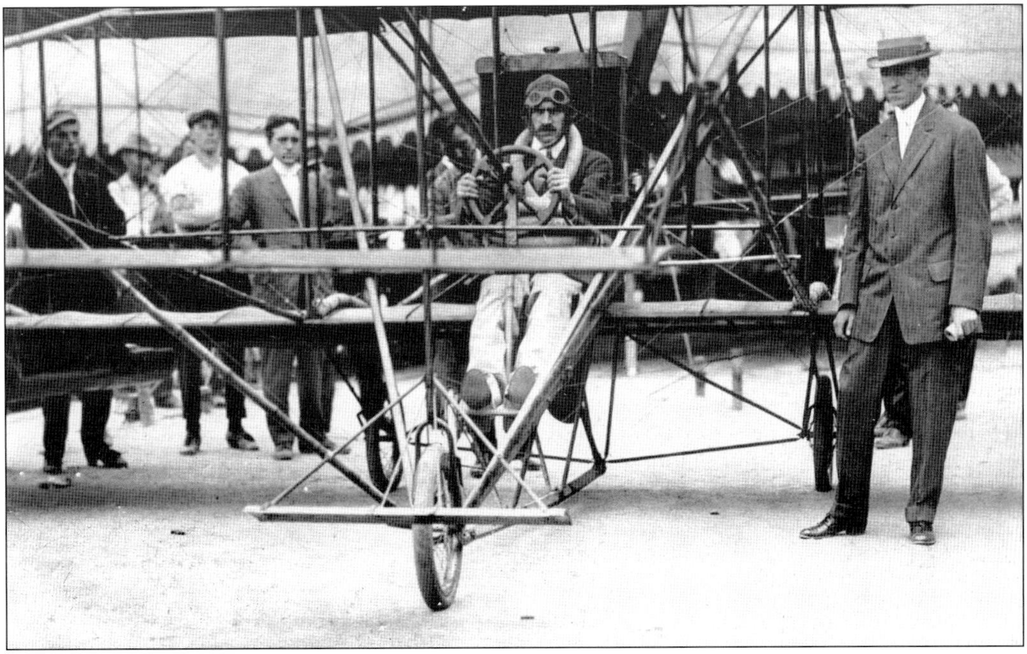

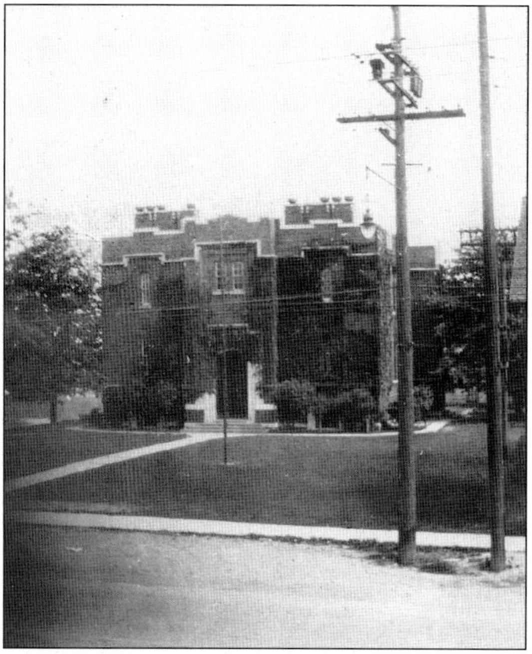

South Euclid High. By the second decade of the 20th century, the South Euclid hamlet was beginning to suburbanize separately from Euclid Village and Nottingham Villages to the north. In 1912, the township trustees built South Euclid High School to face Green Road, just south of Mayfield. The school was demolished in 1957, and the land was sold to commercial interests. (SEHS.)

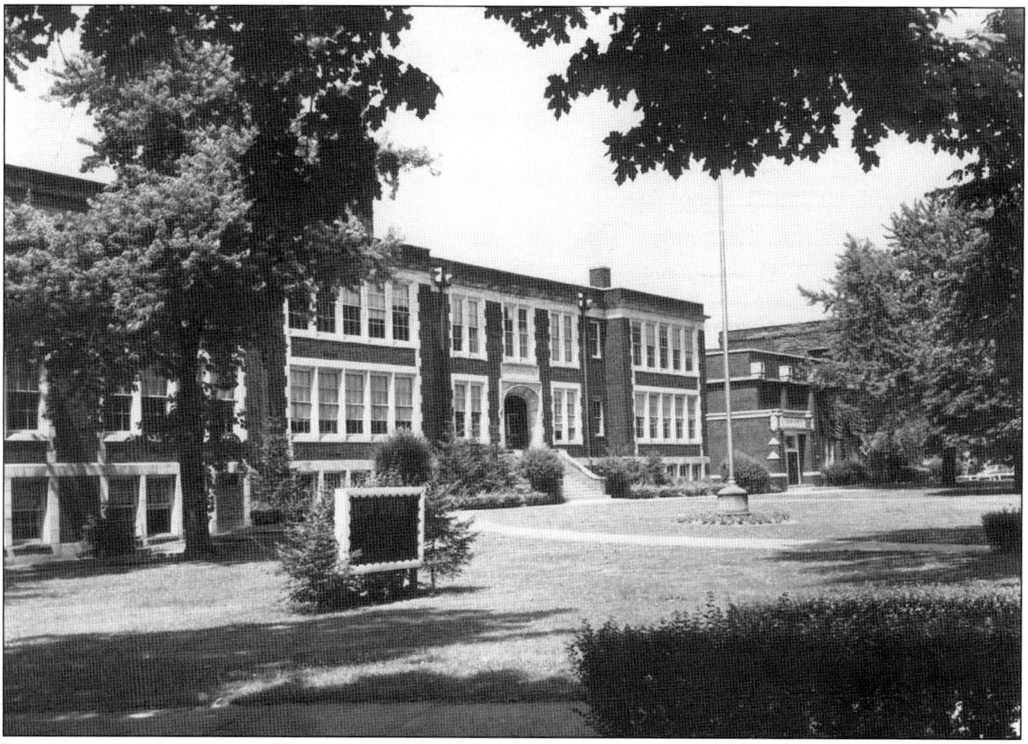

Central High. In 1913, Euclid Village built Central High School at Euclid Creek. Central was the twin to Shore High on the lakeshore. Central received numerous additions over the years, including a magnificent auditorium. Central became a junior high in 1949, when Euclid High arose outside the watershed. Central was considered too big and outmoded in 1967, when it was replaced with the Central Middle School. (EHS.)

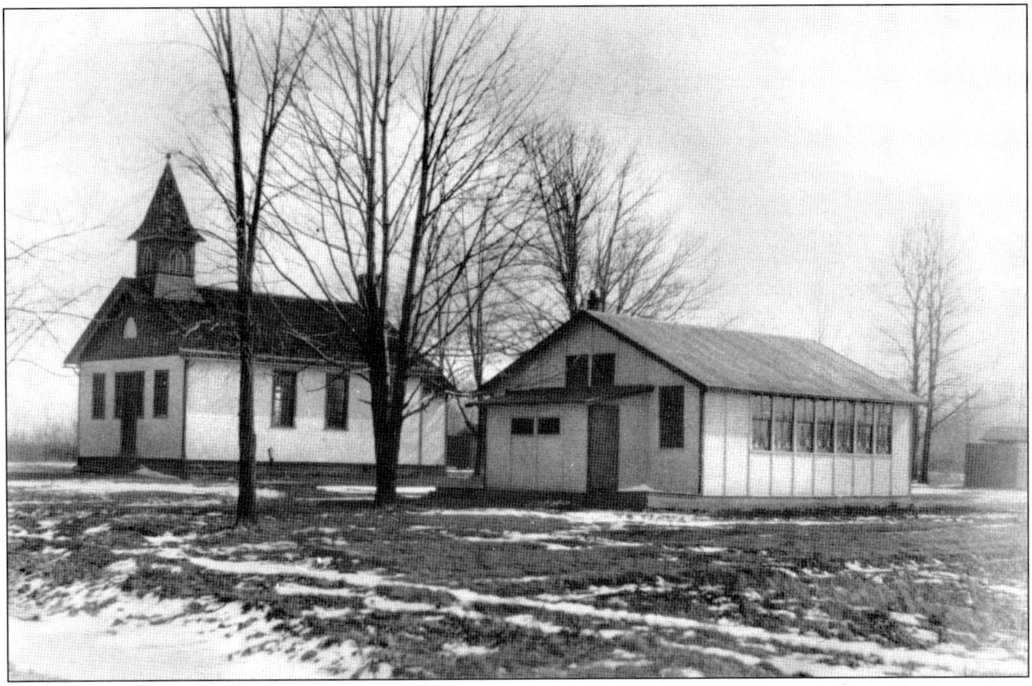

RIEDEL SCHOOL. Not much is known about early schools in western Mayfield Township. The earliest surviving photograph depicts the Riedel school, built in 1900 at 5826 Highland Road across from the current municipal complex. The photograph also shows the unheated, portable annex that was quite unpopular with students and teachers. The Riedel school closed in 1926. (MTHS.)

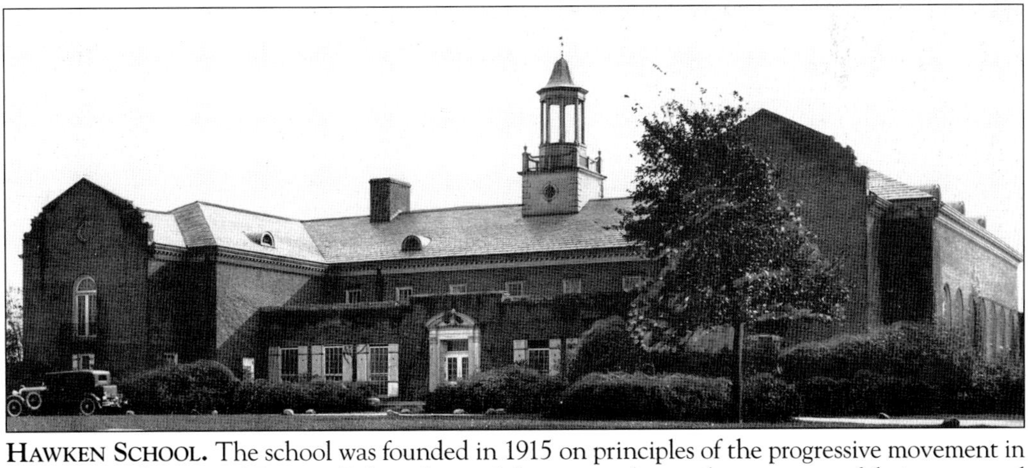

HAWKEN SCHOOL. The school was founded in 1915 on principles of the progressive movement in education. Chester and Frances Bolton donated the site on the northeast corner of their estate and funded the building, later named Bolton Hall. Today, Bolton Hall houses the library, lower and middle-school classrooms, and several administrative and academic offices. (CPL.)

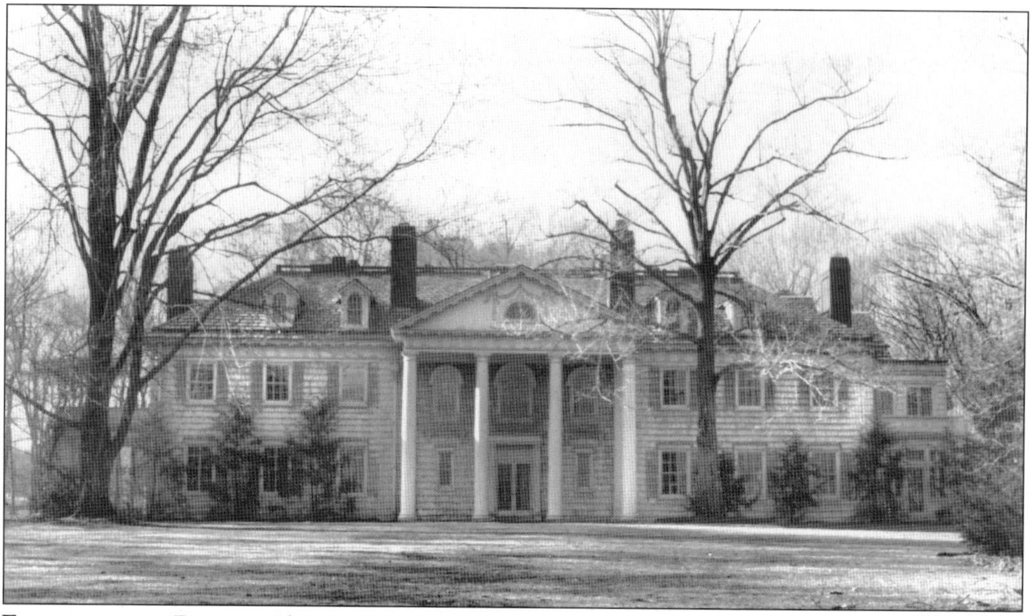

FRANCHESTER PLACE. Chester C. and Frances P. Bolton built this superlative Georgian Colonial–style house in 1917. It was designed by Sanger, Prentice, Architects. One living room contains the paneling from a 17th-century English manor house parlor. When TRW acquired the Bolton estate in 1982, the house was used to host corporate events and guests. Franchester Place was listed on the National Register of Historic Places in 1986. (Rudy Tretera.)

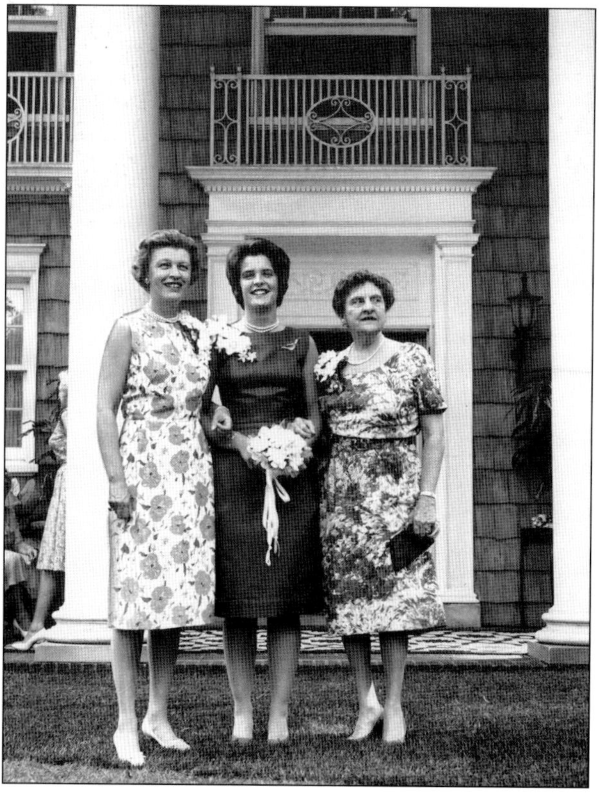

CONGRESSWOMAN BOLTON. Frances Payne Bingham Bolton took over her husband's U.S. Congressional seat upon his death in 1939. She held that seat continuously through 1968. Bolton served on the House Foreign Affairs Committee from 1941 and also legislated on education and working conditions for nurses. At Franchester Place in 1962, Bolton poses with daughter-in-law Adelaide Bolton (left) and debutant granddaughter Barbara Bolton. (CPL.)

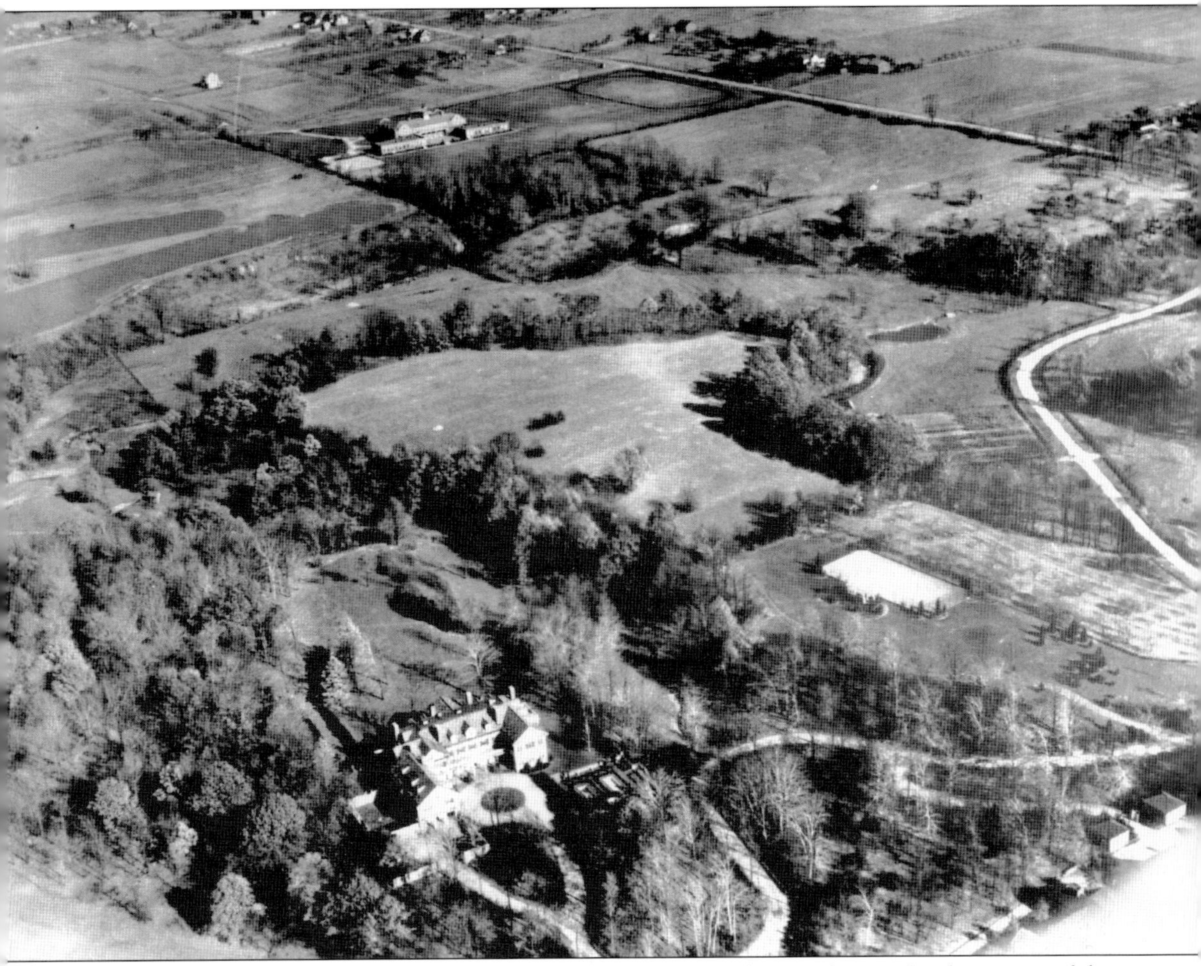

Bolton Estate. In this early-1920s aerial photograph, Franchester Place is the showpiece of the 55-acre Bolton estate. Hawken School appears in the mid-ground, on the northeast corner of the estate. Just out of view at lower right is the Blossom house, now the site of Legacy Village. Euclid Creek's principal headwater, the Acacia branch, traverses the estate in mid-ground. (WRHS.)

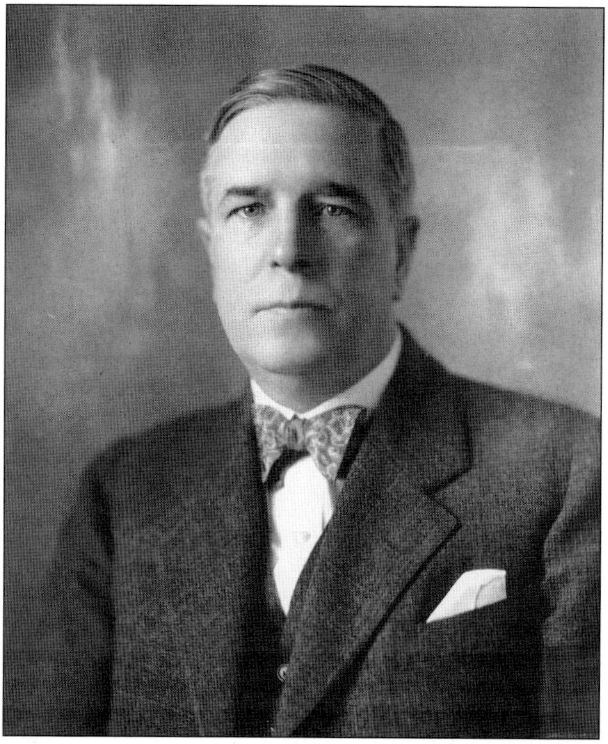

Charles K. Arter. With degrees from Amherst College and Harvard Law School, Charles K. Arter (1875–1957) began a distinguished Cleveland law career in 1901. He also served on the boards of Amherst, Allegheny, and Baldwin-Wallace Colleges; the Cleveland Welfare Federation and the Community Chest; and the First Methodist Church and the Church of the Savior. He was president of the Cleveland Chamber of Commerce in the late 1930s. (CPL.)

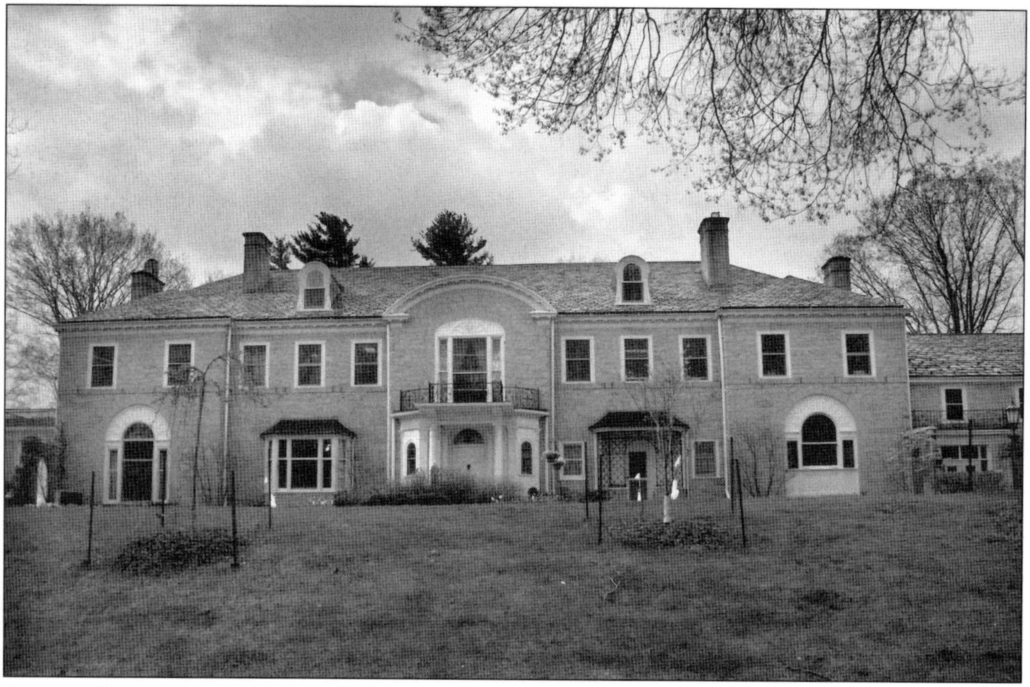

Arter House. In 1913, Arter built this stunning Georgian Colonial–style house on current Clubside Road in Lyndhurst. The house sits on the north bank of a small Euclid Creek headwater. Upon his death in 1957, Arter's heirs sold the house to the Sisters of Notre Dame, who then installed their Julie Billiart School there. (Patrice Havreberg.)

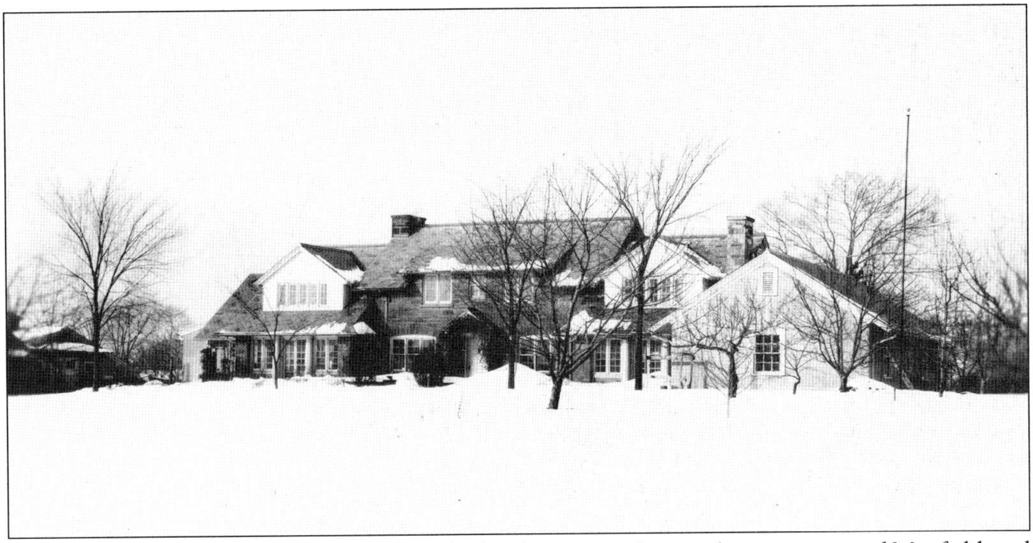

Ford House. In 1913, Horatio Ford built this house on the northwest corner of Mayfield and Richmond Roads. The California bungalow style was making its way east in the second decade of the 20th century. Ford's house shows bungalow influence—on a massive scale—in its long roof slopes punctuated by dormers, and in its use of rusticated local stone for its main walls and chimneys. The house was demolished in the mid-1950s. (SEHS.)

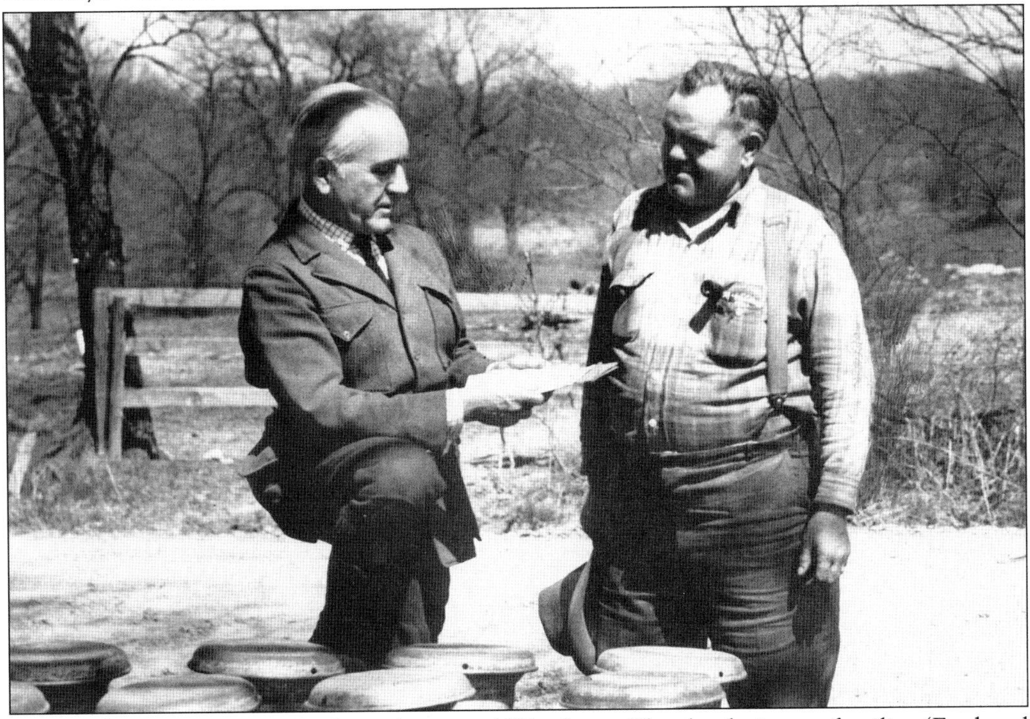

Horatio Ford. Horatio Ford was born in 1881 of two Cleveland pioneer families (Ford and Thorp). With degrees from Yale and Western Reserve University Law, Ford began banking in 1906. In 1910, he helped organize the Cleveland area Boy Scouts. Later in life, Ford became interested in forestry and horses. Here he supervises his 1,500-acre Whitfield Woods in Middlefield, one of Ohio's first tree farms. (CSU.)

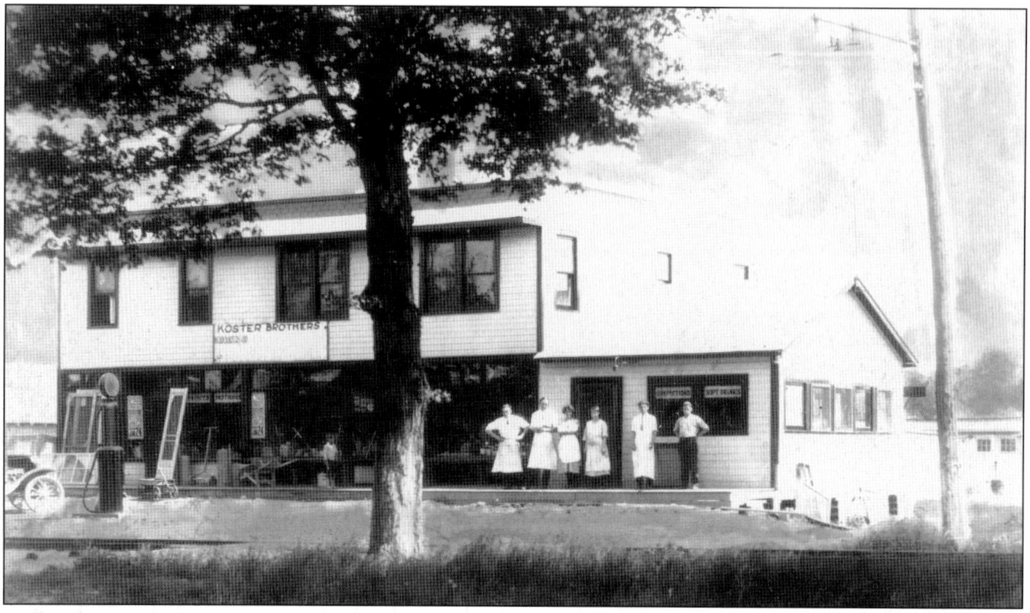

KOSTER BROTHERS. The Koster family opened its hardware store just as automobiles were beginning to populate Mayfield Road. The building itself retains aspects of the Western Reserve–type "upright-and-wing" dwelling. In this photograph, taken during the mid-1920s, the Cleveland and Eastern tracks are visible in the foreground along with an automobile gasoline pump just behind. (MTHS.)

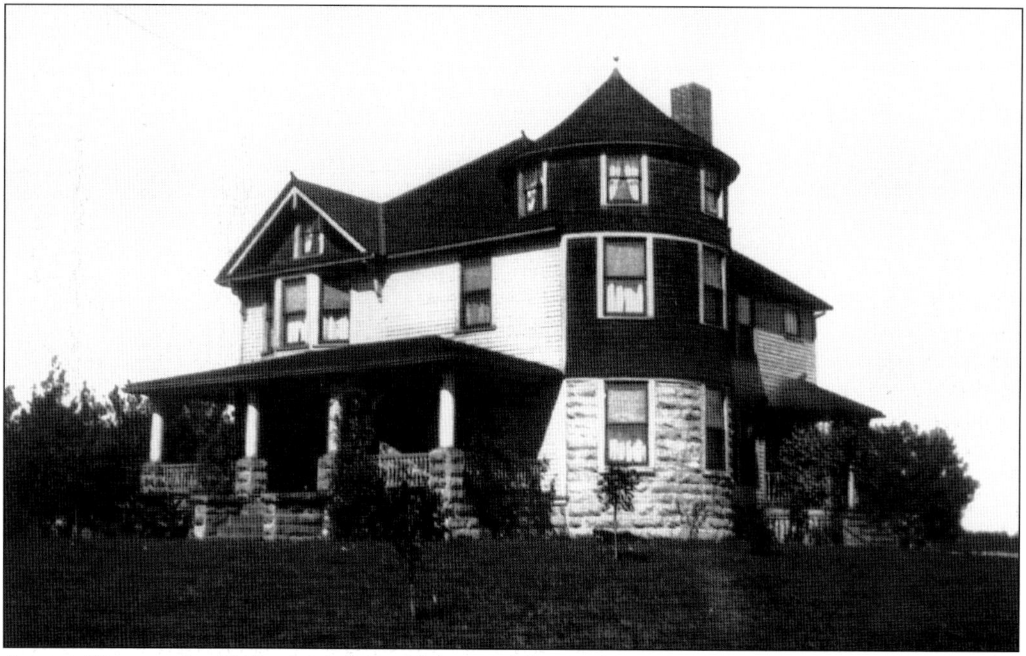

AKINS HOUSE. In 1848, Asahel P. Akins and his wife, Melissa Miner, settled at Whitings Corners (current Mayfield and Lander). Around 1898, son Horton P. Akins built this house just west of the corners, at current 5737 Mayfield Road. The house, still standing, features Euclid bluestone masonry on the ground floor. (MTHS.)

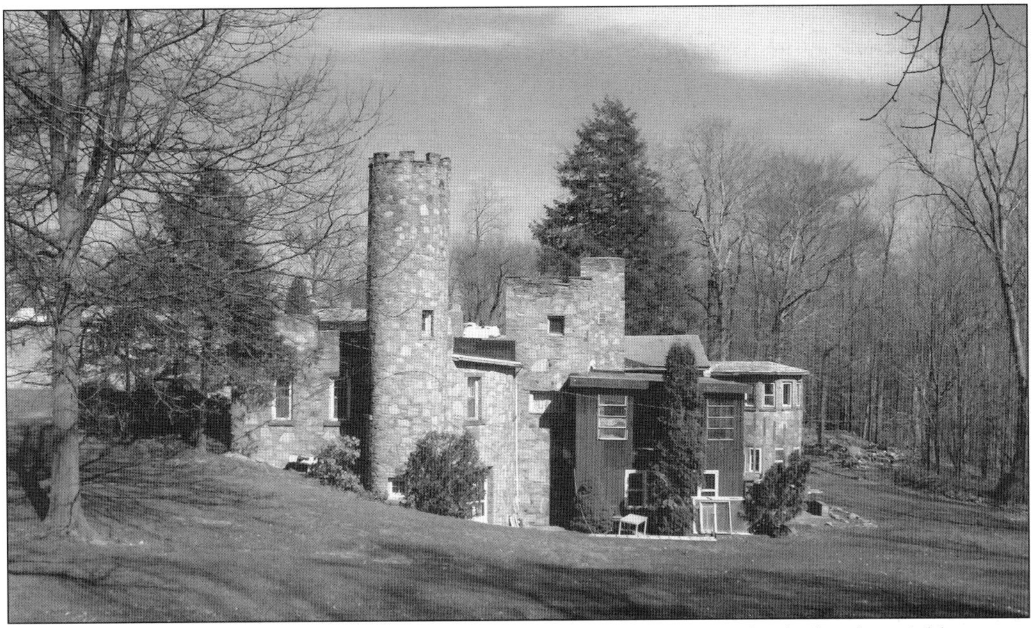

THE CASTLE. Englishman and Shakespearean scholar John Truman built this fanciful house in the second decade of the 20th century. It sits precipitously on the north bank of Euclid Creek's east branch, addressed on Chardonview Road, just west of Richmond. Truman used his own labor and that of servants to quarry stones from the bluestone outcrop on either side of the site. The Sommich family of Richmond Heights later owned the building. (Roy Larick.)

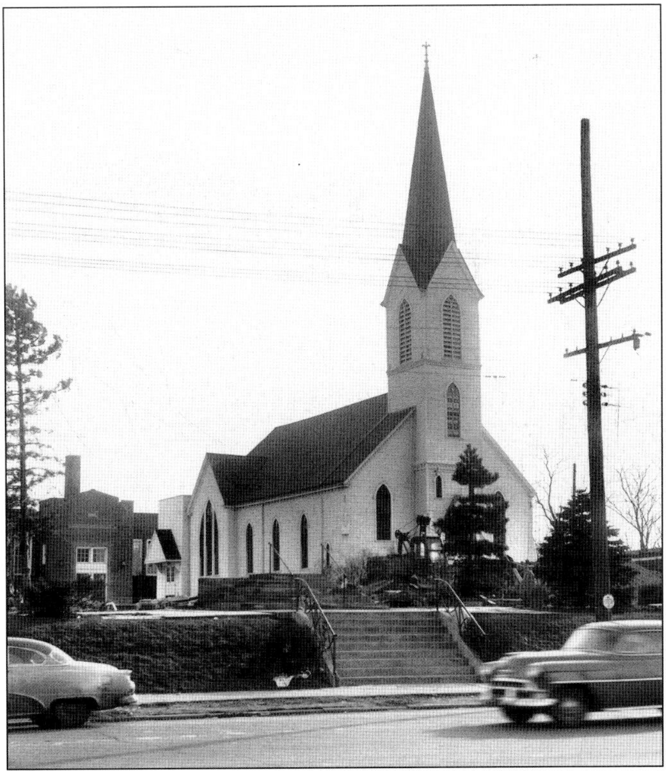

ST. JOHN LUTHERAN. Euclid Township's early Germans organized the St. John congregation (Evangelical Lutheran) in 1853. A meetinghouse and school were built on the north side of Mayfield Road east of Green. New buildings were erected at current 4386 Mayfield in 1862 and again in 1894. This photograph was taken in 1955 upon relocating the 1894 church back some from Mayfield. The building has since been heavily changed. (CPL.)

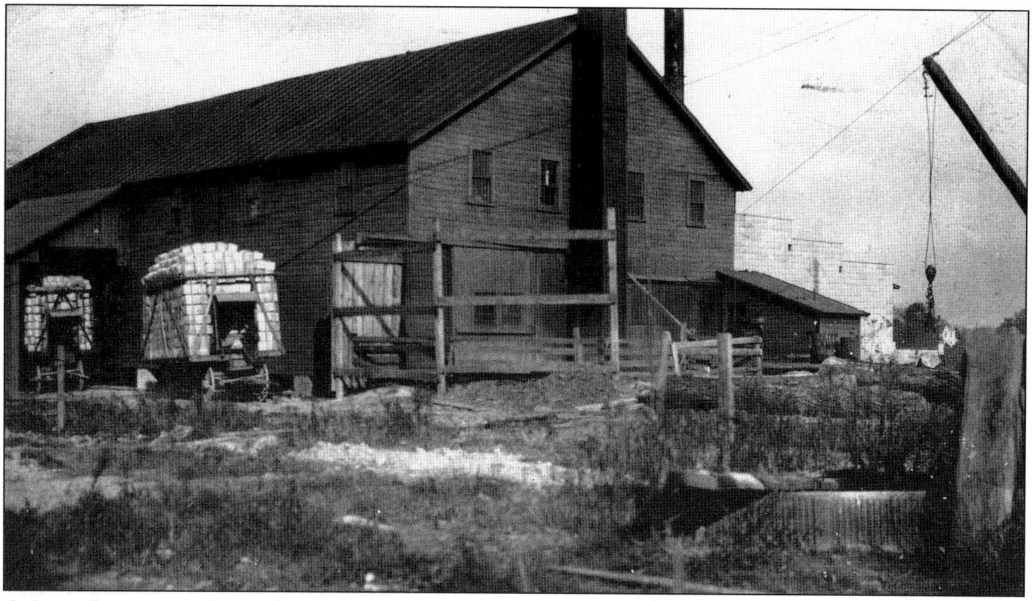

GRAPE BASKETS. The table grape and wine industries demanded specialized equipment. Baskets, for example, were needed in great quantities for picking and shipping. The Stray family operated a steam-powered basket factory at Euclid Creek. The Prasse and Reeker families, whose facilities are shown here, had similar businesses in South Euclid. (SEHS.)

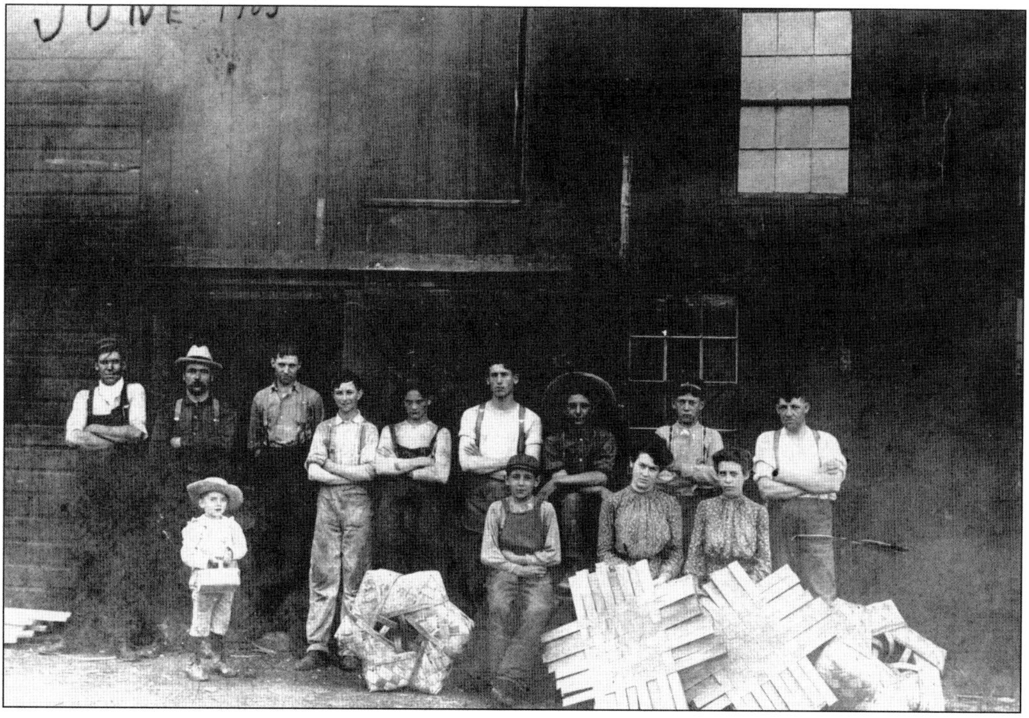

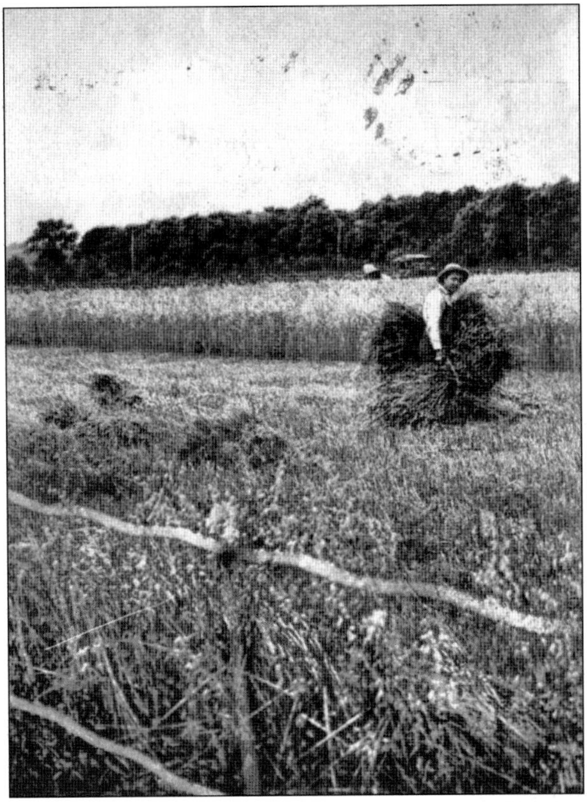

HARVESTS. Not all watershed agriculture was devoted to vineyards. These two shots show haying and threshing in South Euclid, typical scenes anywhere on the plateau in Euclid and Mayfield Townships before 1920. In the era of steam threshing, from 1890 to 1920, the equipment was expensive and cumbersome. Teams were needed. The lower photograph shows a steam team working on the Ernest Prasse farm. For many years, the steam team of Shebanek, Trebisky and Marous would be on the road for weeks at a time doing itinerant work. (NHS, SEHS.)

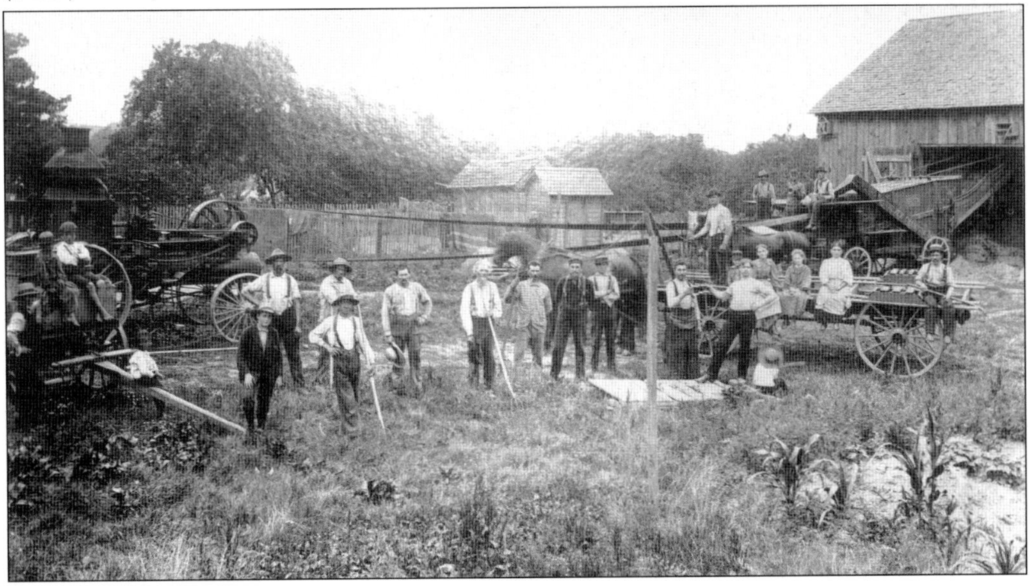

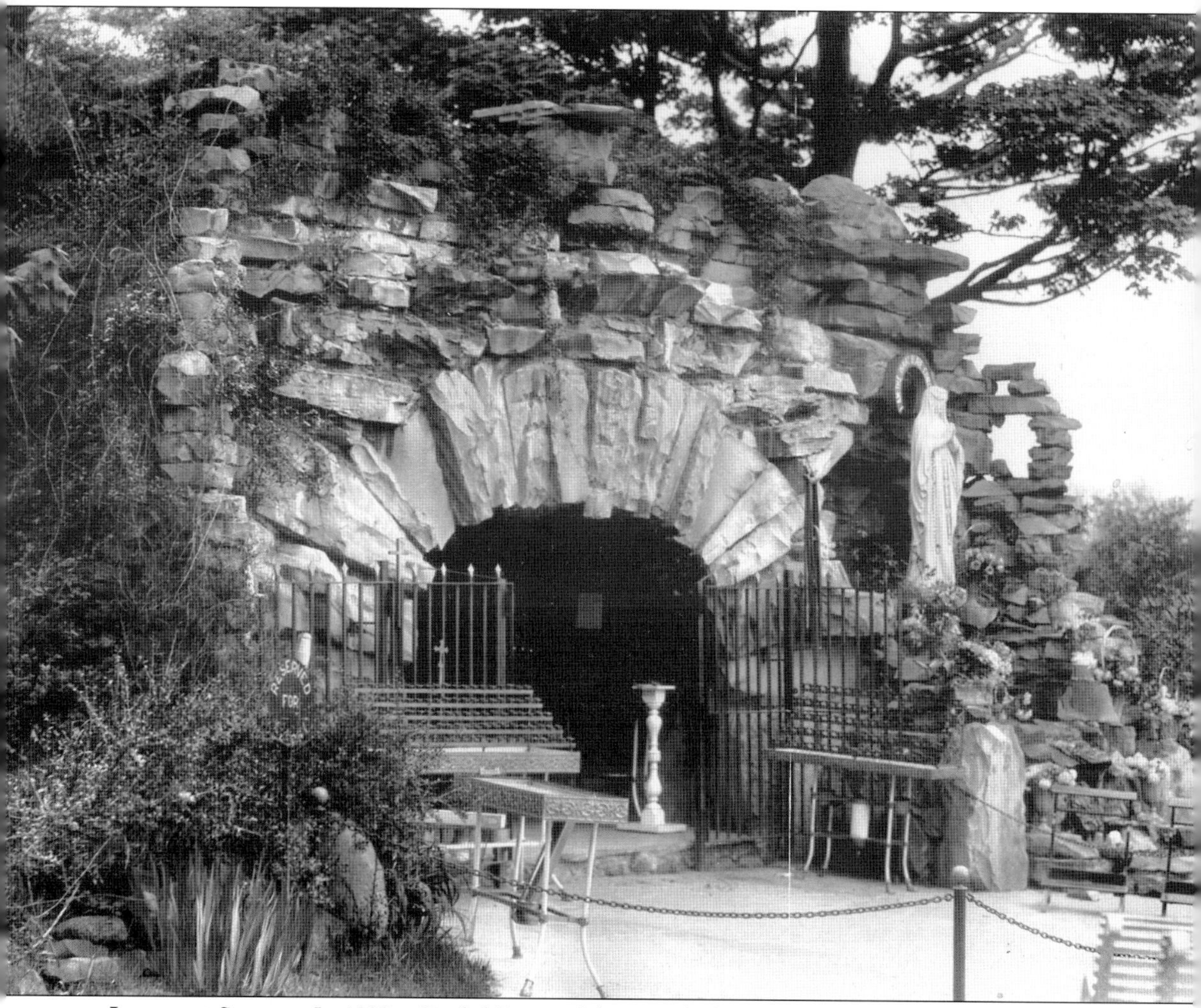

LOURDES SHRINE. In 1922, a Euclid Sister of the Good Shepherd made a pilgrimage to Lourdes, France. She had a vision for a similar shrine at home. The Euclid chapter began its own monument a year later at "Providence Heights, Ohio." They employed local masons to assemble massive bluestone slabs into a grotto over a natural spring on the old Harms property. (CPL.)

Five

AUTO-MOBILE
1918–1962

By the end of the second decade of the 20th century, automobiles had transformed life in the watershed. In short, middle-class city dwellers were driving to Euclid Creek's green space in search of an American Dream home. The old Native American trails now constituted an extensive county road system and, in opening hundreds of residential streets, a truly dense transportation network was emerging. Suburban development also brought the end of agriculture. By 1920, profit from selling farm fields outsized any possible return from cultivating the land.

Automobiles and airplanes developed together early in this era, and Cleveland was a center for both. In 1918, Glen L. Martin moved from California to set up aircraft production in Nottingham Village. His famous MB-2 bomber was made there for 10 years. Martin Field was Cleveland's transcontinental airport until Hopkins was dedicated in 1929. The aircraft industry lingered on St. Clair Avenue through the Depression and rose to importance again during World War II.

Amidst the rush to purchase and subdivide in the second decade of the 20th century, the Cleveland Metropolitan Park Board acquired the creek's west branch gorge lands from a small number of private owners, including the Welch and Pickands families. The Euclid Creek Reservation, then billed as Cleveland's "Grand Canyon," quickly became the most used park in the four-county system.

Euclid's vineyards and wineries suffered a deathblow with national Prohibition in 1920. The Harms Brothers sold everything to the Sisters of the Good Shepherd, a French order recently installed in the United States. The sisters quickly converted the winery into a convent and school, and soon added the Our Lady of Lourdes national shrine. In 1922, Caesar Grasselli donated his country estate on Euclid Avenue to the Cleveland Catholic Diocese. The Sisters of the Humility of Mary then operated it as the Rose-Mary Home for Crippled and Convalescent Children.

Estate building slowed as middle-class suburban development accelerated. William E. Telling began the watershed's last grand structure in 1928. Nearby, the Sisters of Notre Dame bought 50 acres of farmland next door to Rainbow Cottage. They opened the magnificent Notre Dame College building in 1928.

The Great Depression then brought down several of the older streamside estates—and where one falls another may rebuild. Telling suffered heavily but held on until his death in 1938. His family could not, however, and by 1951, the Cuyahoga County Library had moved in. The Sisters of St. Joseph bought most of the Pickands estate in 1942 and used it for their Mount St. Joseph Nursing Home. The Rose-Mary Home received the gift of a neighboring summer estate in 1943. The Depression also brought temporary economic recovery institutions, such as Camp Euclid in the Euclid Creek Reservation.

Despite the slow economy, the middle class kept arriving to take up new homes on new side streets. Tudor Revival was among the more popular architectural styles. Supplying water to the new developments was always a problem. During the mid-1930s, the Cleveland Water Department decided on a lake intake line and filtration plant to serve the burgeoning East Side. A large amount of land was purchased in the Euclid Creek lake plain floodplain. It took another 10 years to complete the Nottingham Water Intake and Filtration Plant.

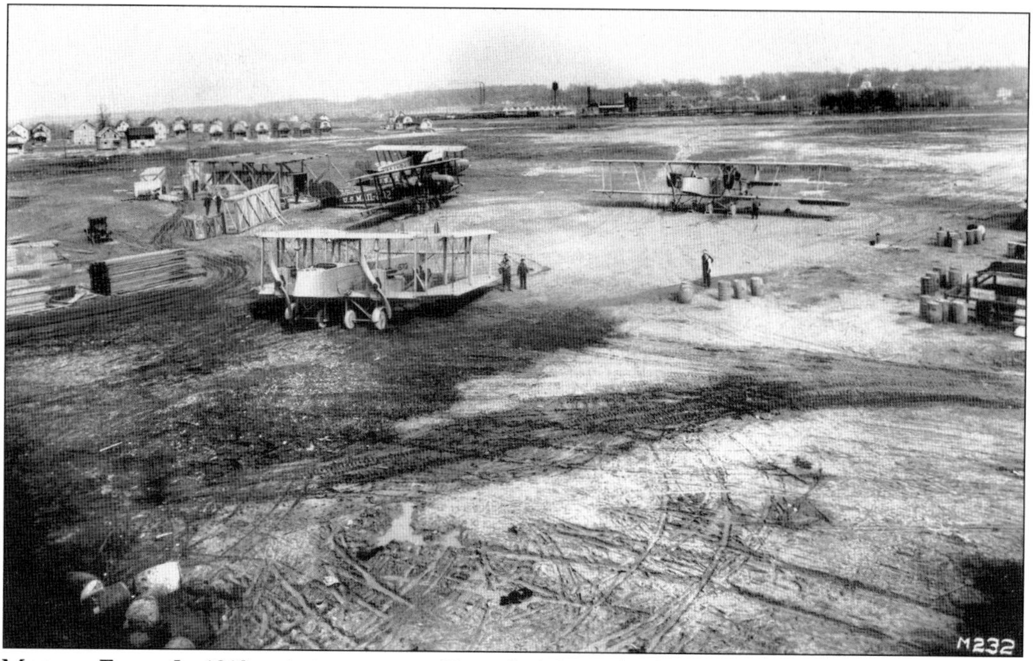

MARTIN FIELD. In 1918, aviation pioneer Glenn L. Martin built a factory at 16800 St. Clair. Here, the famous Martin MB-2 was manufactured for military, U.S. Postal Service, and commercial use. The first truly transcontinental airmail flights began in September 1920, with Martin MB-2s making their Cleveland stop at Martin Field. When Martin moved to Baltimore in 1929, the Great Lakes Aircraft Company operated a portion of the facility into the mid-1930s. (WRHS, CPL.)

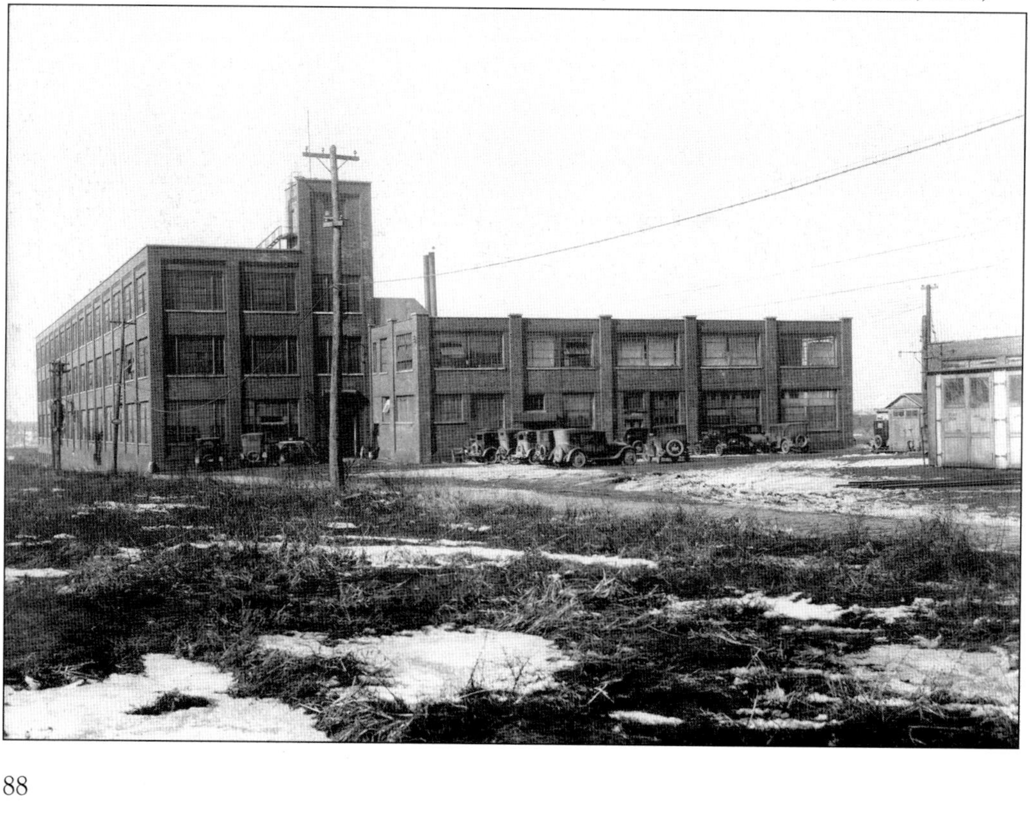

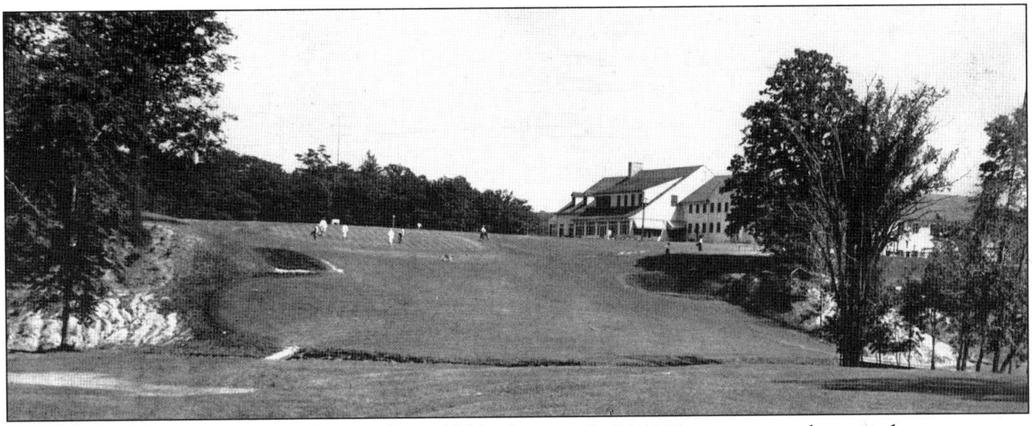

Acacia Country Club. Opened in 1921, Acacia held 300 acres on the northwest corner of Richmond and Cedar. The membership was originally limited to Masons. Donald Ross designed the course around Euclid Creek's main headwater, which neatly bisects the property. The clubhouse opened in 1922 and was expanded in 1963. Acacia now encompasses about 175 acres. (CSU.)

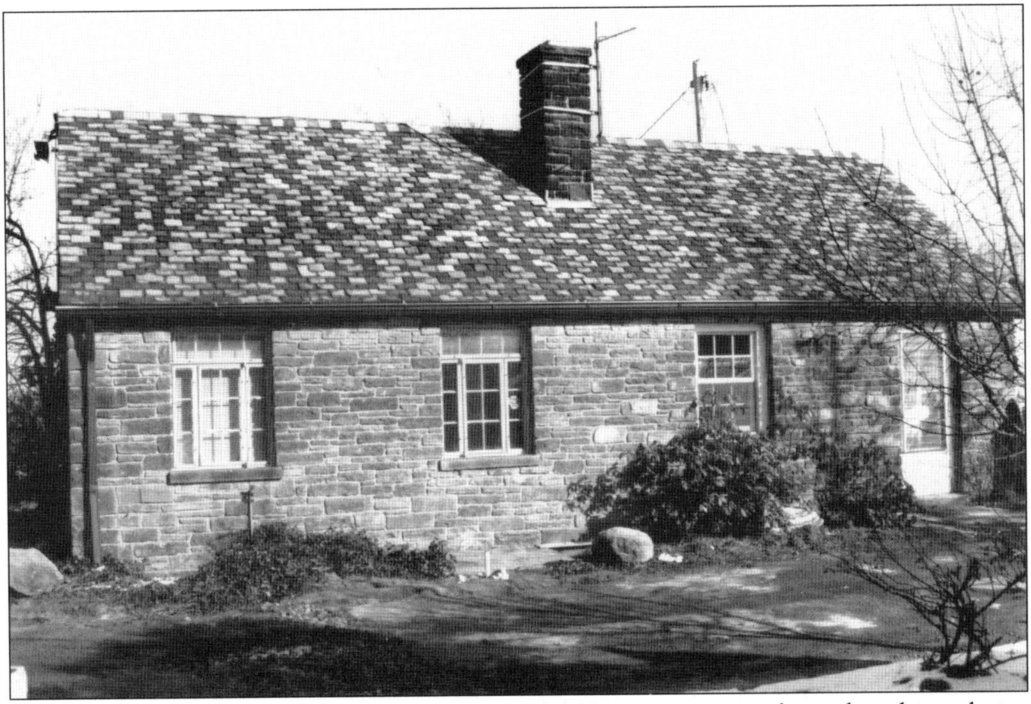

Bluestone Cottage. As it was expensive, Euclid bluestone was rarely used as the exclusive building material in local structures. In the early days, bluestone was used mostly for basements and foundations. During the middle-class suburban development between about 1910 and 1930, the stone was used locally for accenting. This 1920s bluestone cottage is therefore unique. It is located on Wilson Mills Road in South Euclid. (SEHS.)

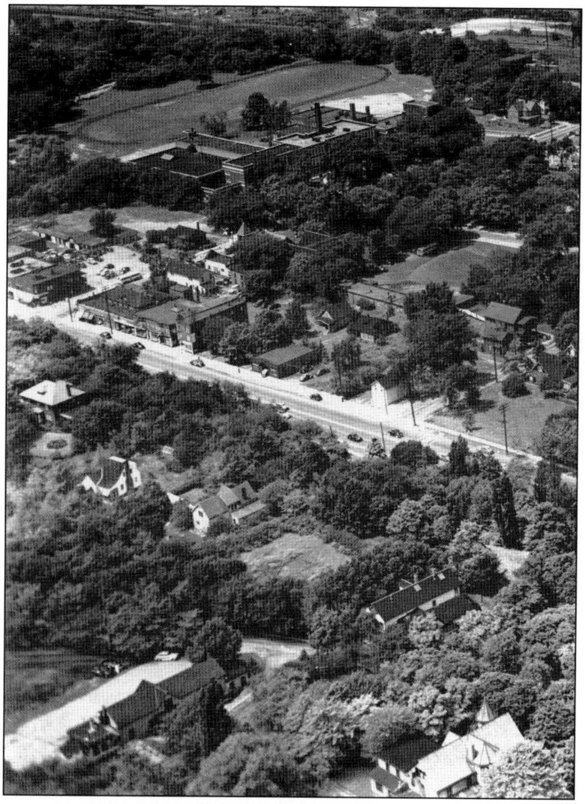

SISTERS OF THE GOOD SHEPHERD. In 1920, the Harms Brothers sold their winery to the Sisters of the Good Shepard, a French order then recently established in the United States. The sisters converted the structures into a convent school and shrine. The 1949 aerial view shows the three largest buildings: the 1890s towered residence (lower right), the teahouse (lower left), and the 1867 Harms house (with long roof). (EHS.)

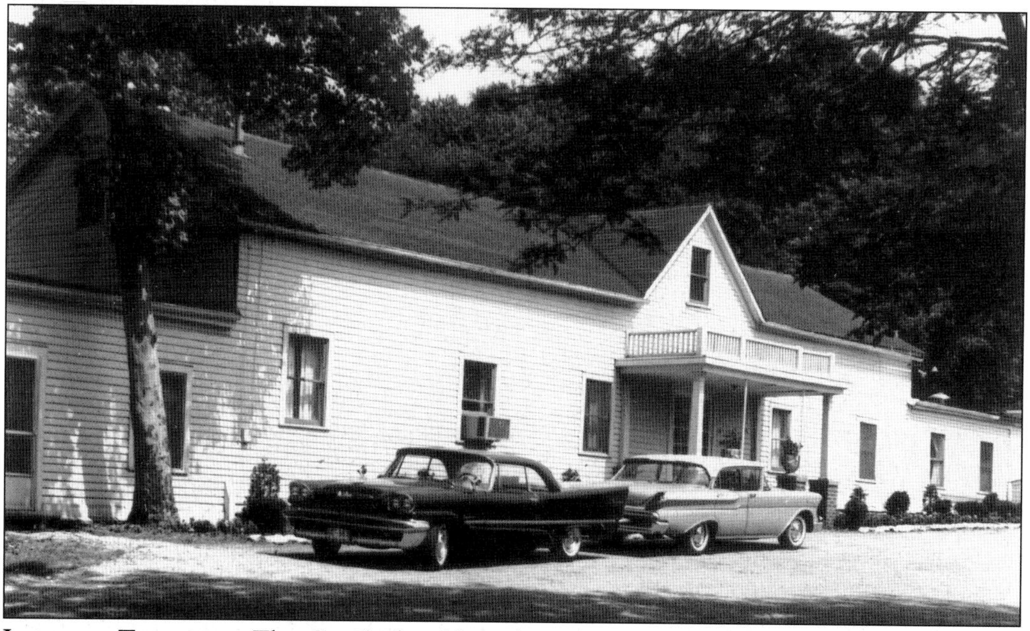

LOURDES TEAHOUSE. The Our Lady of Lourdes grotto and shrine opened in 1925. It was immensely popular. The Good Shepherd Sisters soon built this teahouse to provide refreshment for pilgrims and visitors. In 1953, a few years before this photograph was taken, the Sisters of the Most Holy Trinity bought the entire facility. (SMHT.)

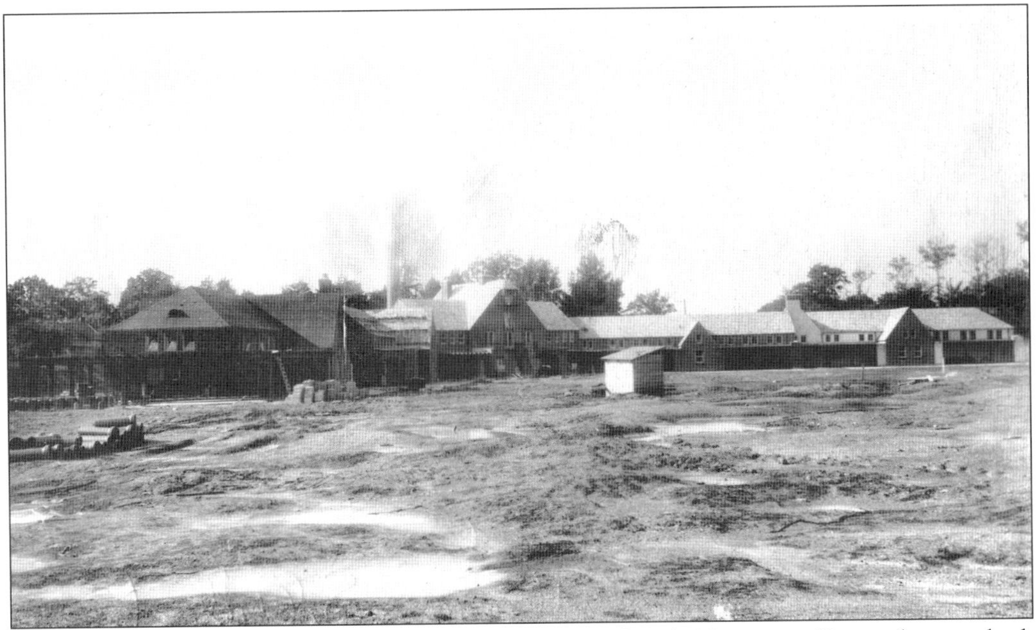

RAINBOW HOSPITAL. In 1927, Rainbow Hospital united with University Hospitals to embark on a $6 million capital campaign. A completely new facility thus arose near Ardendale in 1928. Architects Warner, McCormack, and Mitchell designed a "great home-like cottage" to accommodate 100 children in specialized care. Wards and hospital operations were set on the ground floor so as all patients could be taken outside in good weather. For nearly 40 years in South Euclid, Rainbow maintained high standards of care for children with bone infections, rickets, poliomyelitis, rheumatic fever, tuberculosis, and other crippling conditions. Below, patients and staff pose next to a Bell helicopter chartered for patients' thrills in 1951. (CPL, SEHS.)

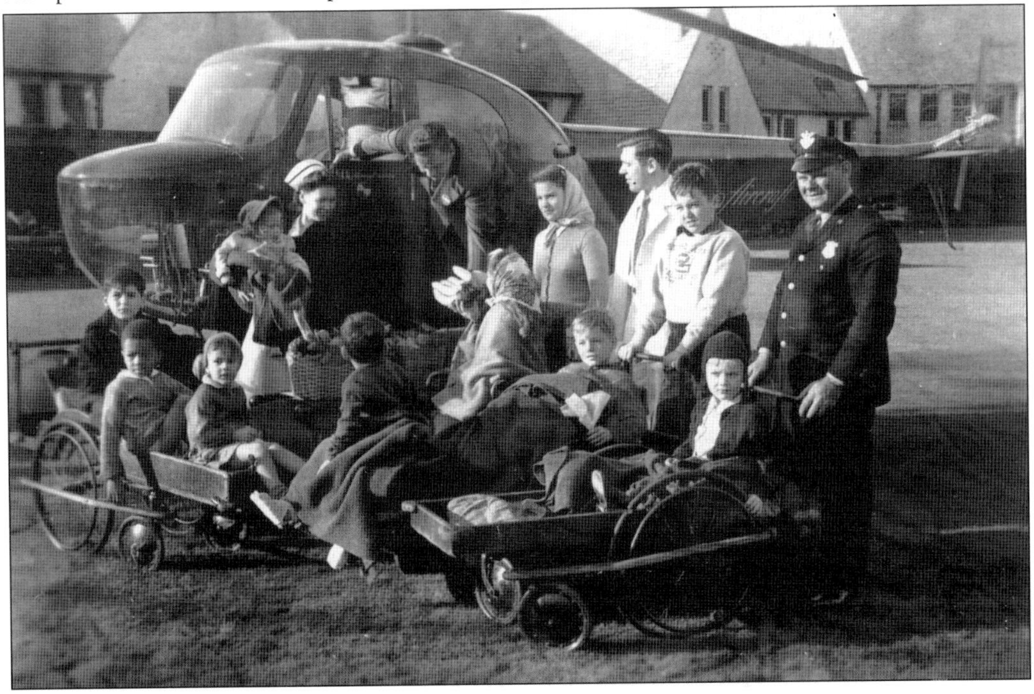

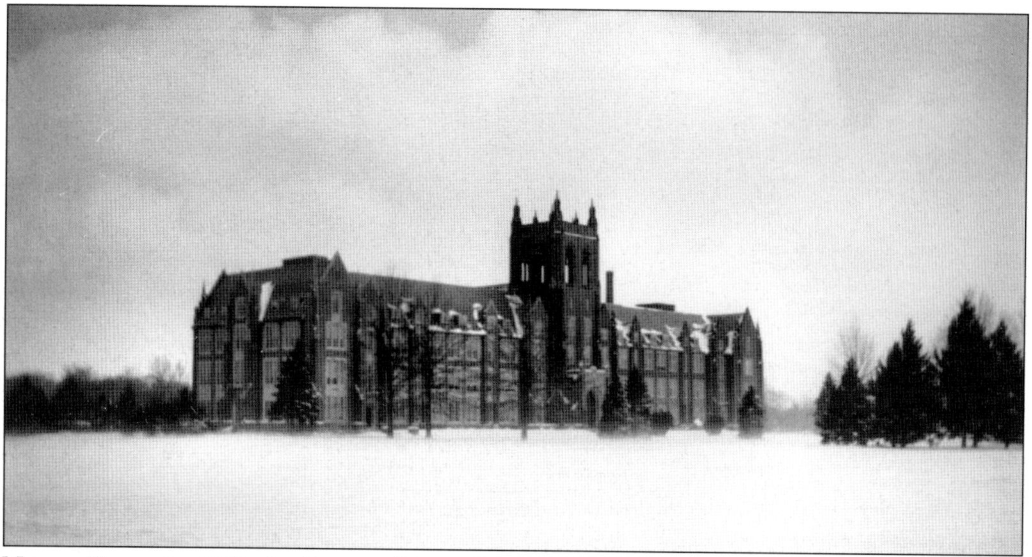

NOTRE DAME. In 1922, the Sisters of Notre Dame opened a women's liberal-arts college at 1324 Ansel Road, Cleveland. In 1928, the college moved to this 53-acre campus east of Green Road, just south of Rainbow Hospital. Both institutions lie on the South Green headwater branch. Recent additions include an administration building, the Connelly Student Center, the Clara Fritsche Library, and the Joseph H. Keller Athletic Center. (SEHS.)

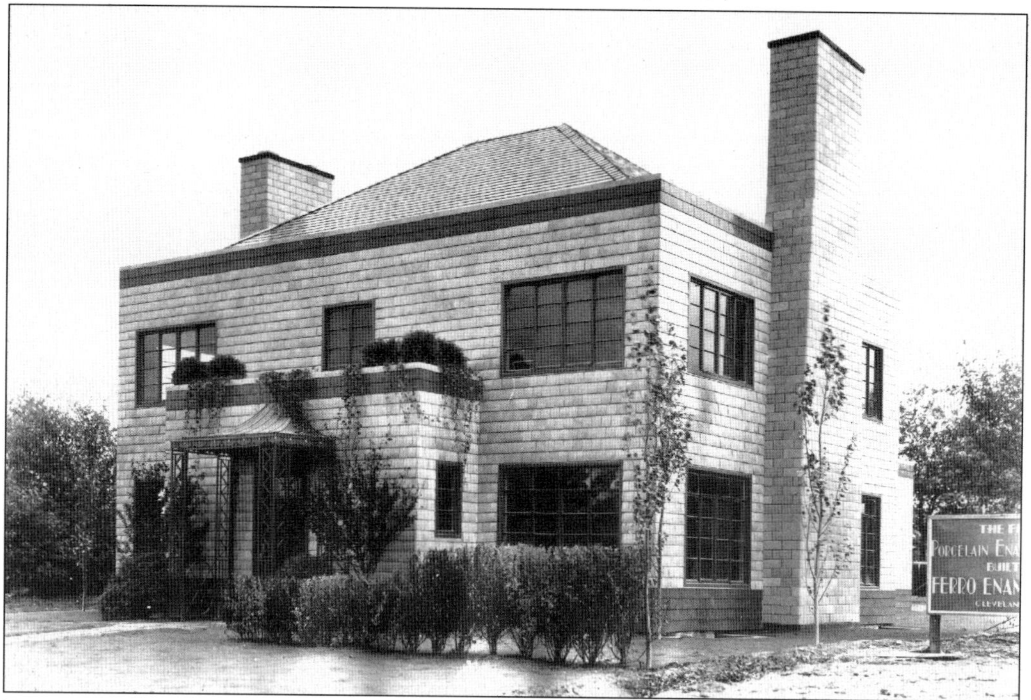

FERRO-ENAMEL. In 1932, Cleveland's Ferro Enamel Company built this house on Campus Drive to showcase steel house construction and its porcelain-enamel steel sheathing shingles. Architects Charles Bacon Rowley & Associates penned the contemporary Colonial design. George L. Dublin was the general contractor. The site was just south of the then new Notre Dame College on a subdivision owned by the Van de Boe-Heger Company. (CPL.)

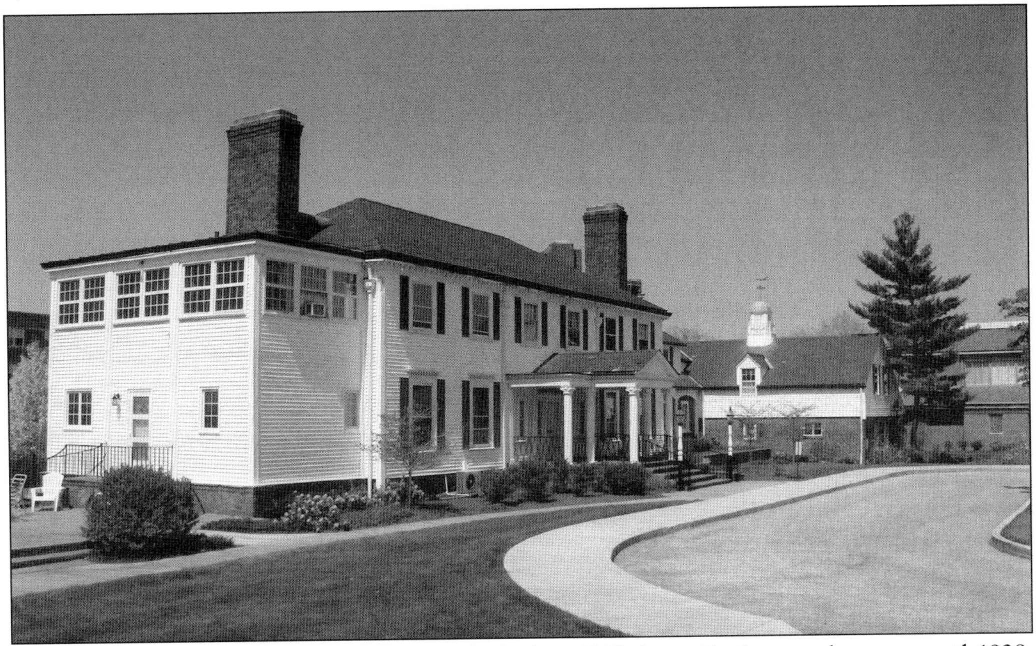

Mount St. Joseph. After Henry Pickands died in 1929, his wife, Jeanne, kept on until 1938, when she demolished the brick house and built this neo-Georgian dwelling in its place. At Jeanne's death in 1942, the Sisters of St. Joseph, a Roman Catholic order of Alsatian origin, purchased the estate. The sisters began their nursing home in Jeanne's house, calling it Mount St. Joseph. (Roy Larick.)

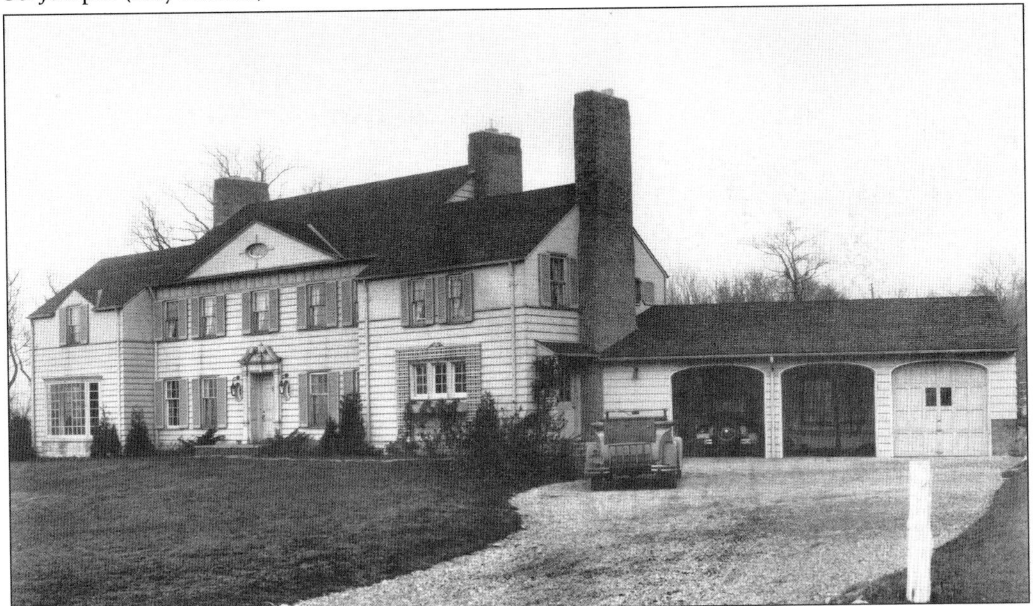

Chestnut Hills. Around 1930, F. P. Ryan was hired to build this lovely neo-Georgian for Pickands daughter Caroline and her husband Robert Cass. The house sat just down the hill from the big brick house. The Sisters of St. Joseph bought it in the 1940s and demolished it in 1950. Sadly, another significant Ryan-built Pickands house—a handsome 1931 rambling Cape Cod—was demolished in 2001. (EHS.)

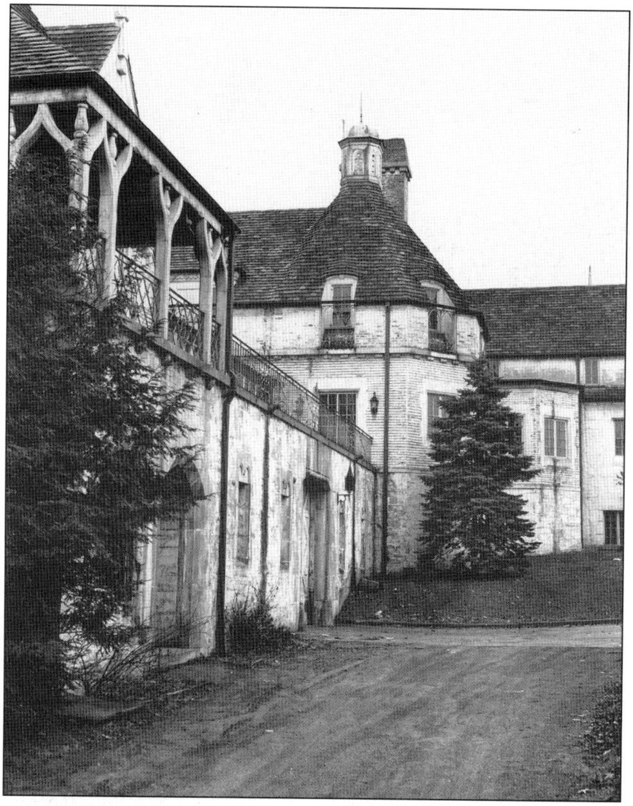

Telling House. William E. Telling (1869–1938) rose from the family farm to be the baron of South Euclid. As a boy he sold strawberries, worked the quarries, conducted horsecars, and even built houses on speculation. In 1892, he started in the dairy business. With the help of his family, Telling's retail business grew into the giant Telling-Belle Vernon, which, in 1928, was the largest dairy in northern Ohio. In 1928, Telling commissioned architect John Sherwood Kelly to design a 26-room dwelling in the Norman French style. The 20,000-square-foot house cost $700,000. The national Depression devastated Telling's finances, but he did not lose the house. The DeTirro family bought the estate in 1945 and sold it to Cuyahoga County for library use in 1951. It was listed on the National Register of Historic Places in 1974. (CSU.)

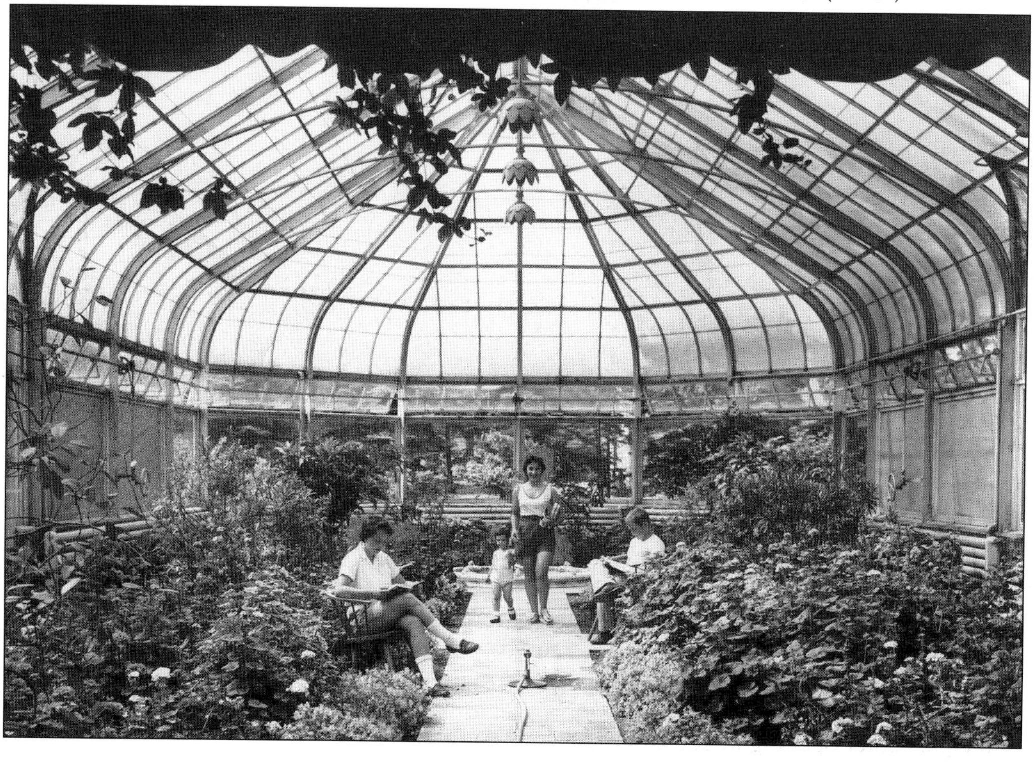

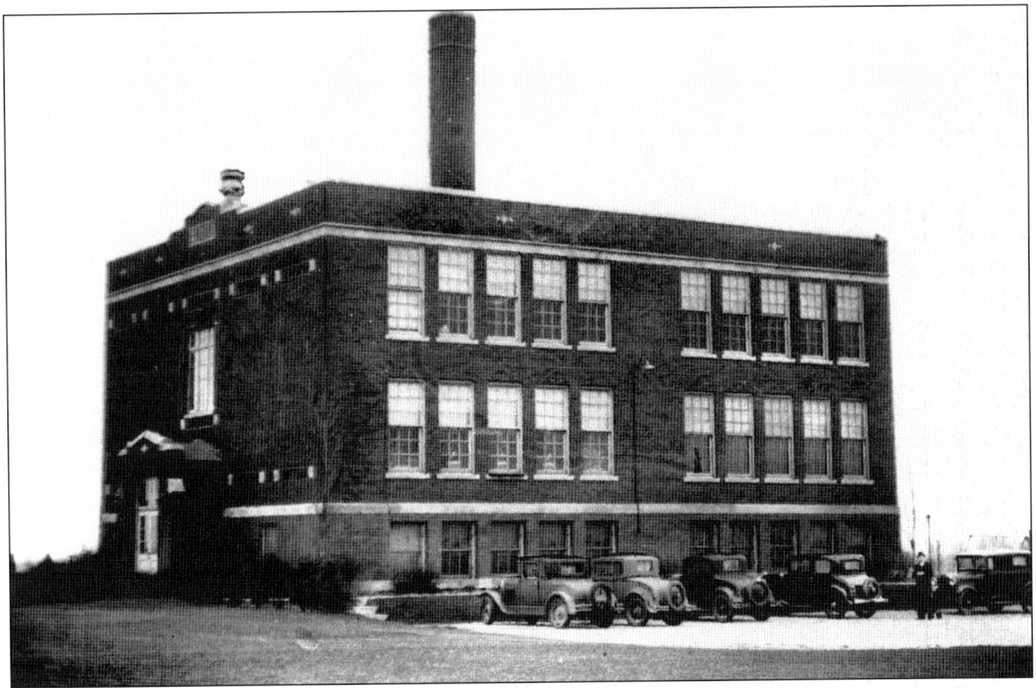

BEECHWOOD SCHOOL. As Beachwood Village suburbanized, the old 19th-century schoolhouses became inadequate. In 1926, the board of education built a frame annex behind the Lewis schoolhouse; it served until this eight-room brick building was completed in 1928. The village incorporators chose the name Beechwood to honor the native Appalachian Plateau beech-maple forest. However, the state charter application inadvertently misspelled it "Beachwood." The school retained the original name. (Jeffrey Morris.)

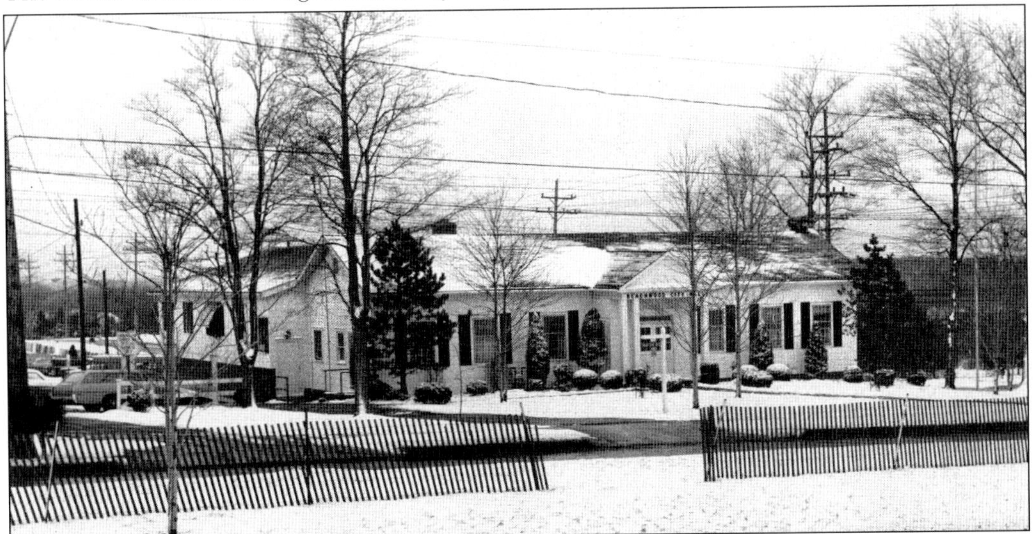

BEACHWOOD VILLAGE HALL. Upon opening Beechwood School in 1928, the Beachwood Board of Education sold Lewis and its annex to the village, which demolished the school and converted the annex into the village hall shown here. When a new city hall arose in 1973, the Beachwood Arts Council came to occupy the old village hall. All was demolished in 2003 for the new municipal center opening in 2005. (CSU.)

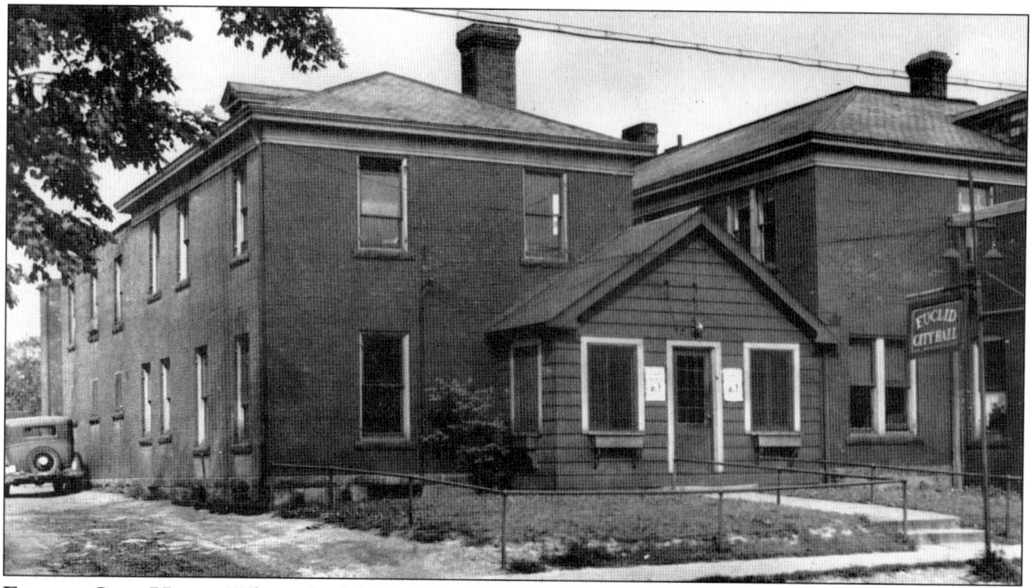

EUCLID CITY HALL. When the North Street township hall burned in 1929, the Village of Euclid moved its offices a few hundred feet west to the Euclid Inn rear wing. An independent entrance was built to front on Chardon Road. The city of Euclid was chartered here in 1931, and the city hall remained at these digs until the bluestone building was completed on East 222nd Street in 1938. (EHS.)

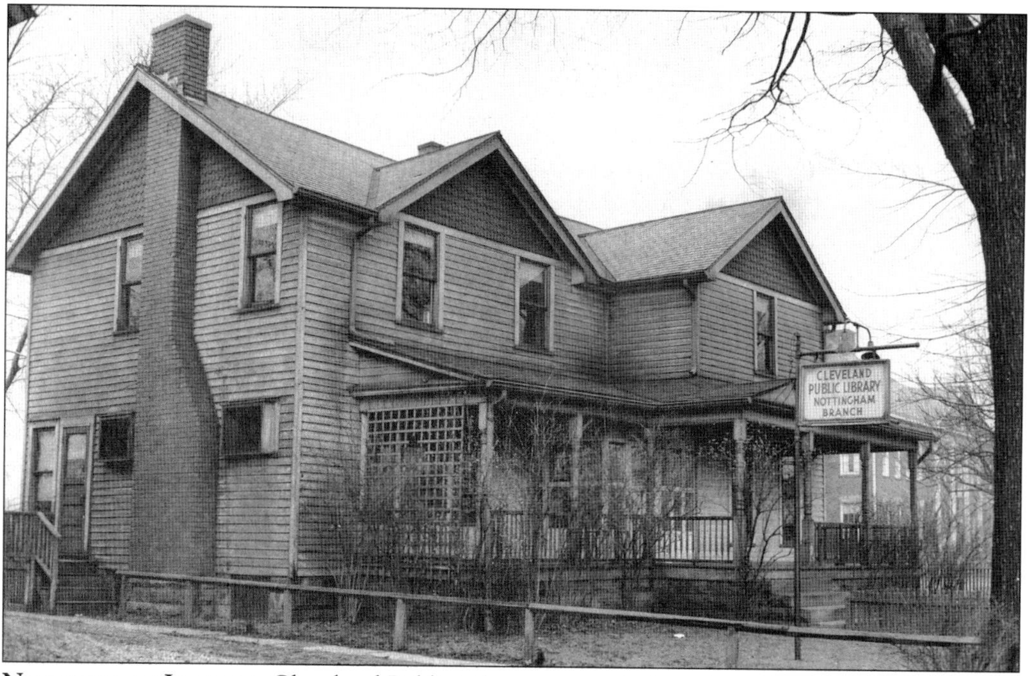

NOTTINGHAM LIBRARY. Cleveland Public Library opened a branch in the Nottingham School in 1921. In 1928, the library was moved to this small, two-story frame house at 18412 Nottingham Road. A study determined that the branch would serve Americans and naturalized foreigners, mostly Slovenes, and that it would complement activities in the neighborhood's public and parochial schools. In 1948, the branch moved to 760 East 185th Street. (CPL.)

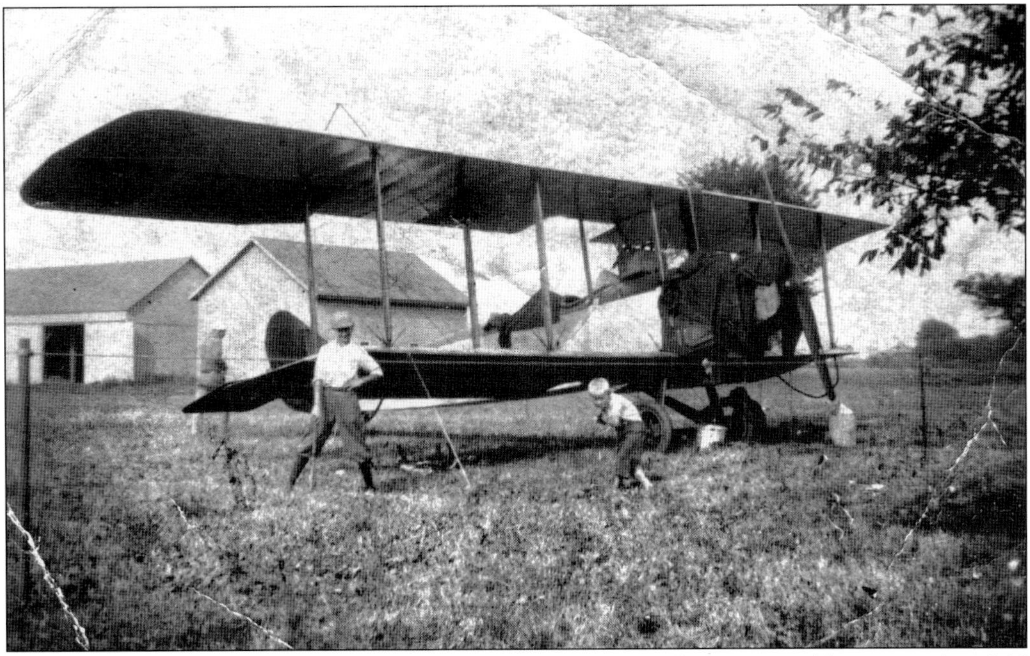

COLE AIRFIELD. In 1927, Ken Cole and his family built a small commercial hangar and airfield in Lyndhurst, in the area of current Blanchester Road. The airfield operated until 1937 and was the seat of operations for Cole Aeronautical Service and Mayfair Air, both catering to aerial photography and contract freighting and ferrying. (SEHS.)

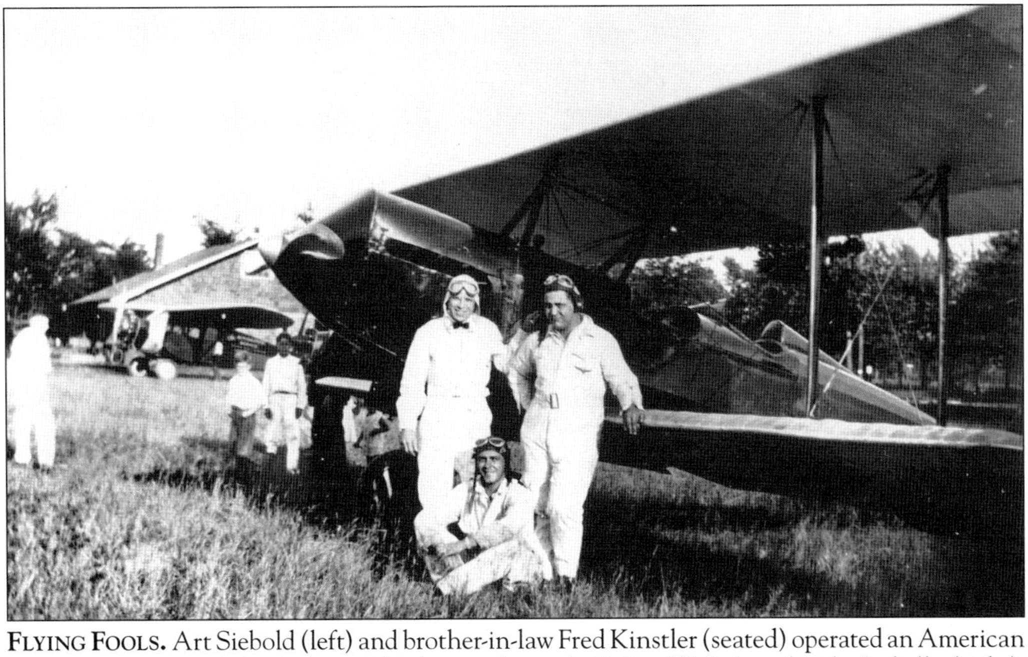

FLYING FOOLS. Art Siebold (left) and brother-in-law Fred Kinstler (seated) operated an American Eagle biplane out of the Cole airfield during the early 1930s. With friend Mike Isabella (right), the "3 Flying Fools" delivered small freight and generally barnstormed around northeast Ohio. A nonfatal crash in 1934 ended the Fools' activities and began to change public sentiment about an airfield in a growing residential area. (SEHS.)

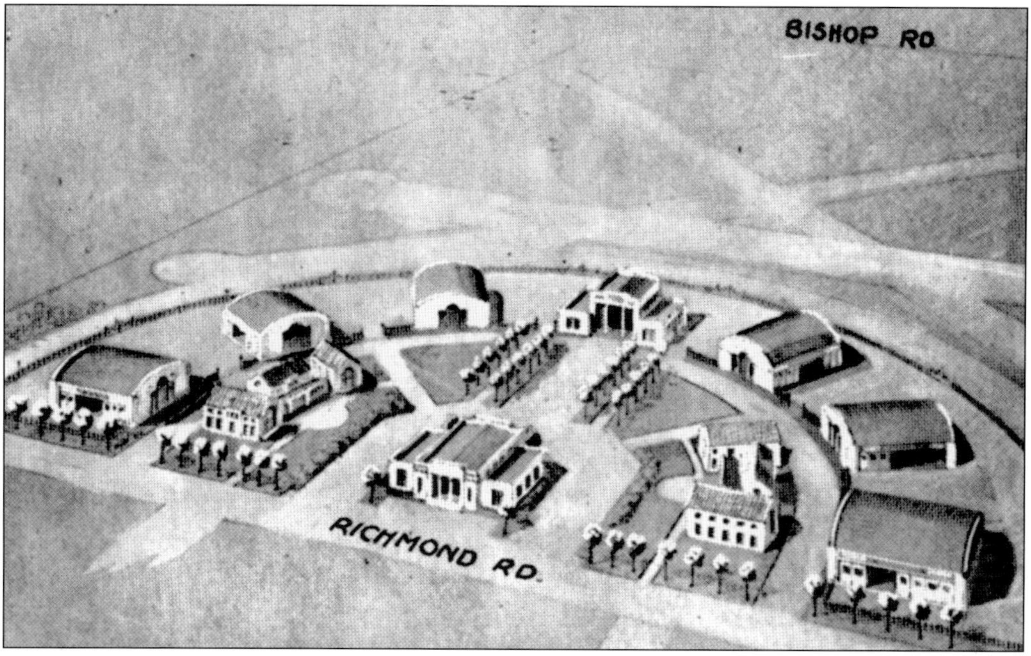

HERRICK AIRPORT. In June 1929, the Curtiss Aeroplane and Motor Company announced plans for a major airport between Richmond and Brush Roads. The name honored Myron T. Herrick, Clevelander, ambassador to France, and aviation enthusiast. The airport was to have 10 Colonial Revival–style buildings serving all aspects of aviation, including showrooms for major manufacturers and a flying school. Local opposition and the national Depression doomed the plan. (CSU.)

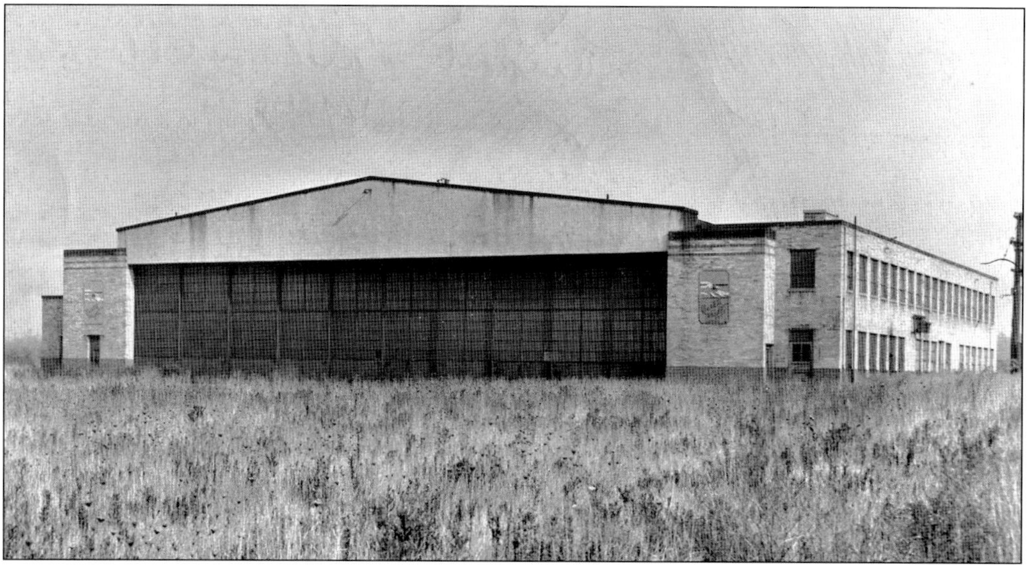

CURTISS-WRIGHT. One Herrick Airport building arose in 1929. This hanger, built at a cost of $150,000, contained space for 30 airplanes and the regional offices for Curtiss-Wright aircraft distribution. The Swetland family, who held a large summer estate on the west side of Richmond Road, filed suit against construction and, in 1931, obtained a federal injunction to close the airport. (CSU.)

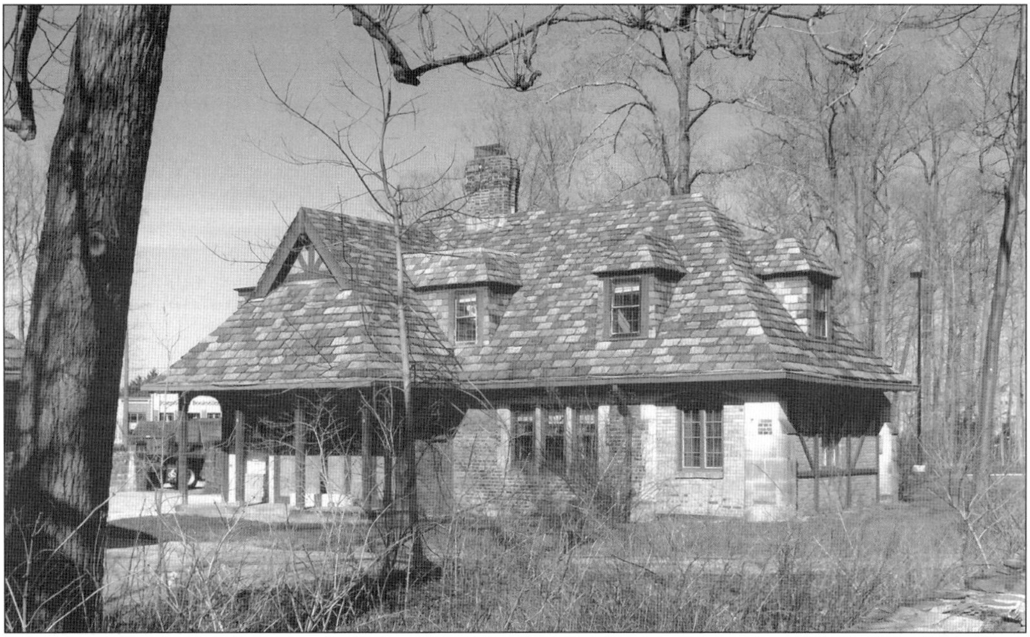

Blossom Estate. Elizabeth Bingham Blossom and Frances Payne Bolton were sisters. About 1920, the Blossoms acquired the southeast corner of the Bolton estate. A large Tudor-style house and service compound were erected. Later, Henry Stoddard Sherman lived on the estate until his death in 1956. The house was demolished shortly thereafter, but the service compound survives and was listed on the National Register of Historic Places in 2004. Legacy Village now occupies the site. (Roy Larick.)

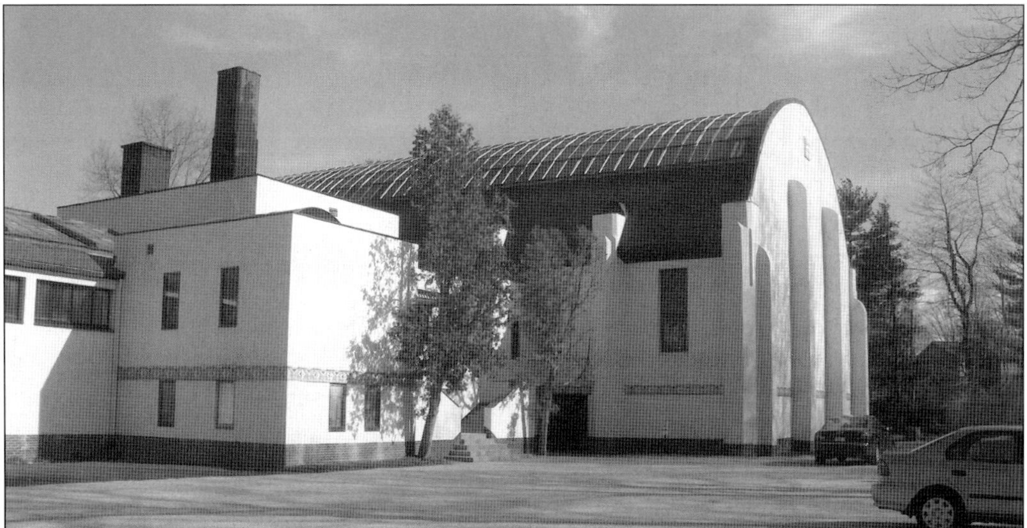

The Hangar. In 1936, Elizabeth Blossom developed a private residential enclave on the southwest corner of Cedar and Richmond Roads (Community Drive and Union Circle). Architect Adam Garfield designed this Art Deco–style recreation facility to front on Cedar. "The Hangar" passed out of family hands in the late 1940s to become the Hangar Recreation Association, a private swim and tennis club. It was listed on the National Register of Historic Places in 1986. (Roy Larick.)

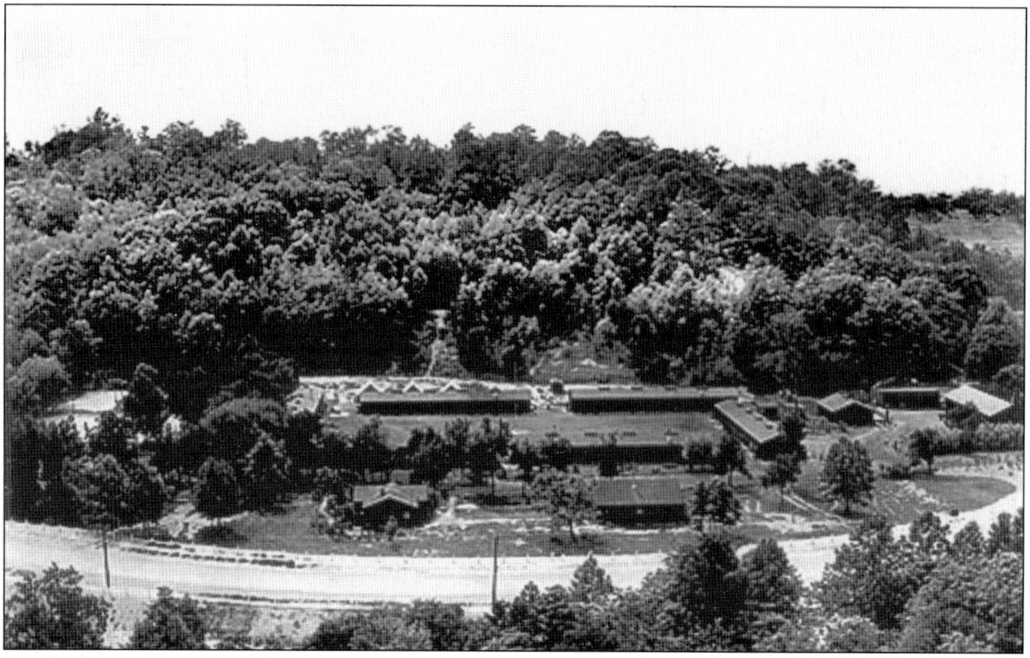

CAMP EUCLID. With his landslide 1932 victory, Pres. Franklin D. Roosevelt was determined to fight economic depression and environmental degradation with an army of unemployed city dwellers. Thus was born the Civilian Conservation Corps. In November 1933, the CCC established Camp Euclid to help the Cleveland Metropolitan Park Board in maintaining and expanding facilities. Projects centered on clearing corridors for roads and utilities, on building retaining walls and pavilions, and on planting trees. The *Camp Euclid Surveyor*, a regular newspaper, was published here from 1934 until the camp closed in 1937. (NARA, CPL.)

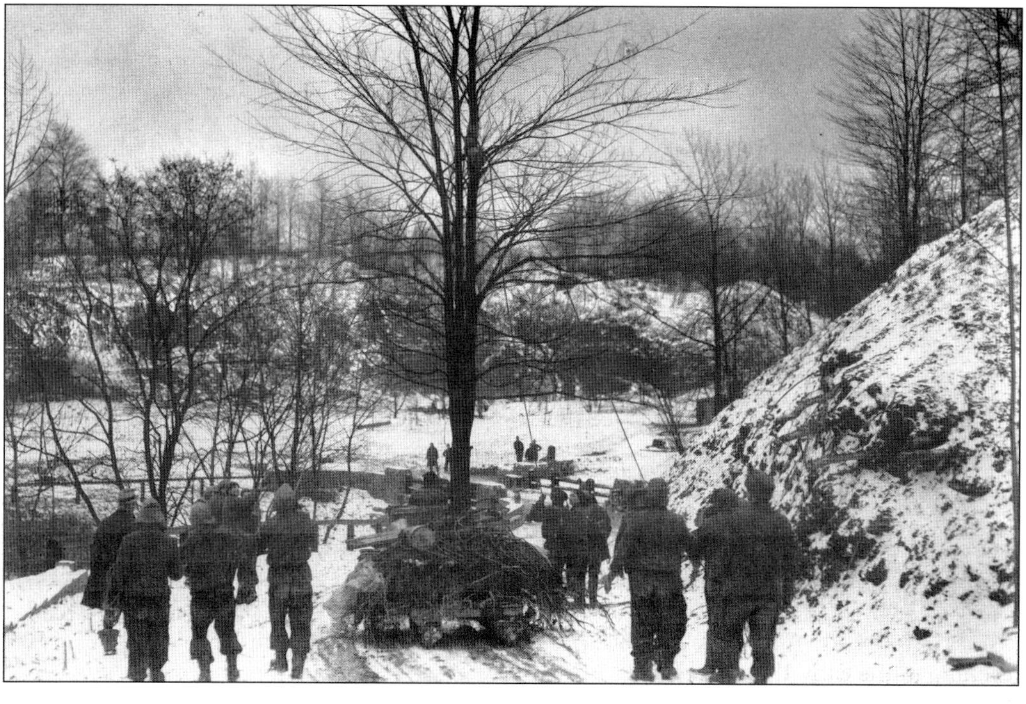

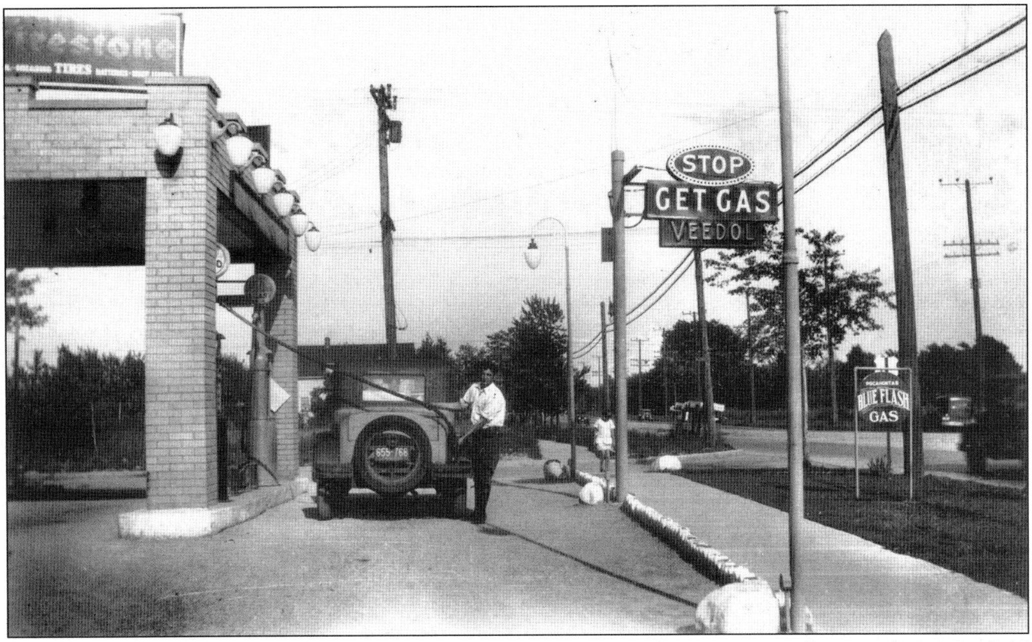

VEEDOL. The Yafanaro family operated a franchise of this early gas station chain at 5851 Mayfield Road. The photograph looks east from the corner of Belrose and Mayfield about 1932. Mayfield road was quickly changing from rural to suburban in the early 1930s. Rows of mailboxes still line the way. (MTHS.)

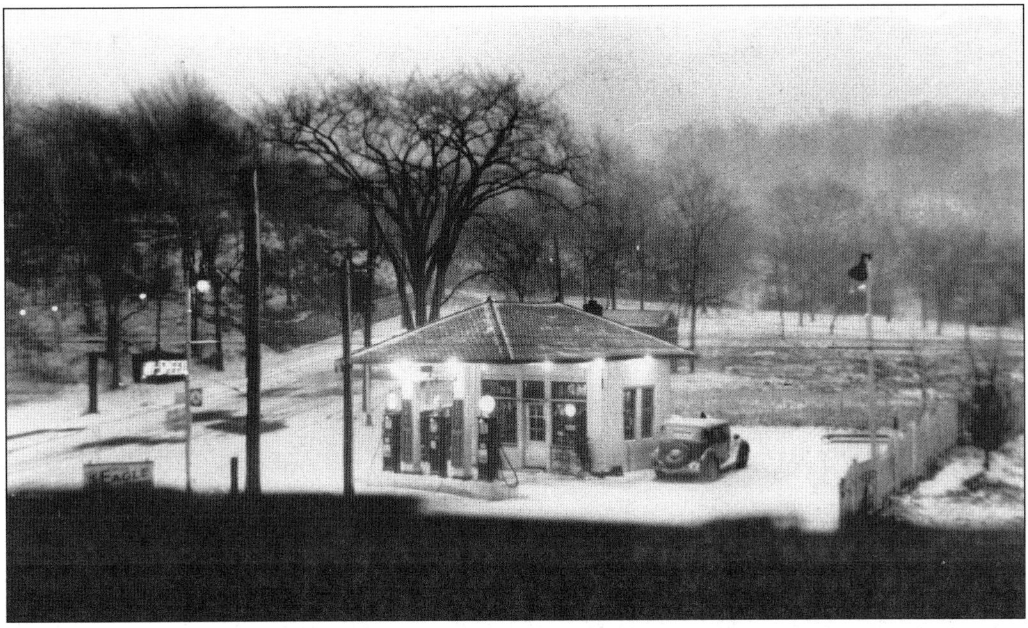

HI-SPEED. This gas station was a fixture on the southwest corner of Euclid Avenue and Chardon Road during the 1920s and early 1930s. The view looks up Chardon Road on a still winter evening in the early 1930s. (EHS.)

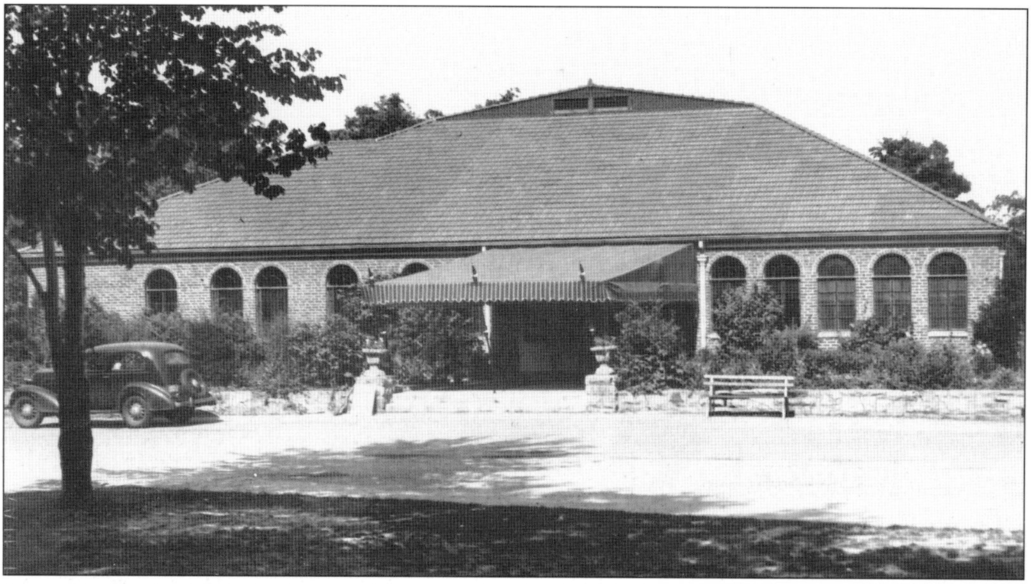

Ohio Villa. In 1933, the Italian-American Brotherhood Club opened a 100-acre country club on Highland Road just west of Richmond. The plan included a recreation park, nursing home, hospital, and arts-and-crafts school. What came was the Ohio Villa, featuring two dining rooms, two bars, a large kitchen, and extensive gambling facilities. Morris Kleinman, Louis Northkopf, and Moe Davis managed the gambling. Later, they managed Las Vegas' Desert Inn. (CSU.)

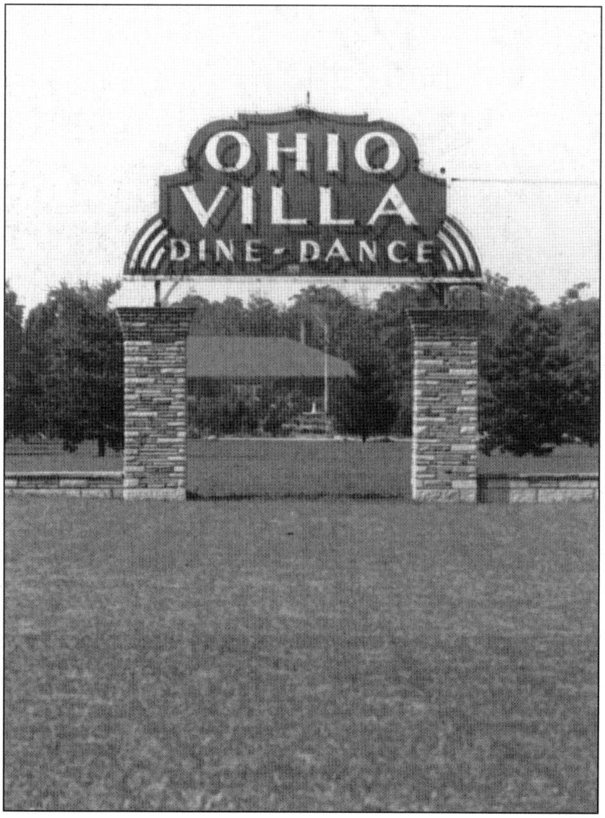

Ohio Villa. Along with the Harvard and Thomas Clubs, the Ohio Villa operated openly but quietly for several years. In 1937, however, the "big three" operators took to bank robbing to pay large debts. A three-year legal battle ensued to shut these operations. In 1942, the Brotherhood Club reopened the facility as a deluxe private restaurant called the Richmond Country Club. The building burned to the ground in 1953. (CSU.)

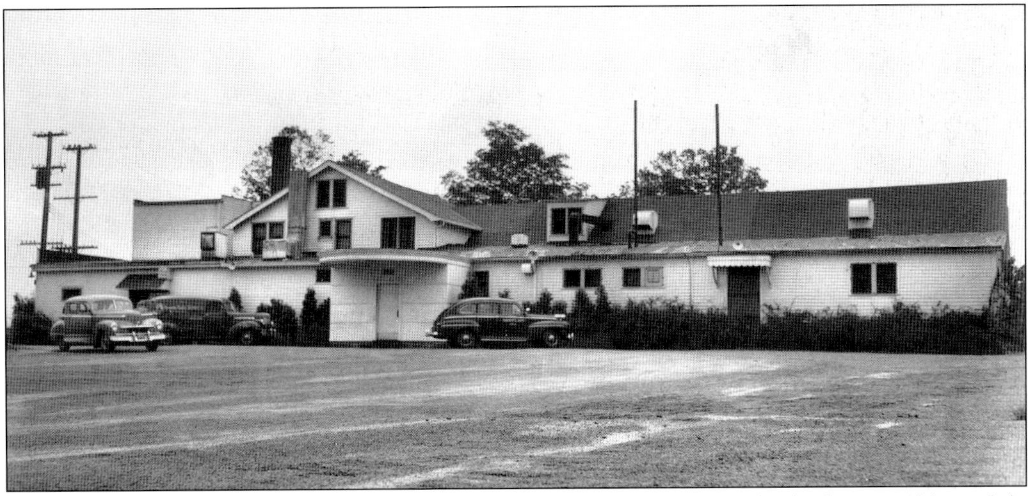

MOUNDS CLUB. In 1933, T. J. McGuinty opened the best remembered suburban gambling club. The Mounds Club lasted 16 years on fine dining and entertainment along with gaming. The beginning of the end came on September 29, 1947, when 14 "commandos" invaded to filch the till and patrons for a half-million dollars in cash, jewels, and furs. Closed as a club in 1949, the building is now the La-Vera Party Center. (CSU.)

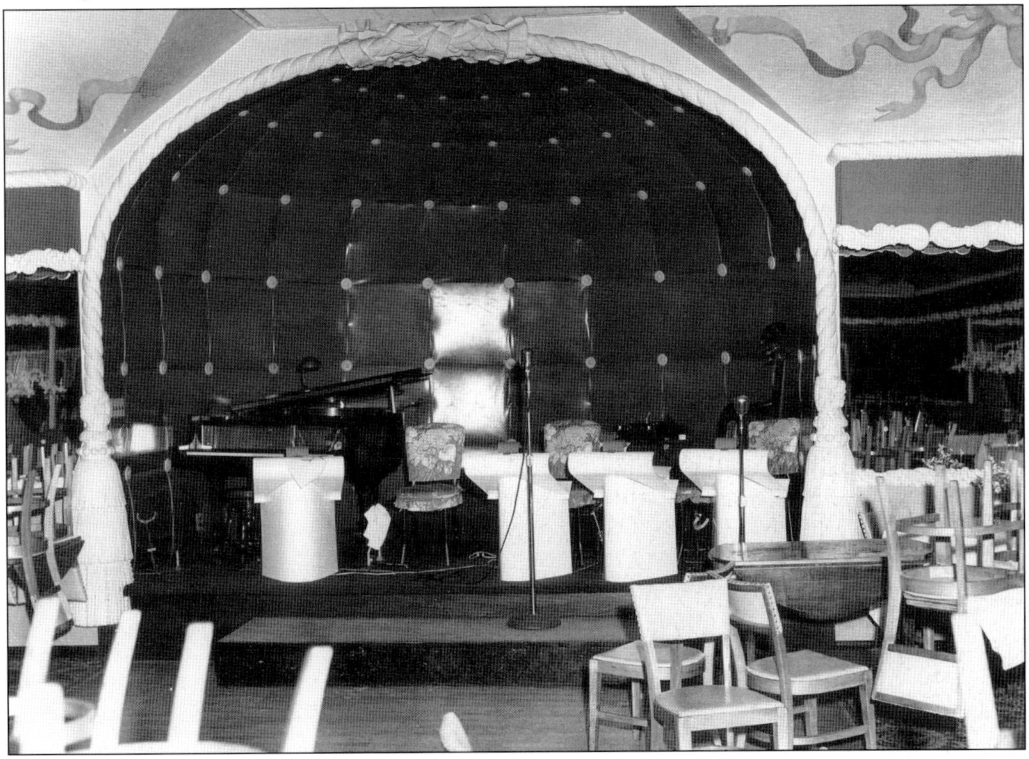

MOUNDS CLUB. Many club-circuit entertainers graced this stage. Dino Crocetti performed here in 1939; a year later, he was calling himself Dean Martin. The 1940s brought Helen Morgan, Sophie Tucker, Hildegarde, and Peter Lind Hayes and wife, Mary Healy. Hayes and Healy were performing on the night of the great robbery. They, and nearly all the patrons, first thought that the event was staged entertainment. (CSU.)

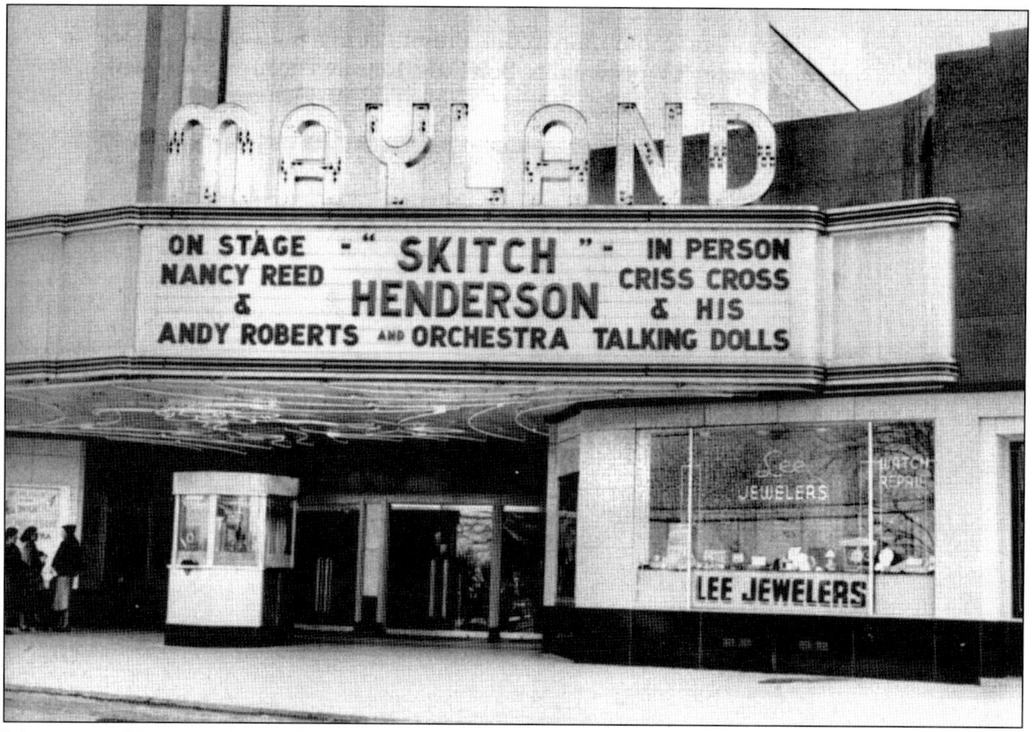

MAYLAND THEATER. Another evolution at Whitings Corners came in 1948 with the opening of the Mayland Shopping Center on the southwest corner of Mayfield and Lander Roads. The Mayland Theater was the anchor attraction. At its start, the theater provided live entertainment as well as movies. (MTHS.)

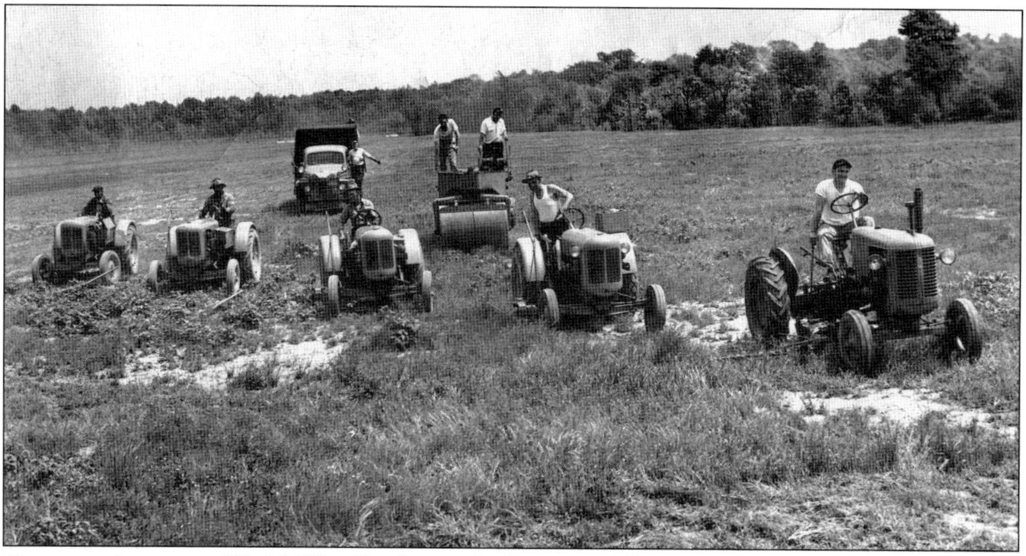

COUNTY AIRPORT. World War II advanced all aviation fronts in the United States. Within this climate, small-plane enthusiasts combined efforts to win voter approval for rehabilitating Herrick Field. The county commissioners bought the facility in 1947 and opened the Cuyahoga County Airport on Memorial Day 1950. Here, a county grounds crew is grooming the field in preparation for opening day. (CSU.)

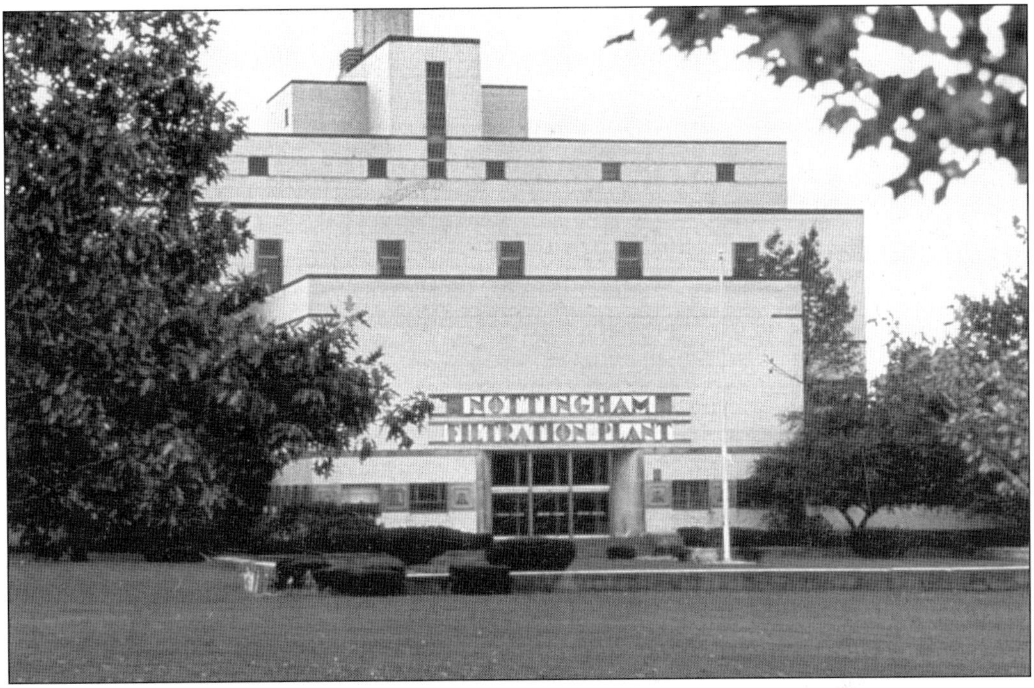

NOTTINGHAM FILTRATION. By the late 1920s, Cleveland's far East Side was growing rapidly and in need of water. The water department considered a number of plans and finally decided on the Nottingham Intake and Filtration plant. Construction began in 1947 with an intake crib, three miles off Wildwood Park, and the filtration plant on Chardon Road, south of St. Clair Avenue. The storage reservoir was excavated into the shale under the filtration plant. (CPL.)

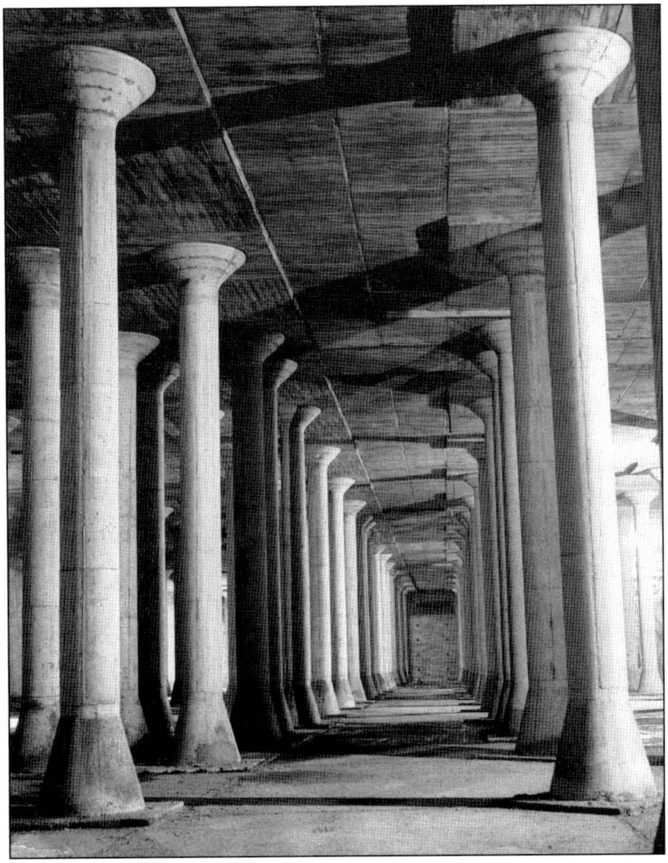

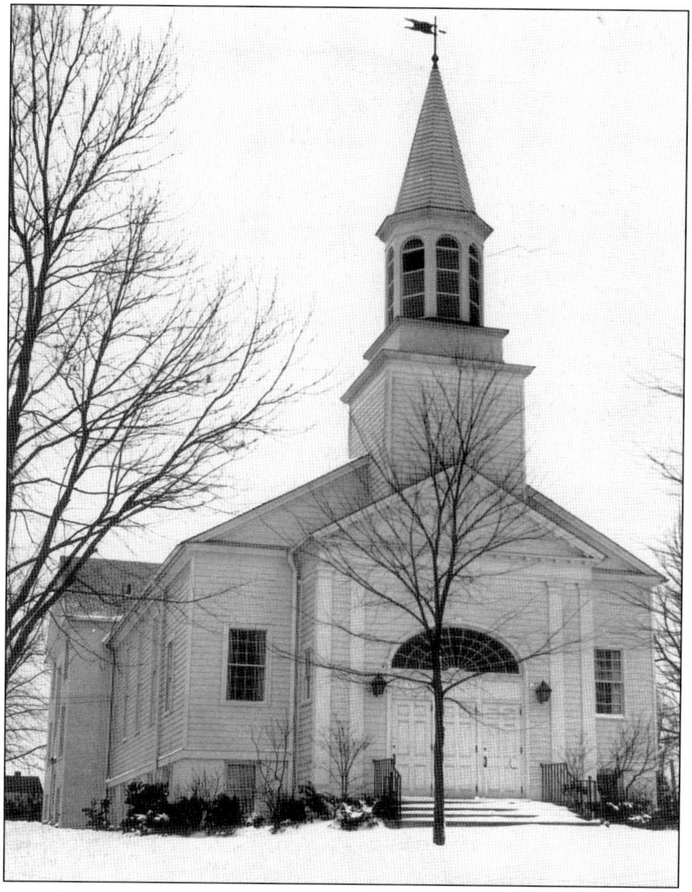

Community Church. In 1928, Dr. George Mackintosh organized a nondenominational church to meet in the Lyndhurst Village Hall. Growing quickly, the church came to hold Sunday school in the jail. In 1939, Frances P. Bolton and her sons seeded a building fund with $10,000. Charles Bacon Rowley & Associates drew up the plans, and in 1941, this handsome Colonial Revival–style church and classroom hall arose opposite the village hall. (CPL.)

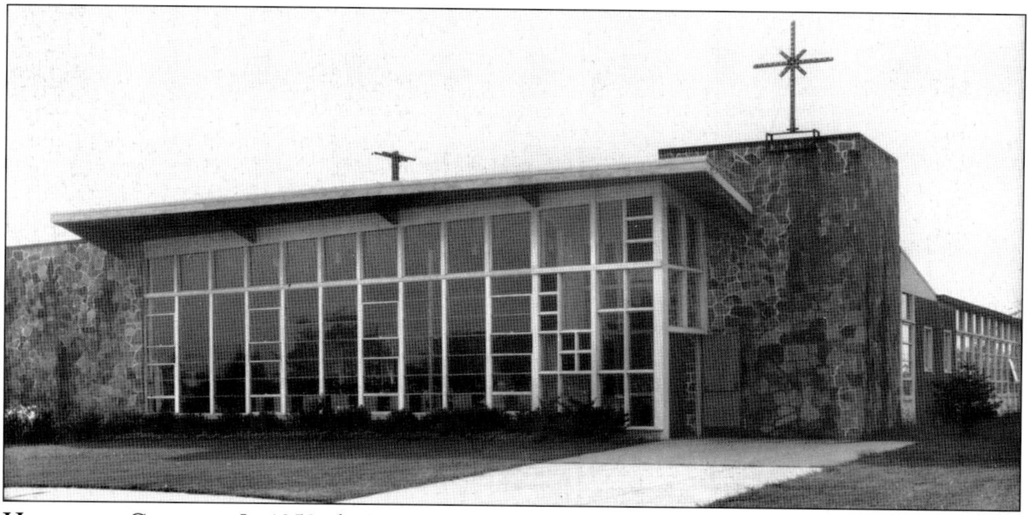

Hillcrest Church. In 1950, the Evangelical United Brethren gave a charter and pastor Daniel Lansell to a nondenominational congregation already meeting at Mayfield Heights City Hall. At 1400 Lander Road, Hillcrest dedicated this modernist structure in October 1955. The north-facing window wall gave the sanctuary great indirect natural light. The church became United Methodist in 1968. In 1994, it was sold to the Cornerstone Community Church. (MTHS.)

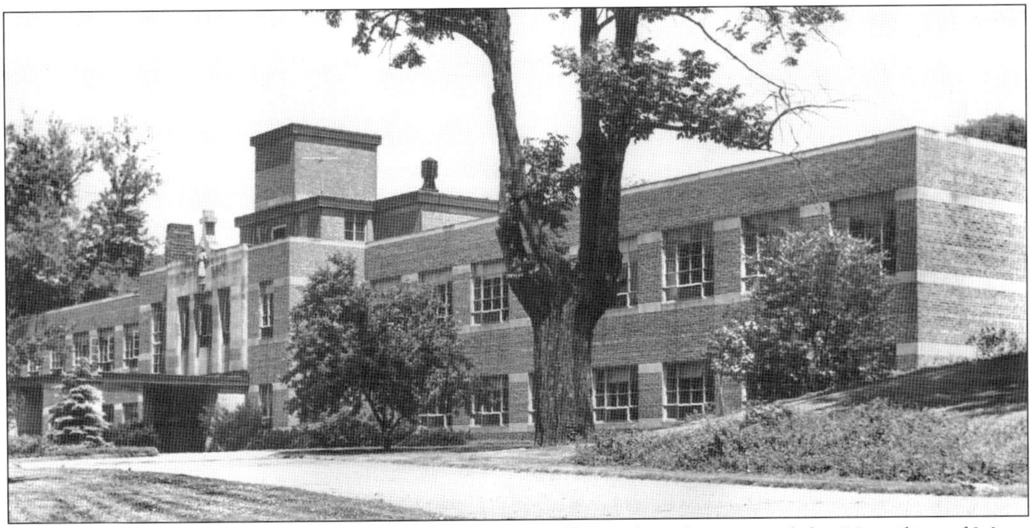

Rose-Mary Center. As a gift from Caesar Grasselli, and under care of the Humility of Mary Sisters, "Rose-Mary" opened in 1922. Even as the Delaney gift doubled its size in 1943, there was never enough room. This 1949 education wing connected the two houses. A staff of 40 was now able to provide treatment, education, and therapeutic programs for 40 residents and numerous outpatients. (RMC.)

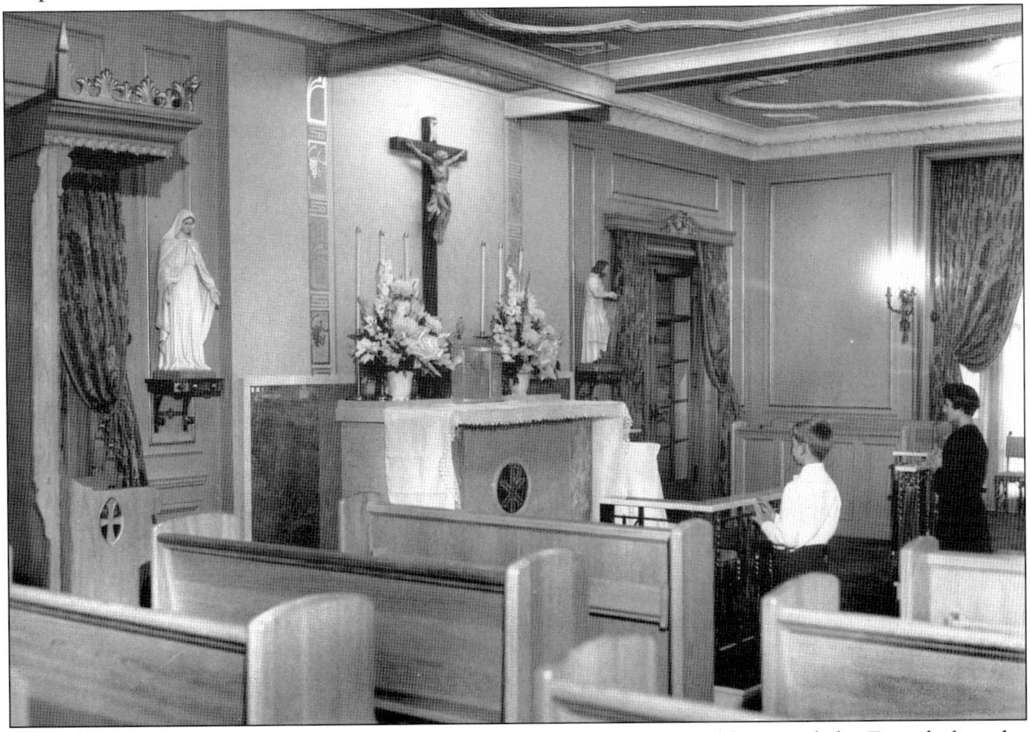

Julie Billiart. Founded in 1954, Cleveland's Julie Billiart School honored the French founder of the Sisters of Notre Dame. In 1958, the school moved into the Charles K. Arter house on Clubside Road, Lyndhurst. The early 1960s saw a new gymnasium, and the late 1970s brought classrooms and athletic facilities. This photograph shows the chapel placed in one of the house's parlors. (CPL.)

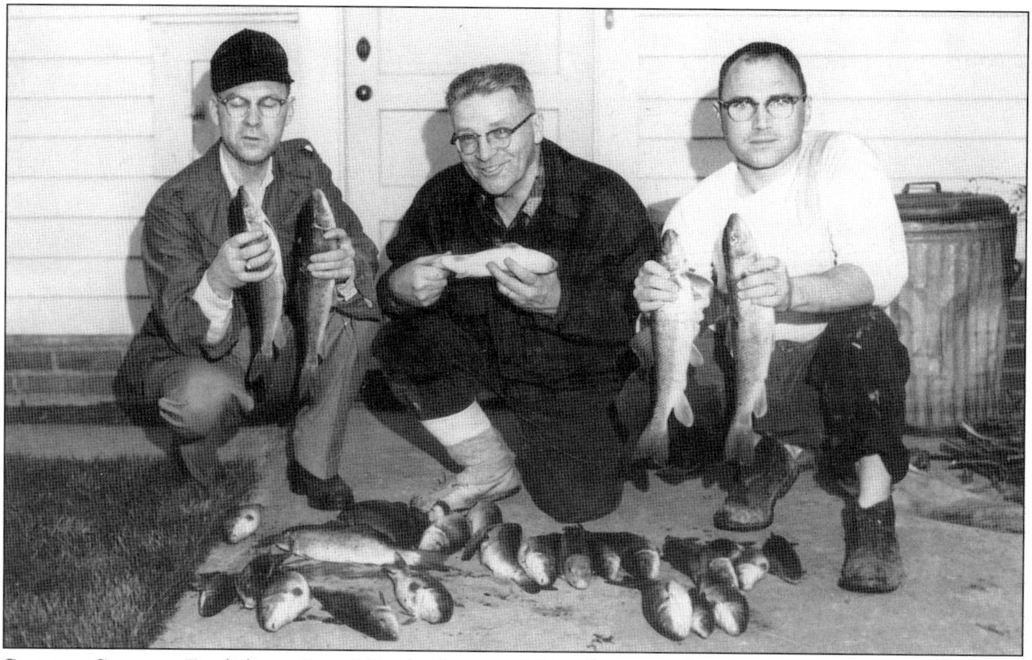

Spring Spawn. Euclidians Roy Hinch, Leonard Voorhees, and an unidentified Miller display their catch of common suckers (*Catostomus commersoni)* from Euclid Creek in May 1959. During the late 19th and early 20th centuries, creek-spawning lake fish included suckers, largemouth bass, sunfish, crappies, and catfish. Suckers held on through the darkest days of chemical and biological pollution in the latter 20th century. (EHS.)

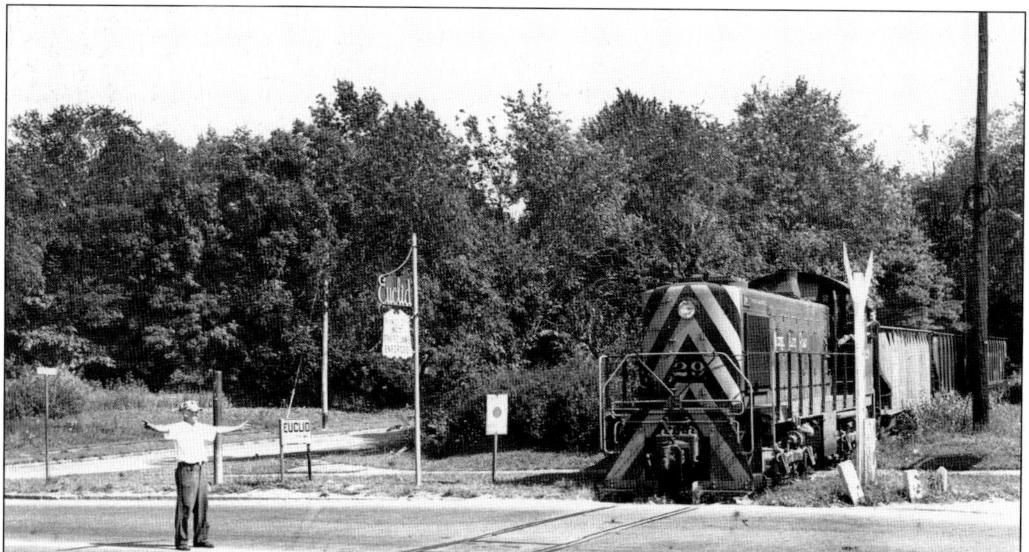

Euclid Railroad. A train descends onto Euclid Avenue from South Euclid in August 1950. Upper Valley Drive lies behind the crossing guard. The small flatland beyond is the probable site for David Dille Jr.'s 1803 cabin. All the signage speaks of a slower time along the avenue. Opened in 1882, the Euclid Railroad closed in 1969. Now, Euclid and South Euclid are working to make the track bed into a trail. (EHS.)

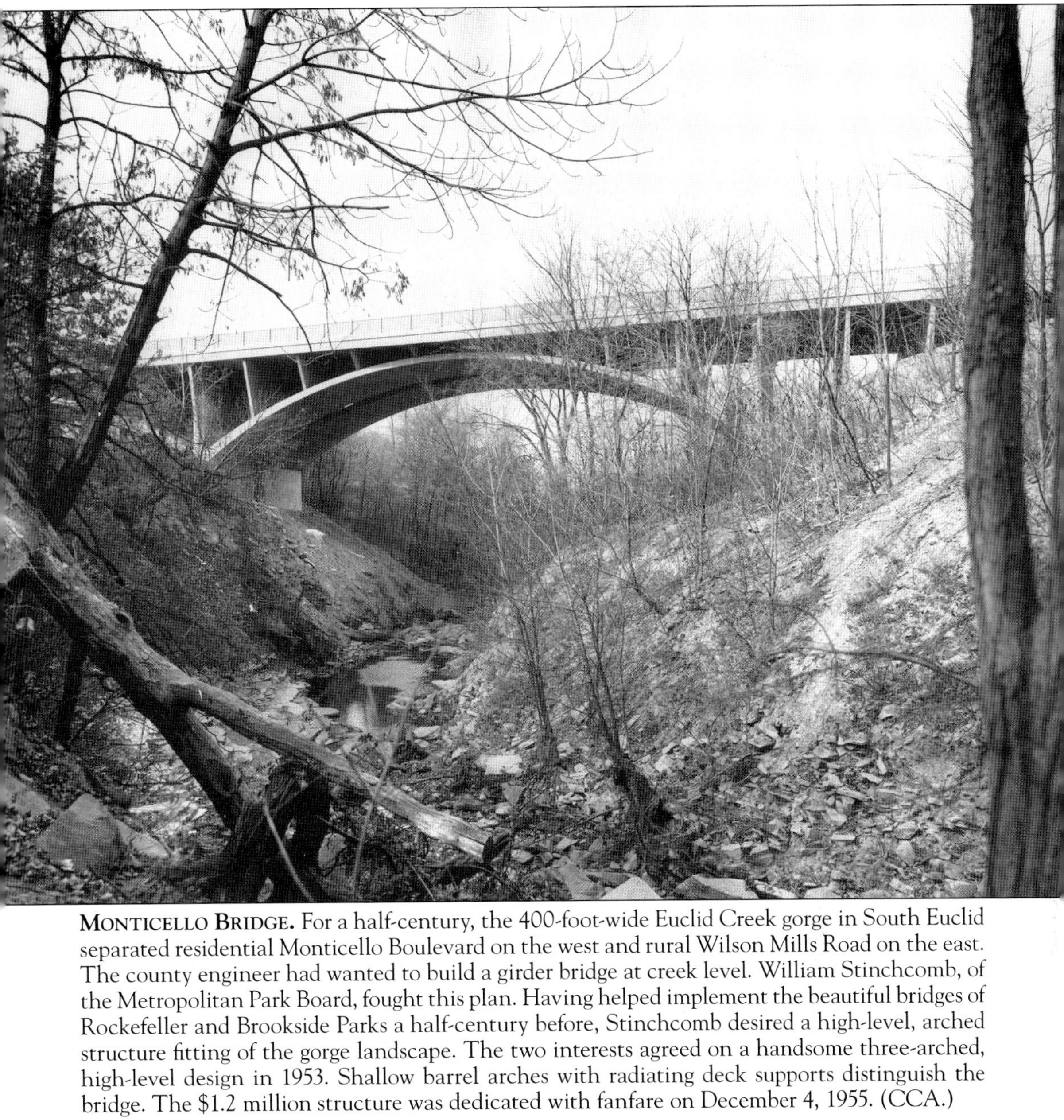

MONTICELLO BRIDGE. For a half-century, the 400-foot-wide Euclid Creek gorge in South Euclid separated residential Monticello Boulevard on the west and rural Wilson Mills Road on the east. The county engineer had wanted to build a girder bridge at creek level. William Stinchcomb, of the Metropolitan Park Board, fought this plan. Having helped implement the beautiful bridges of Rockefeller and Brookside Parks a half-century before, Stinchcomb desired a high-level, arched structure fitting of the gorge landscape. The two interests agreed on a handsome three-arched, high-level design in 1953. Shallow barrel arches with radiating deck supports distinguish the bridge. The $1.2 million structure was dedicated with fanfare on December 4, 1955. (CCA.)

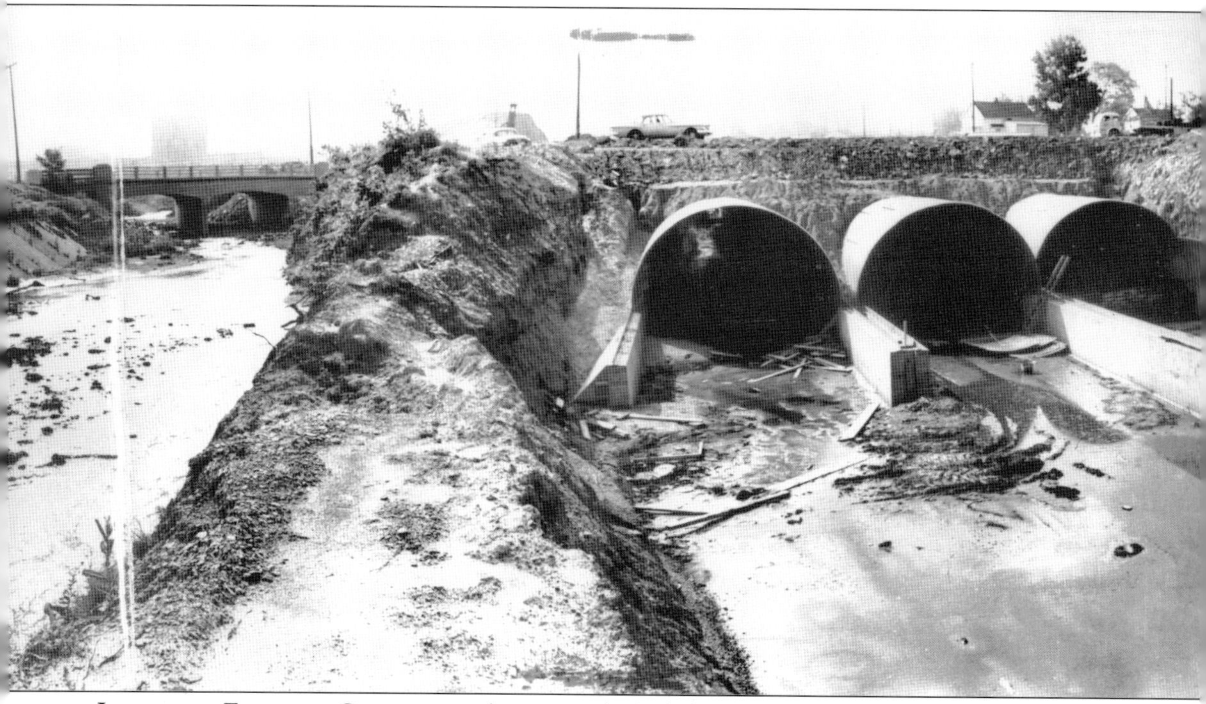

LAKELAND FREEWAY. Construction began on the Lakeland Freeway (Interstate 90/Route 2) in the spring of 1961. Freeway building brought a distinct change to stream engineering—diverting and culverting instead of bridging natural channels. This view looks upstream along Euclid Creek's original channel (left) to East 185th Street. The culvert outlet channel lies on the right. When this work was finished, the old channel, which included a large meander loop, was filled in, and a cloverleaf ramp was built above. (WRHS.)

Six

Interstate Lifestyles 1962–2005

By 1960, northeastern Ohio's industrial output had peaked and was about to commence a long slow decline. General economic activity diminished accordingly. Within the watershed, the trend was barely noticeable as a drop in building starts for industrial, residential, and cultural structures. There was, nevertheless, a disguising growth factor in the arrival of the Interstate Highway System.

The Lakeland Freeway (Interstate 90/Route 2) was completed in 1962 and the Interstate 90/Interstate 271 Euclid Spur followed in 1965. The interstate network had two effects on the watershed. First, the Lakeland Freeway cut directly across Nottingham village to obliterate an entire residential neighborhood centering on Nottingham and Waterloo Roads. Large structures lost included the Nottingham School and the handsome Congregational church. Euclid Creek itself was diverted, shortened, and unceremoniously set inside a culvert under the freeway and its East 185th Street cloverleaf.

Second, the opening of Interstate 271 through the headwater communities (Willoughby Hills, Highland Heights, Mayfield Heights Beachwood, and Pepper Pike) quickly drew development to the watershed's east and south fringes, and well beyond. All remaining rural tracts were built out by the late 1990s. Most interstate-era construction followed new requirements for immense parking lots and strip agglomeration. Housing was dispersed on lots sometimes large in size. This quick and pervasive growth masked the general regional decline.

Much recent building has focused on the retail and service industries and on entertainment. In 1966, the deBartolo firm completed the Richmond Mall in Richmond Heights. In the 1970s, Beachwood Place mall and La Place retail center rose in Beachwood. The Front Row Theater came to Highland Heights in 1974 and then closed in 1993. Highland Heights also saw the arrival of Alpha Park industrial park in 1986 and the Aberdeen Office Park in 1991. The year 2003 saw the retail experience climax at Legacy Village, northeastern Ohio's first and still largest "lifestyle center."

Among the watershed buildings put up during the last 40 years, we salute the designs of Richard Fleischman. Fleishman has been designing buildings for the entire interstate era, with a drive to "sculpt spaces where people can celebrate, meditate, and share their feelings and ideas." The firm has seven significant buildings or building additions in Euclid Creek, all having received national or regional awards. The designs are highly graphical and sculptural, and they are stark and powerful on the landscape.

On the less pleasant side, current building trends are overwhelming the watershed's landforms. The Lakeland Freeway culvert for Euclid Creek set the precedent for unmitigated cutting and filling that typifies the last 40 years. Watercourses large and small are no longer natural features worthy of respect. They are merely engineering obstacles to be dealt away. Remaining riparian areas are under intense pressure for housing as area residents desire to live closer to nature even as nature diminishes in extent.

It is in this latter context that the Euclid Creek watershed action plan is a necessary tool for future development. The plan specifies ways for improving watershed cultural and historic resources as well as the natural habitat. To truly improve our quality of life, future development must maintain the watershed's significant cultural heritage. We want the best of the past—as documented in *Euclid Creek's* historical images—to set the stage for a sustainable future.

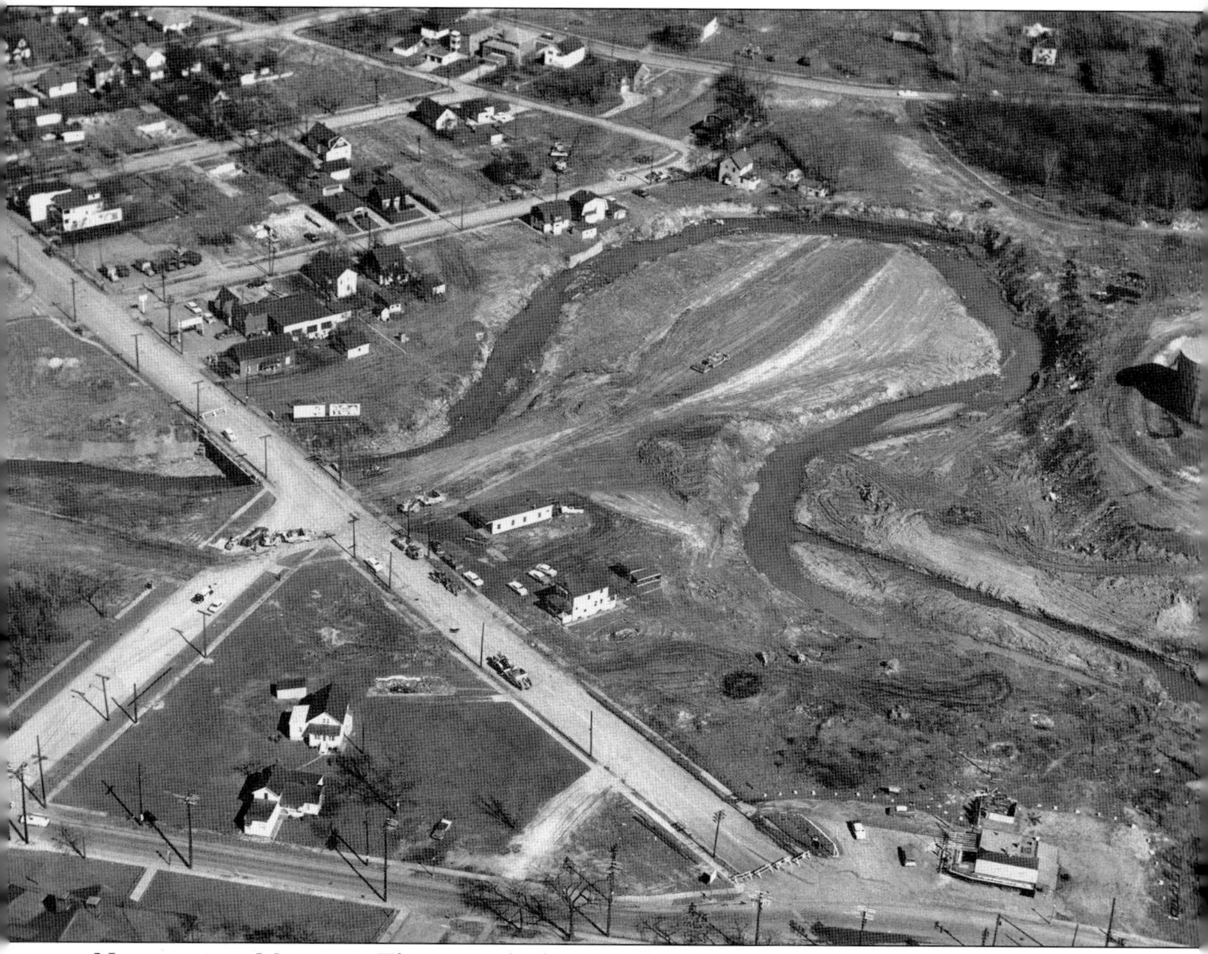

NOTTINGHAM MEANDER. This view is looking northeast in the summer of 1961 during Lakeland Freeway construction. East 185th Street crosses the creek. Old Nottingham Road is barely visible in the lower left. Old Waterloo crosses Nottingham to dead end at East 185th in the middle left. Neff Road crosses the top of the photograph. The Lakeland Freeway culvert eliminated the meander. The old channel is now overlain by the East 185th eastbound off-cloverleaf. (CSU.)

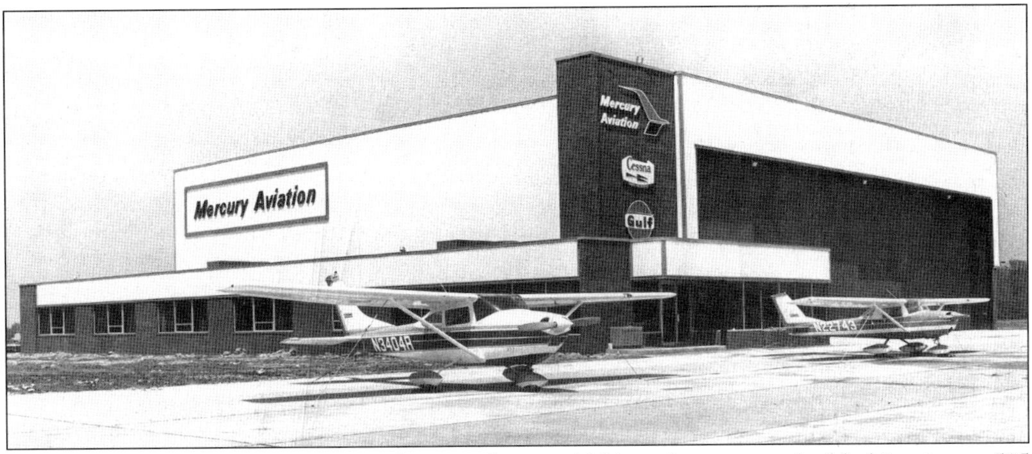

COUNTY AIRPORT. This photograph was taken in 1964 as the airport doubled its size to 585 acres, allowing for future growth. It is now the main county airport servicing private and corporate-owned aircraft and is the regional center for aviation-related industries. There is now a four-story office complex and industrial park. (CSU.)

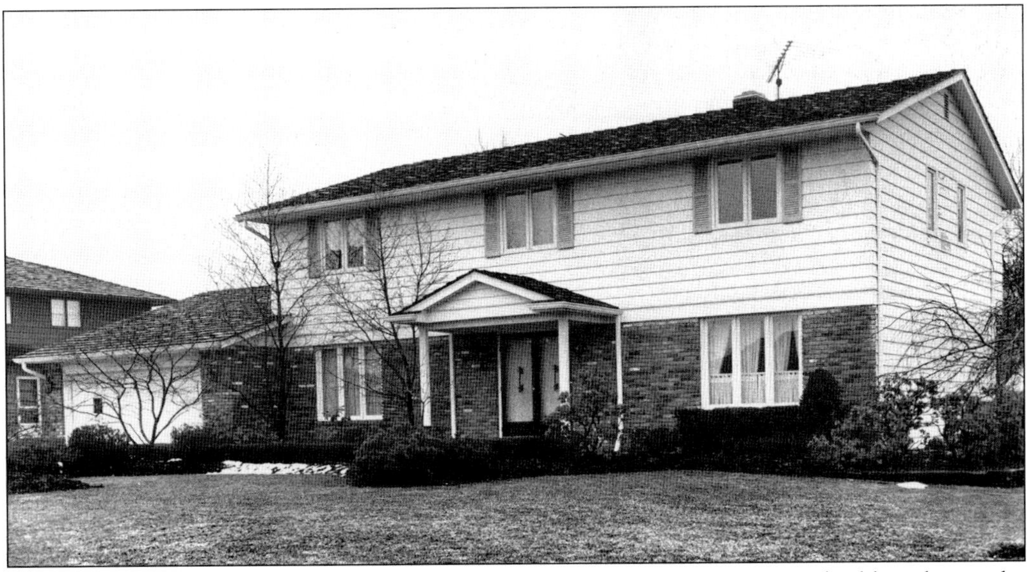

BRIAN DRIVE. Located on Beachwood's Brian Drive, this house typifies tract building during the early and mid-1960s in the still undeveloped parts of Beachwood, Highland Heights, Lyndhurst, Mayfield Heights, and Pepper Pike. With its high main block and lower attached garage, the design still retains elements of the upright-and-wing houses of the early 1800s. (CSU.)

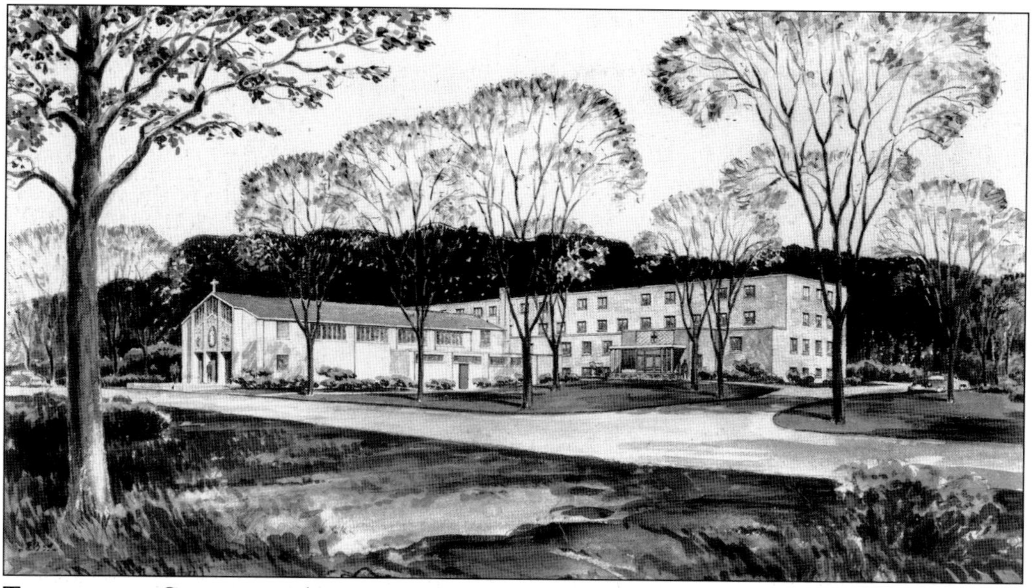

TRINITARIAN CONVENT. The Sisters of the Most Holy Trinity are a Roman Catholic Order headquartered in Rome. The Trinitarians bought the Our Lady of Lourdes Shrine and adjoining convent in 1953 and have operated them successfully for more than a half-century. During the 1960s, the Trinitarians began constructing modern facilities, which included a chapel, convent, gift shop, and restaurant. (SMHT.)

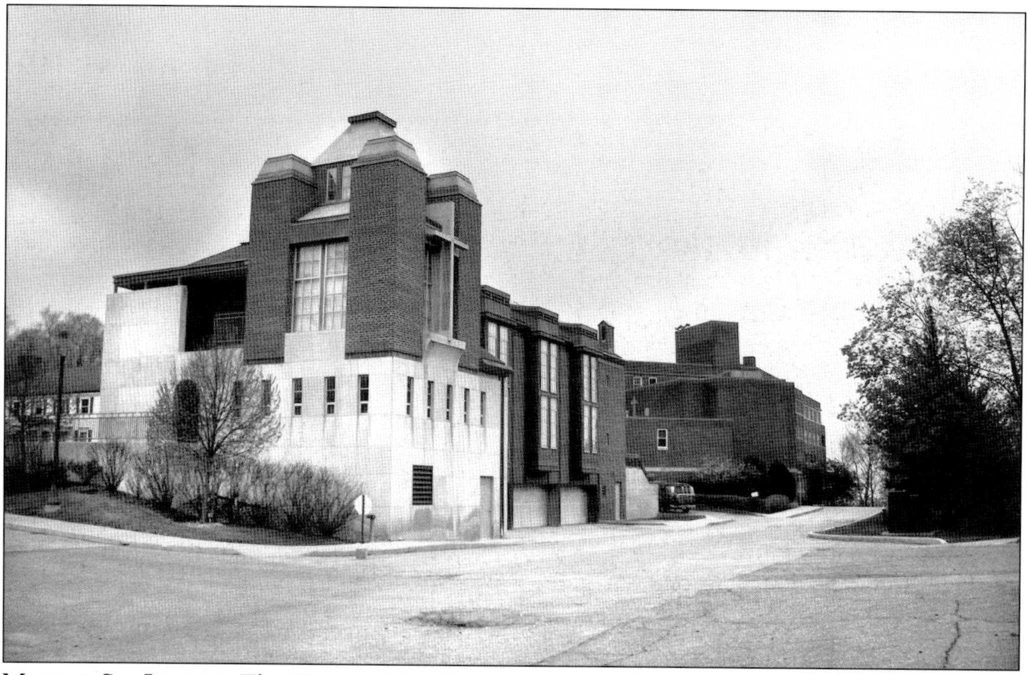

MOUNT ST. JOSEPH. The Sisters of St. Joseph ran their Mount St. Joseph nursing home in Jeanne Pickands's house for a decade before building a large institutional facility next door. By the 1960s, the building had grown to three four-story wings. In 1980, the sisters became independent from the French founders and renamed themselves the Sisters of St. Joseph of St. Mark. Recent additions include residential and operational wings. (SMSJ.)

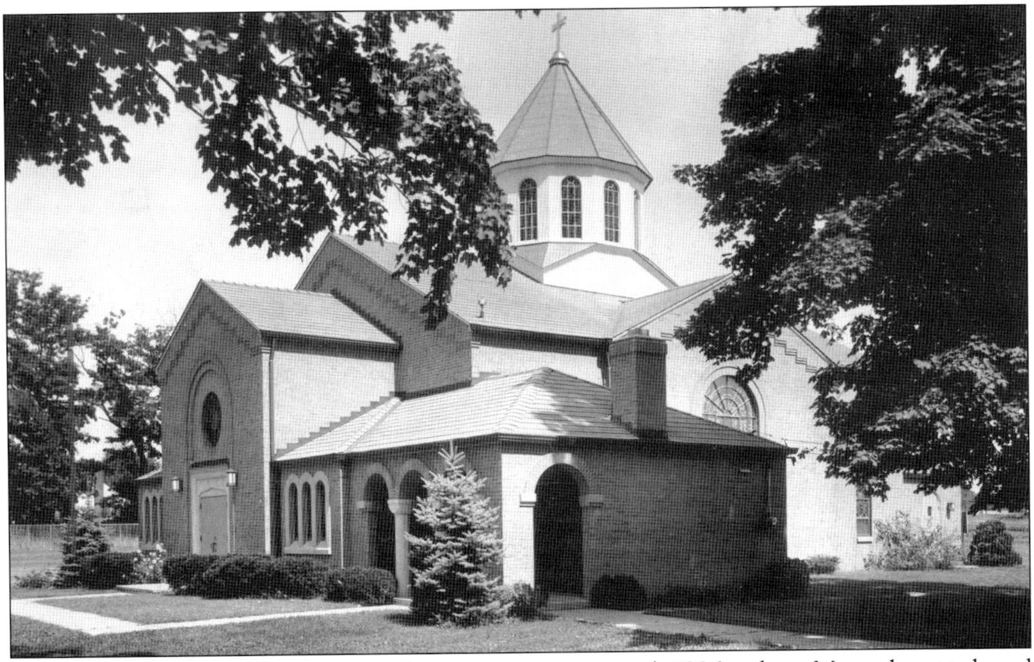

ARMENIAN CHURCH. Armenians began arriving around 1906, when Massachusetts-based American Steel & Wire Company opened a Cleveland facility. Shortly thereafter, the Ramgavars (Armenian Constitutional Democratic party) established a presence. Nearly a half-century later, in 1963, the Ramgavars built St. Gregory of Narek Church on Richmond Road. The domed cruciform structure takes cues from Armenian churches built during Christianity's first 1,000 years. (CPL.)

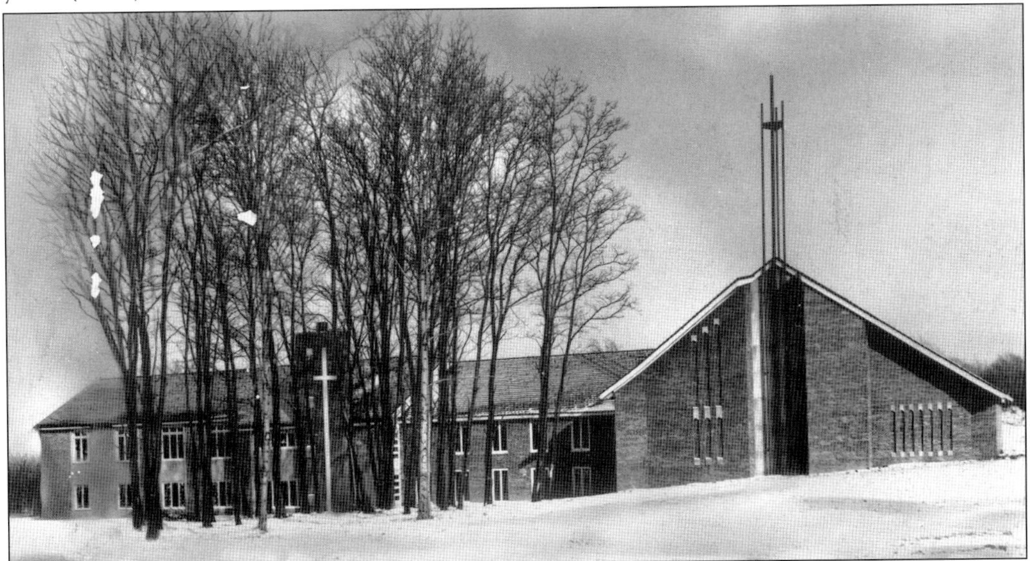

FAITH CHURCH. During the late 1950s, the Congregational Christian Church and Evangelical and Reformed Churches merged nationally to form the United Church of Christ. In 1956, local Congregationalists bought land at 575 Richmond Road. In 1958, the Eddy Road (Cleveland) Evangelical and Reformed Church joined them to build a UCC church on the lot. The building was completed in 1965. (CPL.)

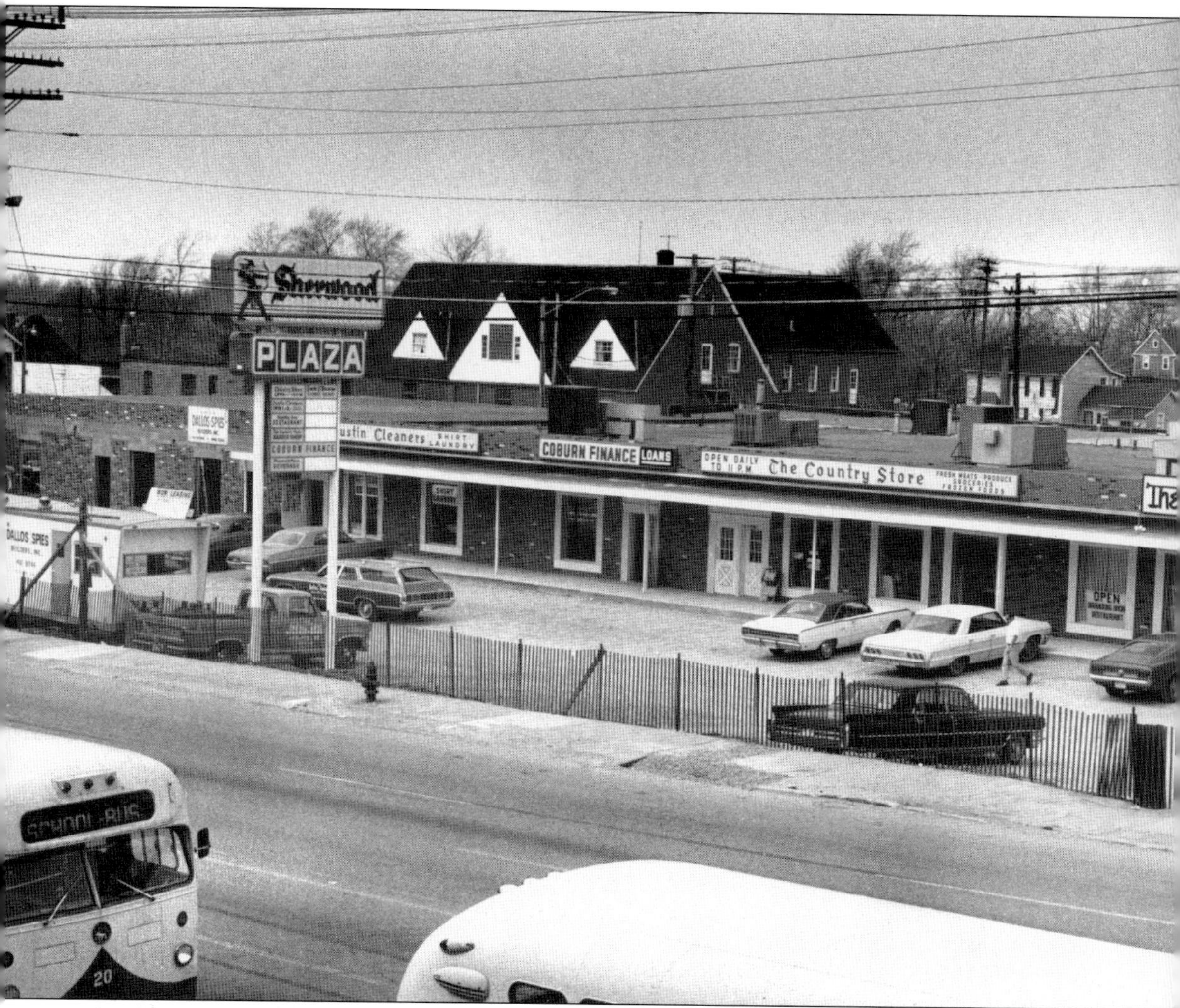

SHERWOOD PLAZA. There were sad days on Euclid Avenue during the mid-1960s urban renewal craze. The bluestone First Baptist Church came down in 1965, and the Euclid Inn and Coit Buildings fell in 1967. These were the last vestiges of old Euclid Creek village. The present brick Baptist building complex rose in 1966 (background), and the Sherwood Plaza came in 1969. (CPL.)

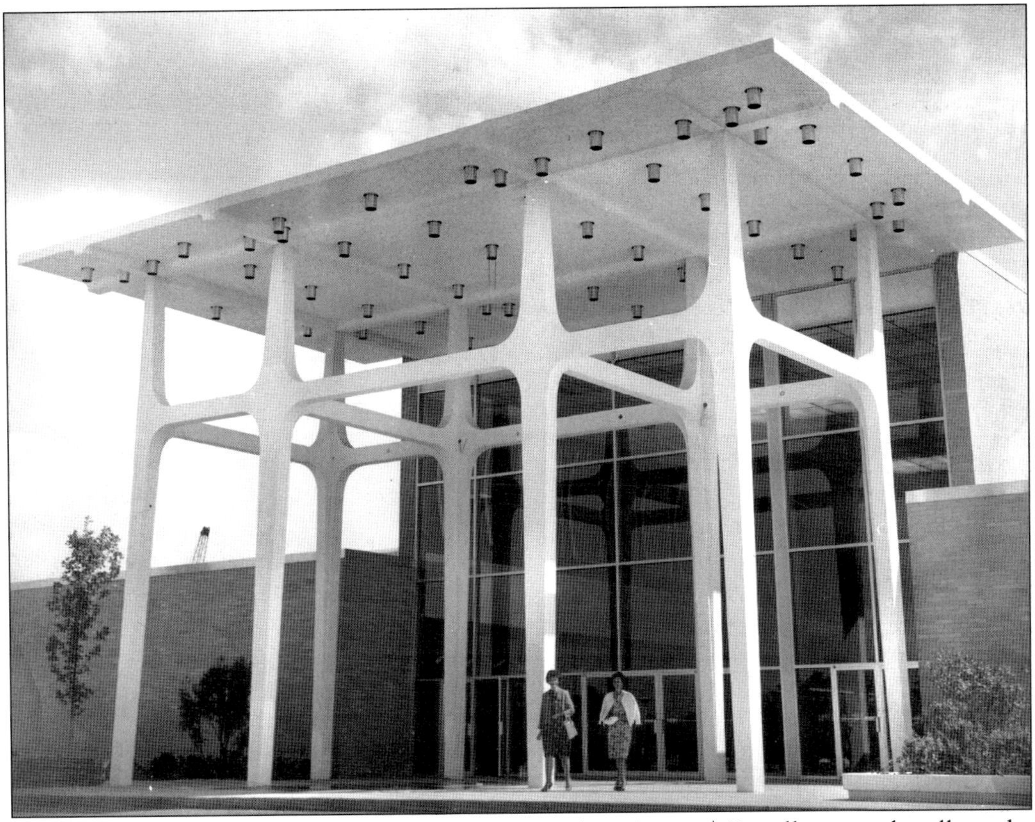

Richmond Mall. In 1963, Glazer-Marotta planned a 65-acre, $42 million retail mall on the northeast corner of Richmond and Wilson Mills. Edward J. deBartolo finished it, in August 1966, as the grandest enclosed mall in Ohio. The Sears Roebuck and J.C. Penney anchor stores were among the largest in the country. In 1996, the Simon Property Group bought the facility and renamed it Richmond Town Square. (CPL.)

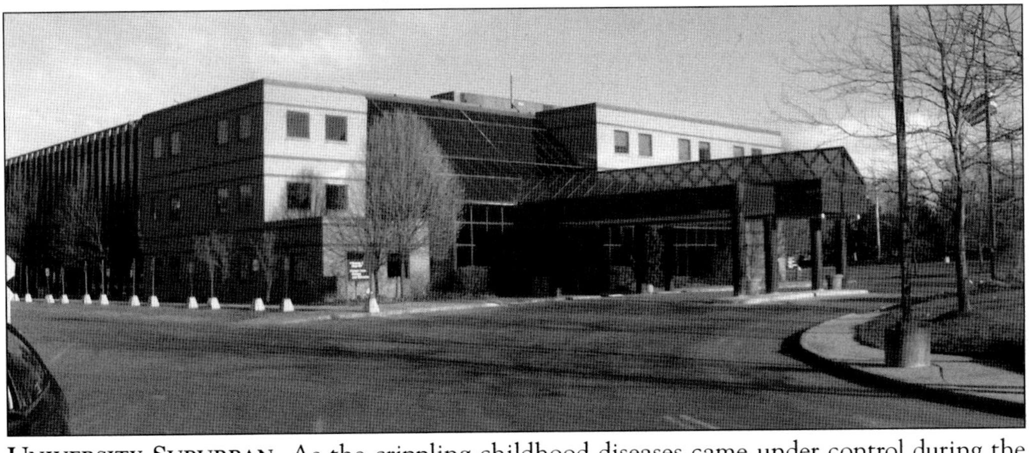

University Suburban. As the crippling childhood diseases came under control during the 20th century, Rainbow Hospital's work changed, and its patient load decreased. In 1971, the facility moved to University Circle to become Rainbow Babies and Children's Hospital. The great rambling cottage was demolished, and the University Suburban Health Center now stands on the Green Road site. (Roy Larick.)

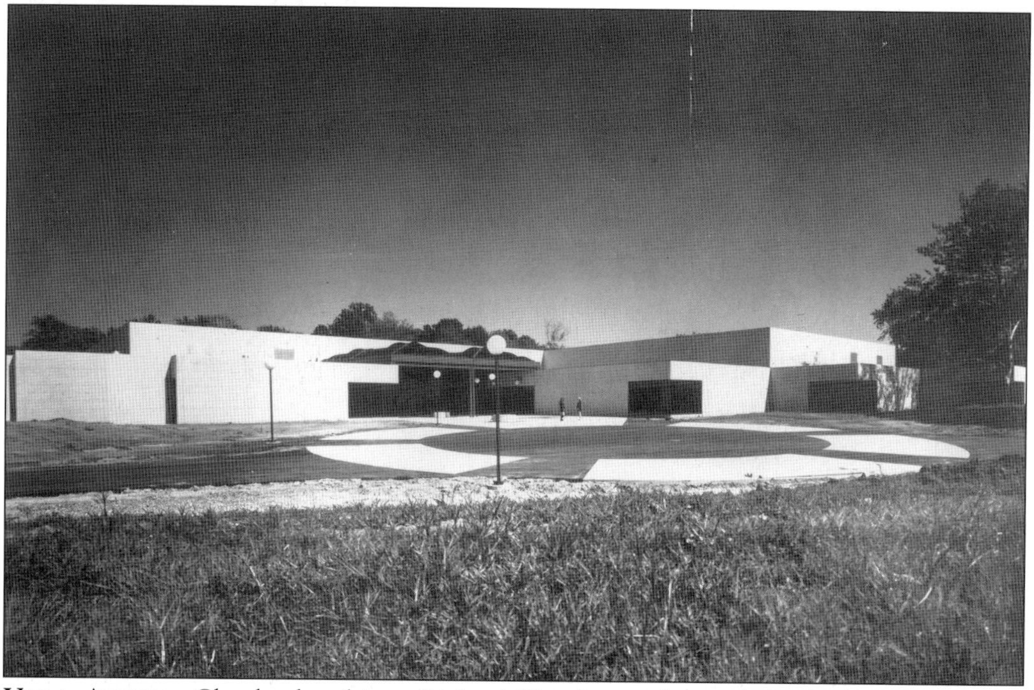

VILLA ANGELA. Cleveland architect Richard Fleischman designed the building in 1973 as the new Villa Angela High School. The architecture received the Greater Cleveland Growth Association Certificate of Merit in the same year. However, the school closed in 1990, when it merged with St. Joseph High School in Euclid. (USC.)

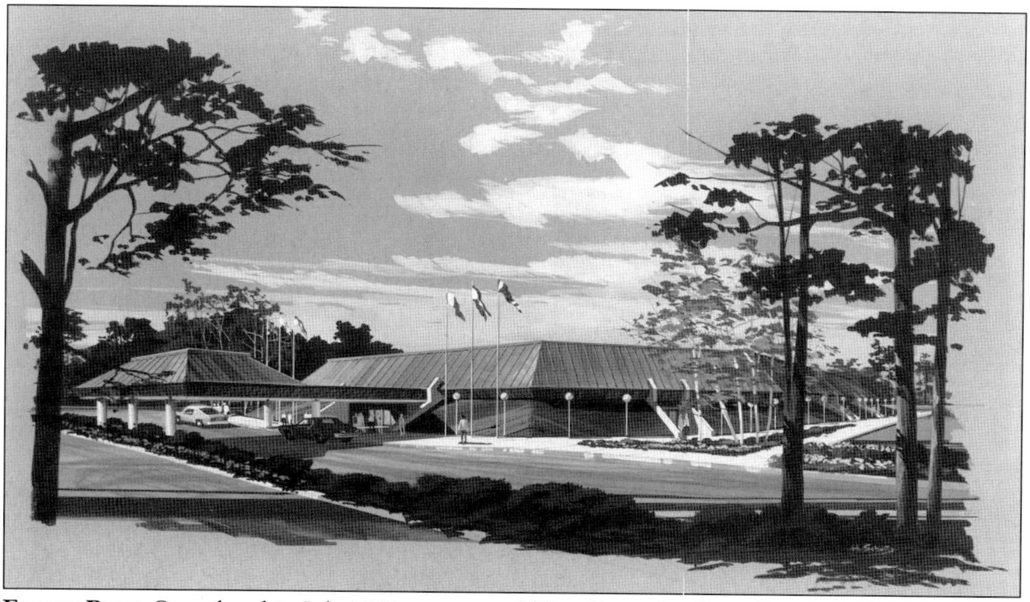

FRONT ROW. Completed in July 1974 at a cost of $3 million, the Front Row was the first indoor theater to be built regionally since the 1927 Cleveland Playhouse. Local architect Richard R. Jencen designed the 300-foot-domed auditorium without pillars. The stage and its encircling orchestra pit slowly revolved during performances. Seating for 3,200 claimed back rows just 60 feet from the stage. The Front Row closed in 1993. (CPL.)

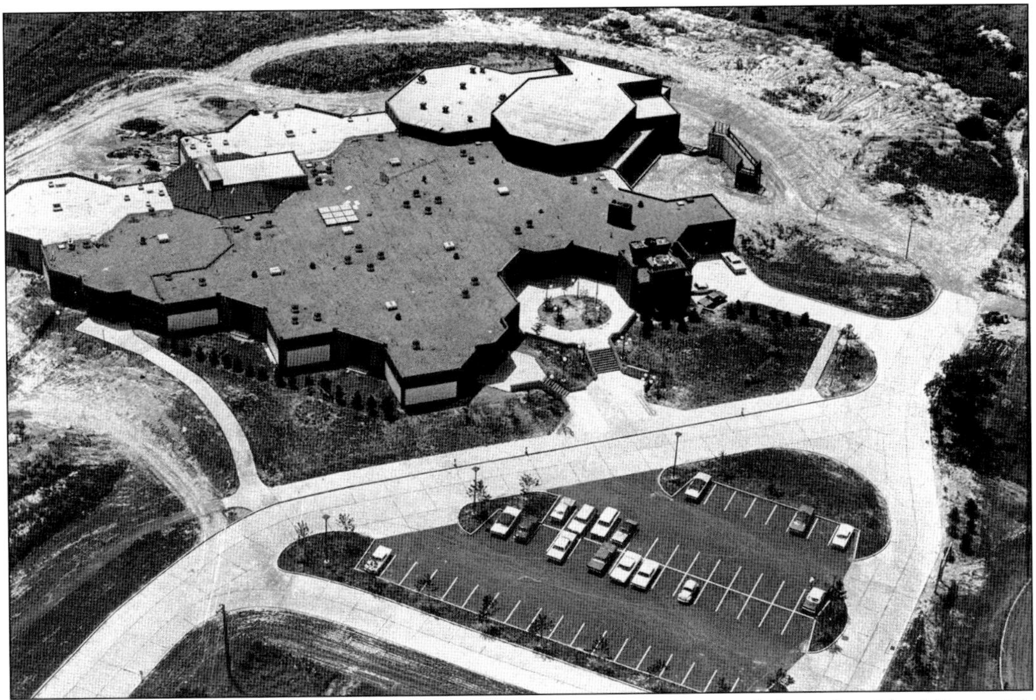

Beachwood Middle School. In 1966, architect Phil Hart designed this school building with the innovative spirit of the times. Classrooms were built open and grouped into "pods." The entire educational process would emphasize openness and communality. Teachers and students would be aware of themselves and of others within the pod. The concept was not a success. Walls were eventually erected to give the classrooms a more traditional character. (CSU.)

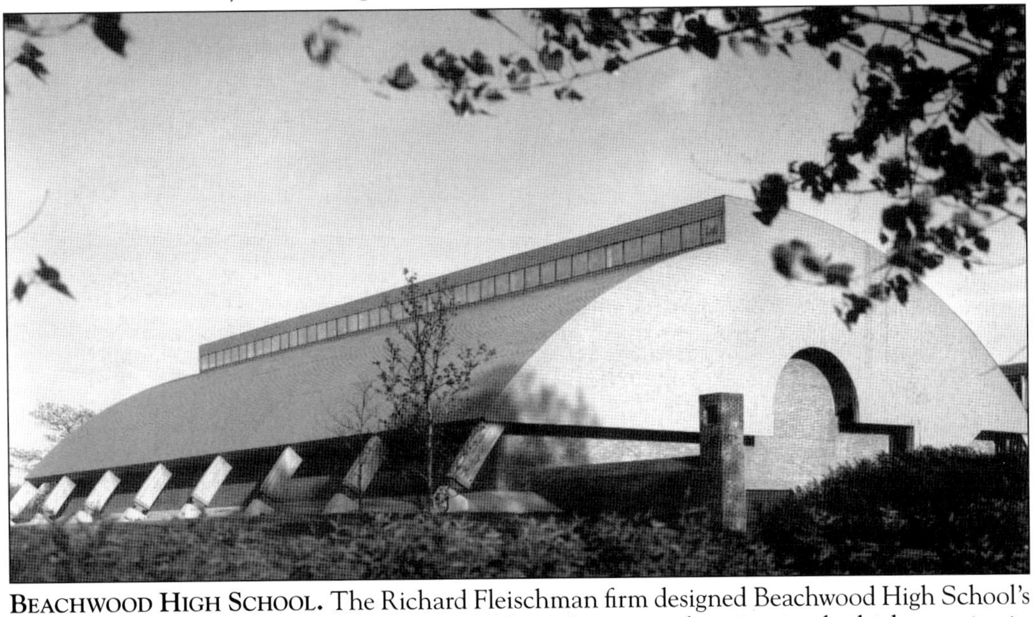

Beachwood High School. The Richard Fleischman firm designed Beachwood High School's indoor pool in 1979. The massive structure takes advantage of its site sits the highest point in the watershed, just south of Fairmount Boulevard and west of Richmond. In 1981, the building won an American Institute of Architects Award of Design Excellence. (RFPA.)

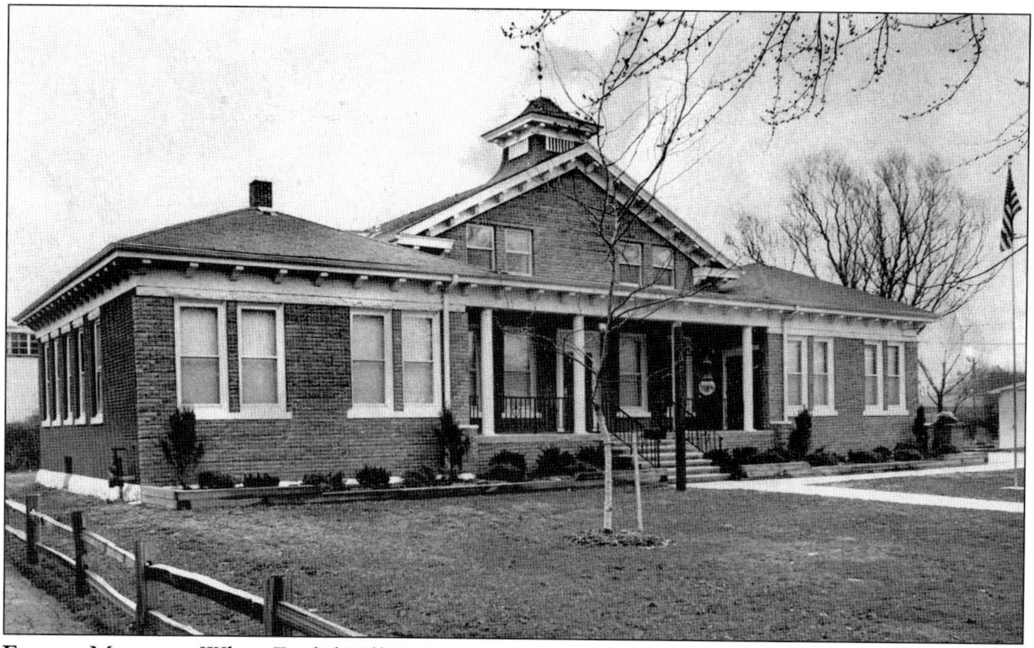

Euclid Museum. When Euclid Village's Central High School opened in 1913, the old township high school was sold for private use. Shortly after, it held 17 small apartments. The City of Euclid bought the building in 1975 and opened the museum in 1984. Displays include township maps from 1796 to 1917, Victorian living spaces, a Charles Brush arc light, old vineyard equipment, and early industrial products. (EHS.)

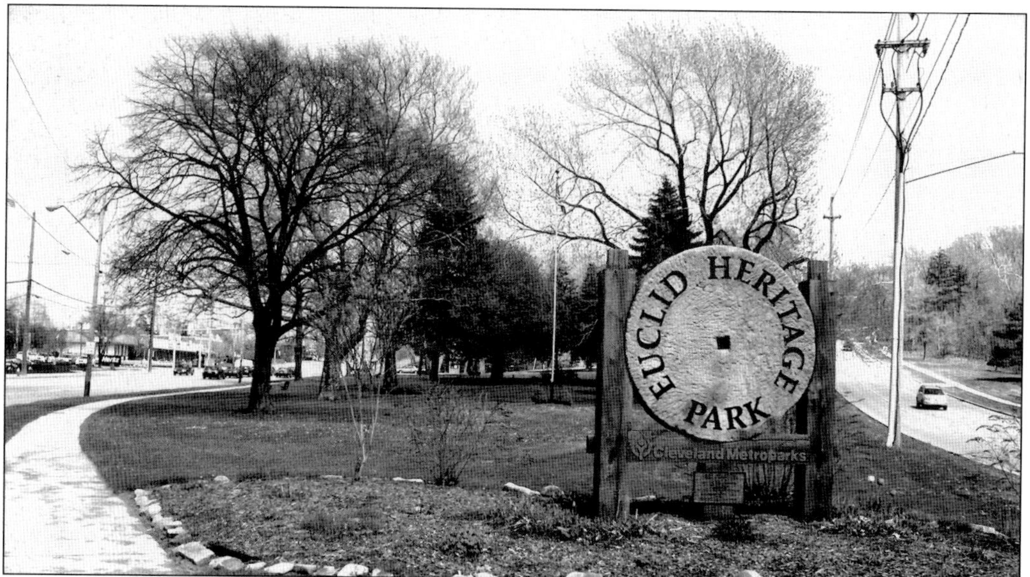

Heritage Park. An important crossroads in prehistoric times, Euclid Creek village saw commercial development in the second decade of the 19th century. The pioneer Pelton family sold the crossroads triangle to the Euclid Creek Reservation in 1916. Metroparks deeded it to the City of Euclid in 1976. A buckeye grove commemorates early settlers and the heroes of September 11, 2001, Flight 93. A large Euclid bluestone millstone recalls the local quarrying industry. (Roy Larick.)

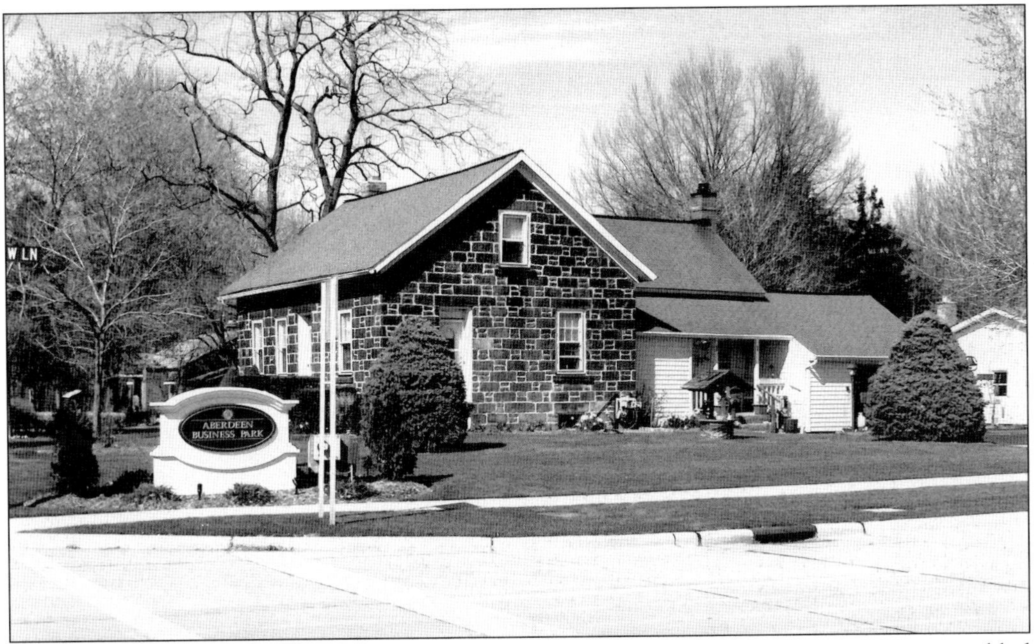

ABERDEEN OFFICE PARK. During the 1990s, the Aberdeen Development Corporation assembled the last remaining clear land in Highland Heights, including most of the Hager and Miner properties. On this 250-acre parcel, Aberdeen has built a 220-unit upscale housing development, and a business park catering to professional offices. (Roy Larick.)

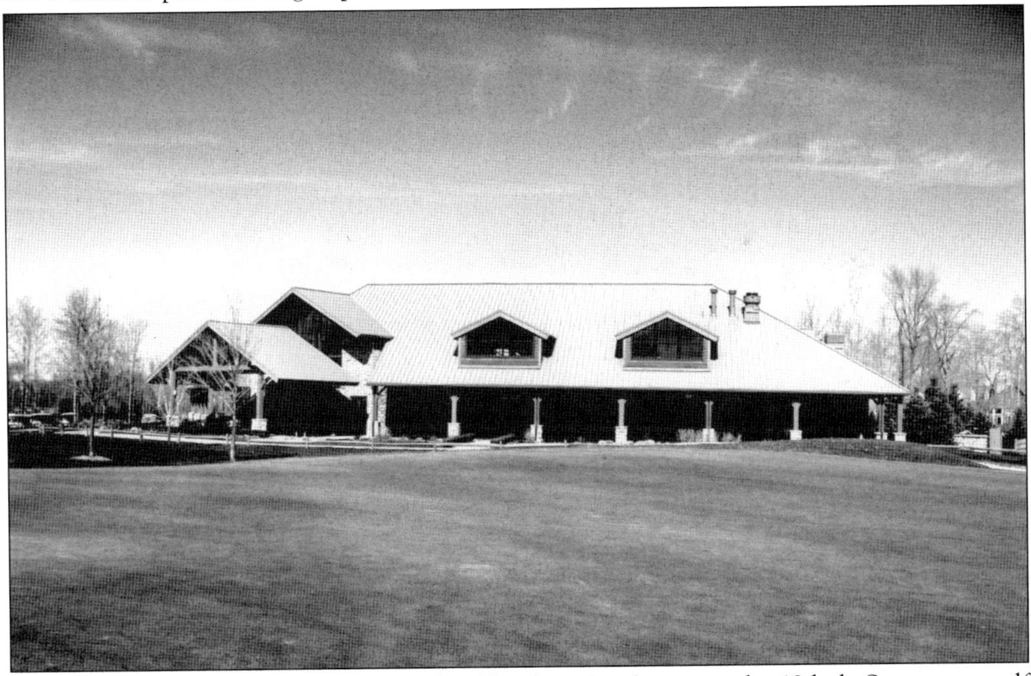

STONEWATER GOLF CLUB. As part of the Aberdeen development, the 18-hole Stonewater golf course was designed by Michael Hudzan and Dana Fry. It opened in 1996. In its 2005 nationwide survey of golf courses, *Golf Digest* ranked Stonewater the best public course in Ohio and the 29th best in the nation. (Roy Larick.)

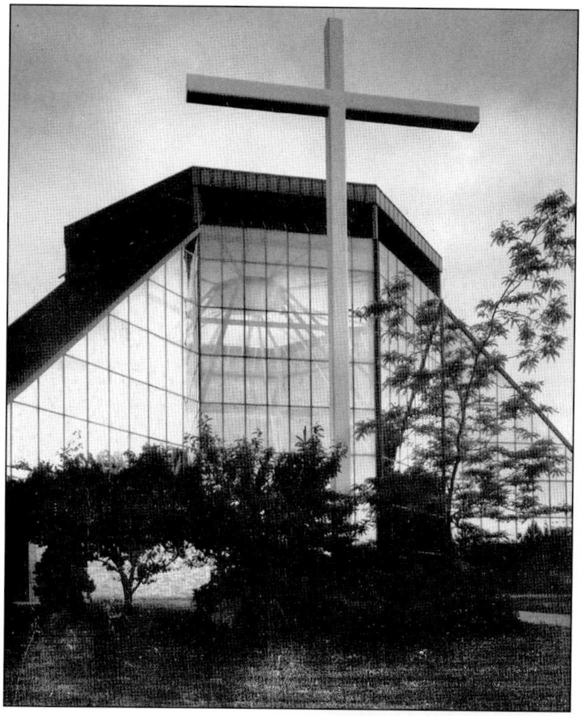

ST. PASCHAL BAYLON. The parish, organized from five others in 1953, built its first church on Wilson Mills Road in Highland Heights in 1955. The present building, opened in April 1971, is a design of the Fleischman firm. The sanctuary seats 1,300. In the year 2000, the structure won the American Institute of Architects 25 Year Building Award. (RFPA.)

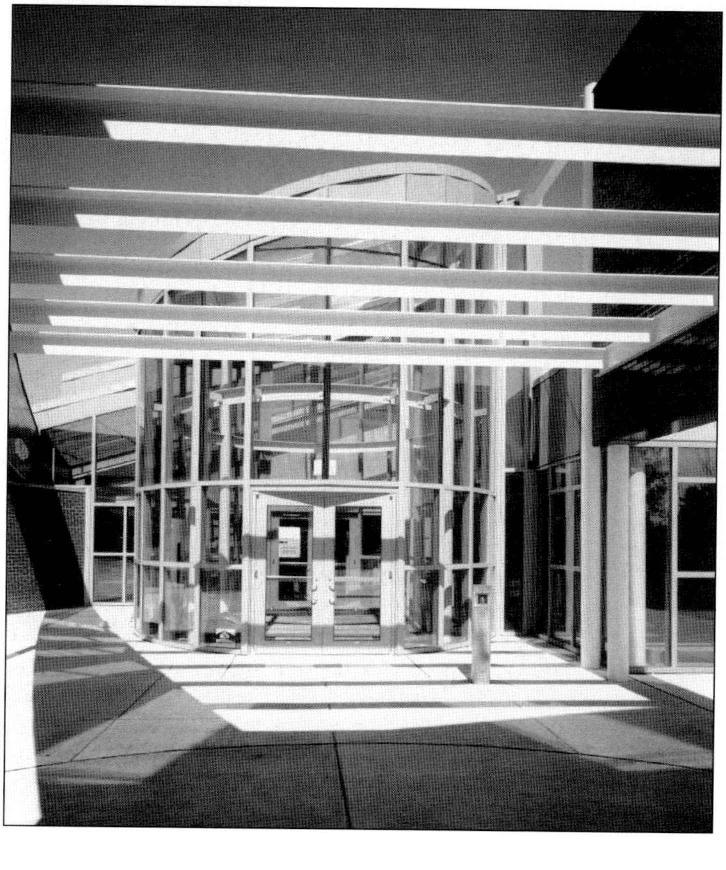

NOTTINGHAM LIBRARY. In 1991, the Cleveland Public Library bought the Villa Angela school building and part of the grounds. The library hired the original architect, Richard Fleischman, to convert the school into its Memorial-Nottingham branch, which opened in 1994. The library is distinguished with a large meeting room and climate-controlled storage for historic documents. The conversion has received awards in Excellence for Library Architecture. (RFPA.)

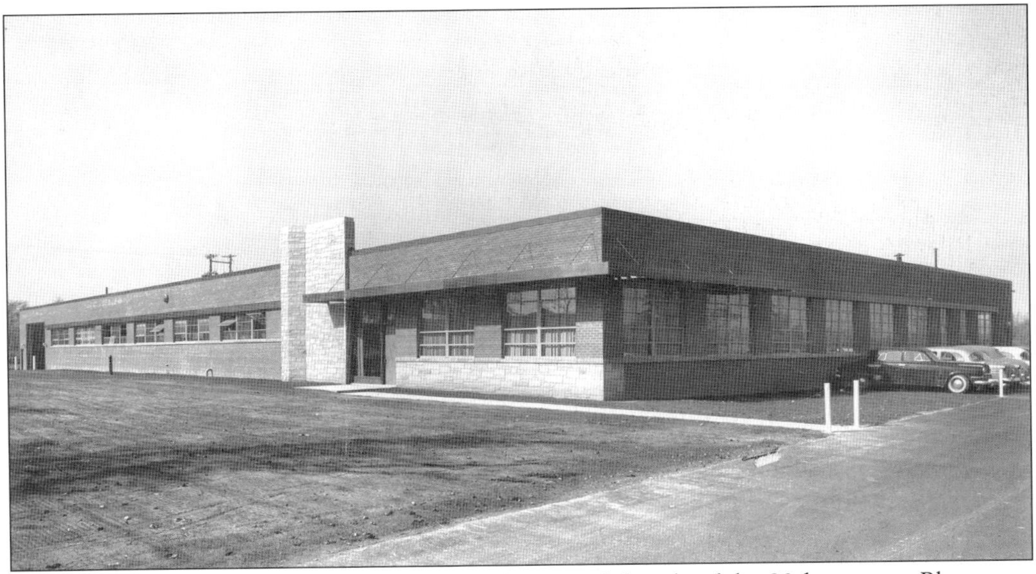

GLASTIC. After the quarries closed down in the second decade of the 20th century, Bluestsone Village was recast as the South Euclid industrial area. Growth was slow and limited. During the 1950s, the Glastic Corporation moved here to produce specialized composite materials for use in electrical, thermal, corrosive, and abrasive environments. The Glenridge Road factory was built in 1955 and expanded during the 1960s. Glastic also has facilities in Clinton, Michigan; Birmingham, England; and Mexico City. (CPL.)

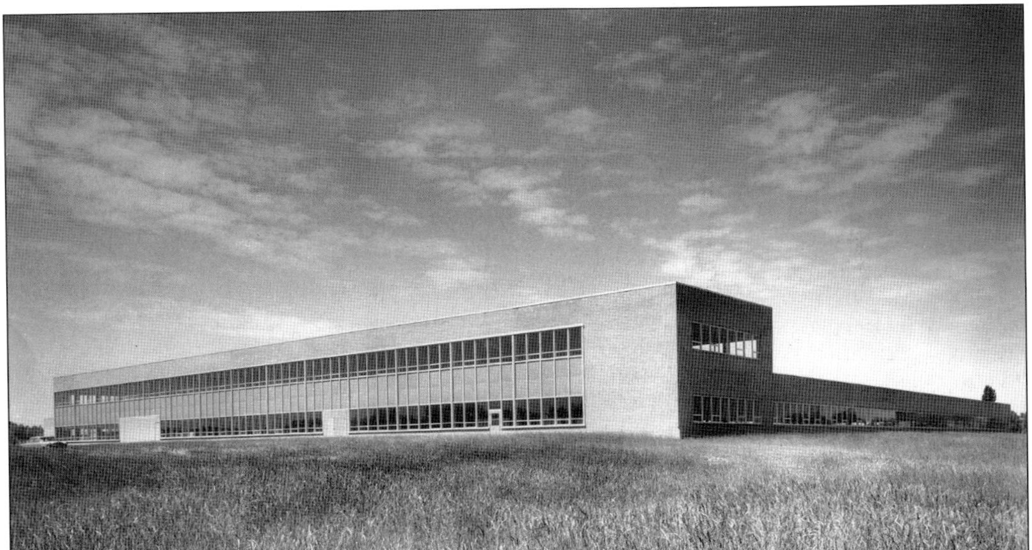

GENERAL ELECTRIC. Since the second decade of the 20th century, GE has manufactured specialized glass in Cleveland facilities, including Nela Park. In 1956, GE bought 76 acres of the Highland Road Verbsky farm, on which to consolidate lamp glass manufacturing. The plant employed 250 people during the 1960s and 1970s. Part of the acreage was sold in the 1980s and then reacquired. Part has been sold again and, in 2005, was under consideration for housing development. (CPL.)

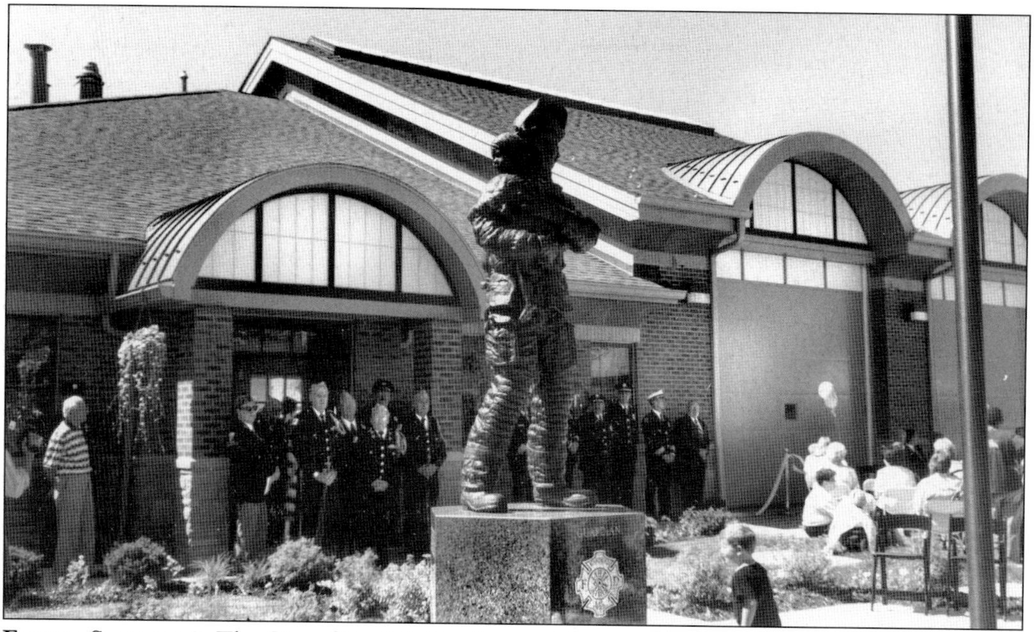

EUCLID STATION 2. The City of Euclid's Fire Station 2 has always served the original Euclid Creek village area. In 1946, the station was moved outside the Chardon-Euclid crossroads. In the late 1990s, it was moved back to Chardon Road, to be central and to help revitalize the crossroads. The new design, by Architecture Resource Corporation, facilitates modern apparatus and firefighter lifestyles, the new Station 2 was dedicated in August 2000. (Euclid Fire Department.)

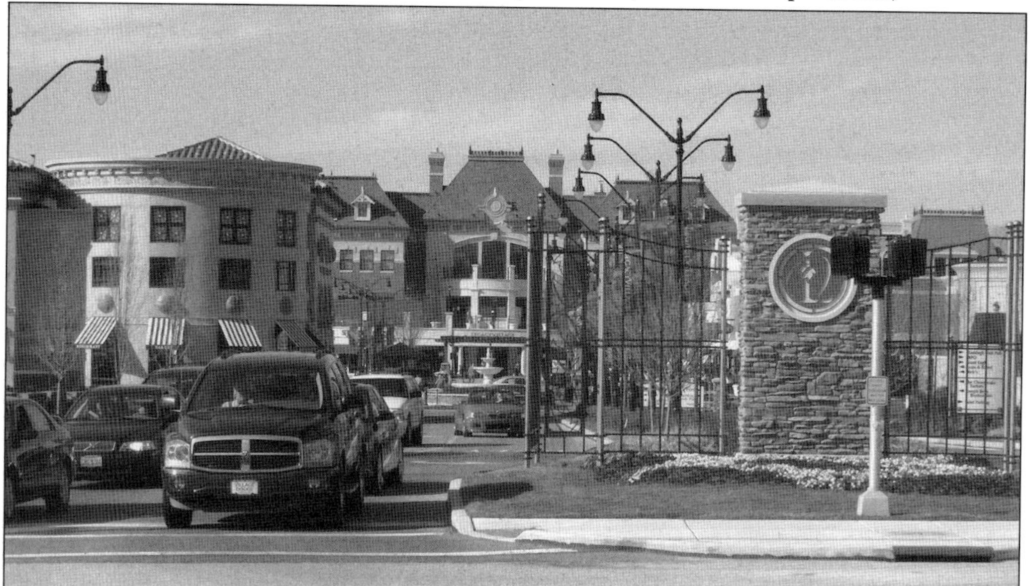

LEGACY VILLAGE. In 1982, TRW bought the Bolton estate and moved its corporate headquarters there from Euclid Avenue. This facility closed as Northrop Grumman acquired TRW in 1998. In 1999, First Interstate Properties bought the Blossom end of the estate and created Legacy Village, Ohio's first and largest "lifestyle center." The City of Lyndhurst is banking on Legacy Village to replace the tax revenues lost with TRW's departure. (Roy Larick.)

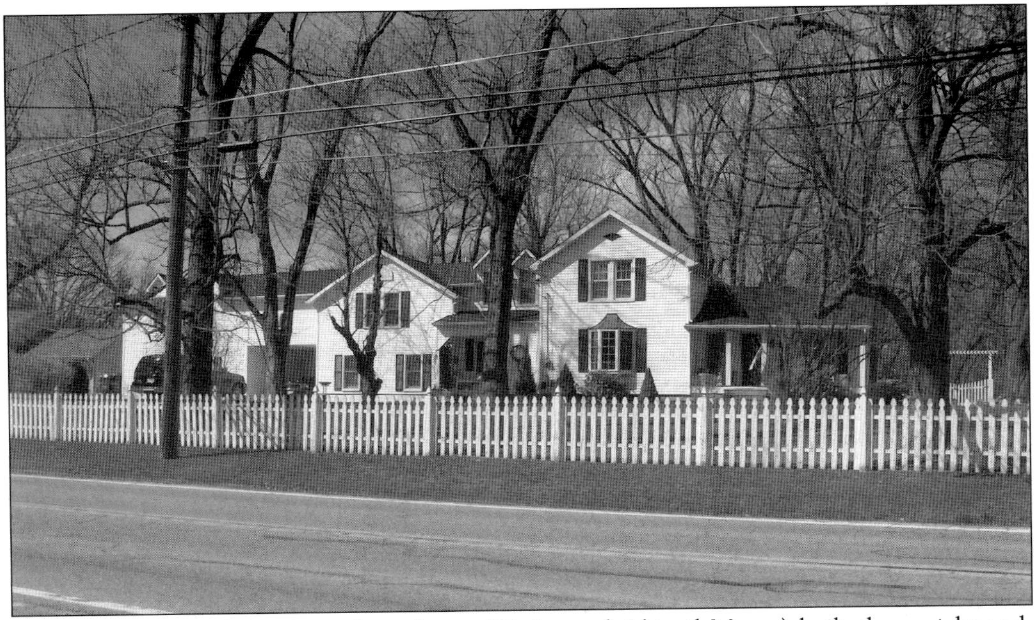

MAPES-BIRO. Obadiah Mapes (grandson of Rufus and Abigail Mapes) built the upright-and-wing (on the right) around 1850. It stands on White Road, west of Rockefeller. Beginning in 1990, the Biro family hired architect Allen Clough to design two additions that greatly expand and modernize the house while leaving the original structure intact. The work treated a valuable cultural resource in a most sensitive way. (Roy Larick.)

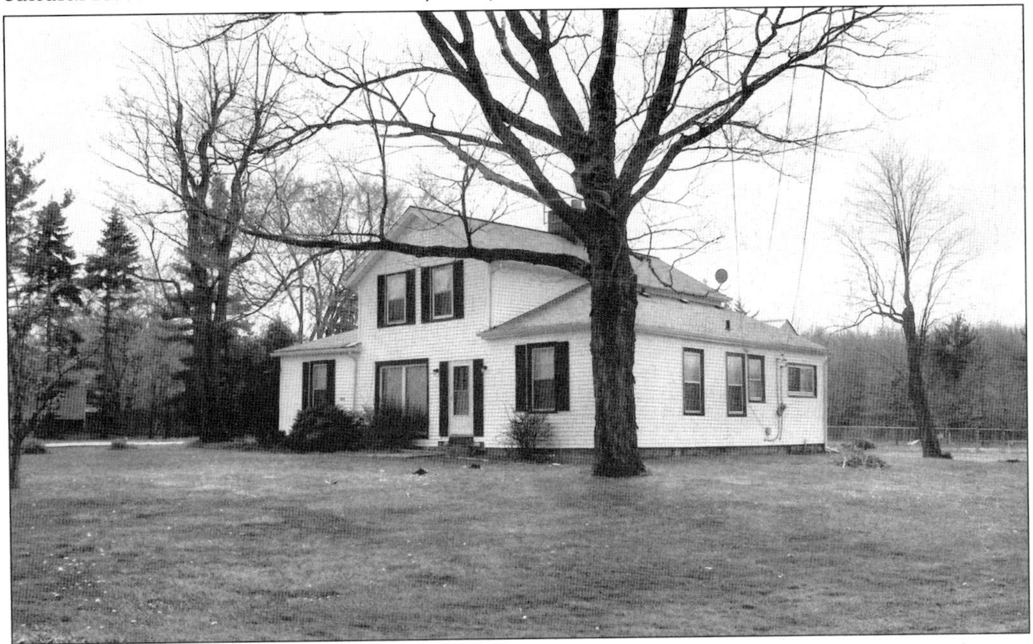

WELCH HOUSE. The Welch family came to Euclid from Connecticut before 1820, purchasing the Euclid Creek gorge north of current Monticello Boulevard. The Bailey family now owns the 1854 Welch house and has worked hard to stabilize the foundation and frame. In 2004, the Euclid Landmark Commission designated the Welch and Pelton houses and the Euclid Cemetery as City-of-Euclid Landmarks within the Euclid Creek watershed. (Roy Larick.)

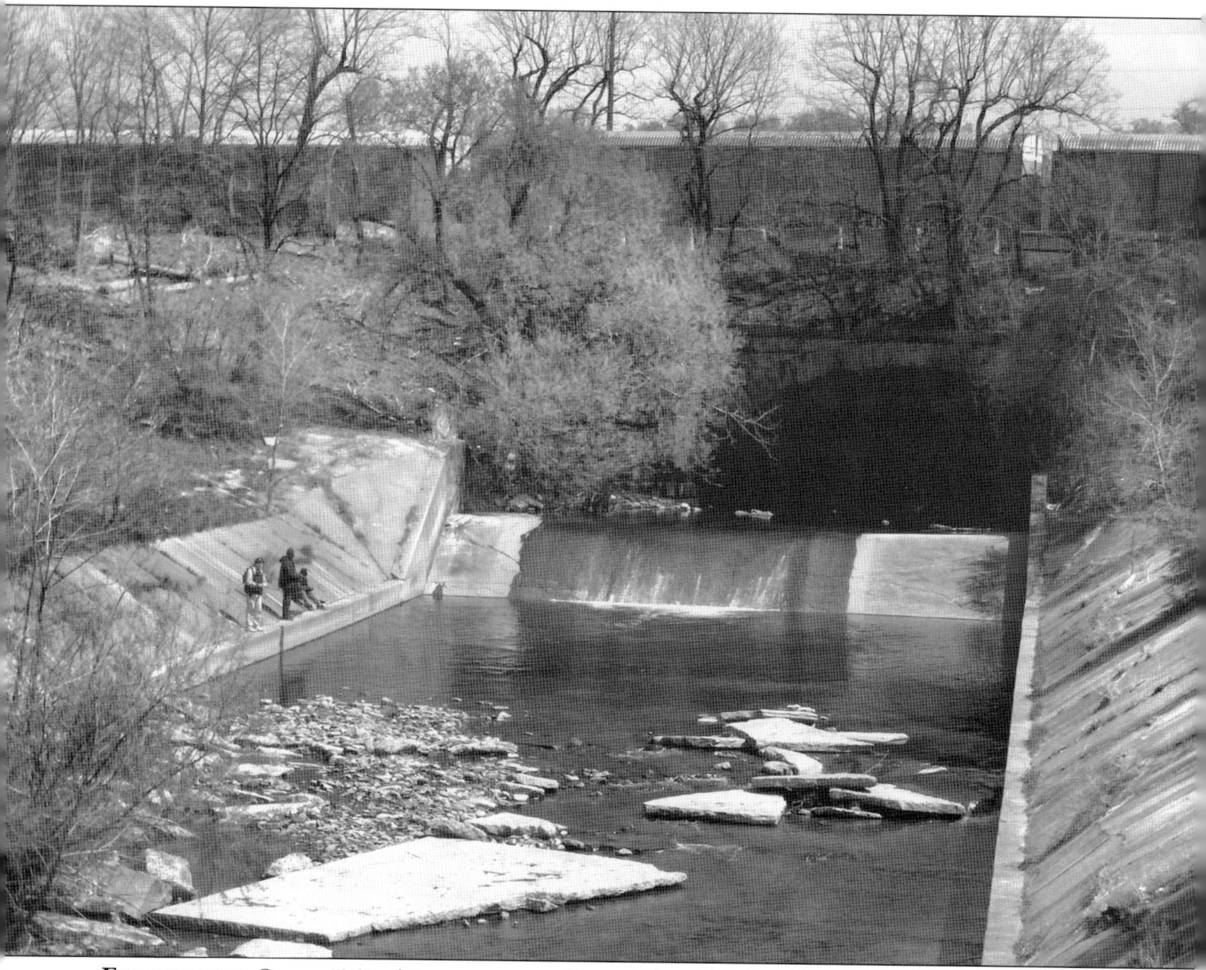

FRUITLANDS. Since 1961, this concrete spillway has taken Euclid Creek from its natural level at the CSX Railroad bridge to the Interstate 90 culvert level below. As the structure blocked the progress of creek-spawning lake fish, Fruitlands (named after the neighboring farm stand) became a reputed fishing hole. In the mid-1990s, steelhead trout (*Oncorhynchus mykiss*) were introduced to the lake. April 2005 brought trout and anglers to Fruitlands. (Roy Larick.)

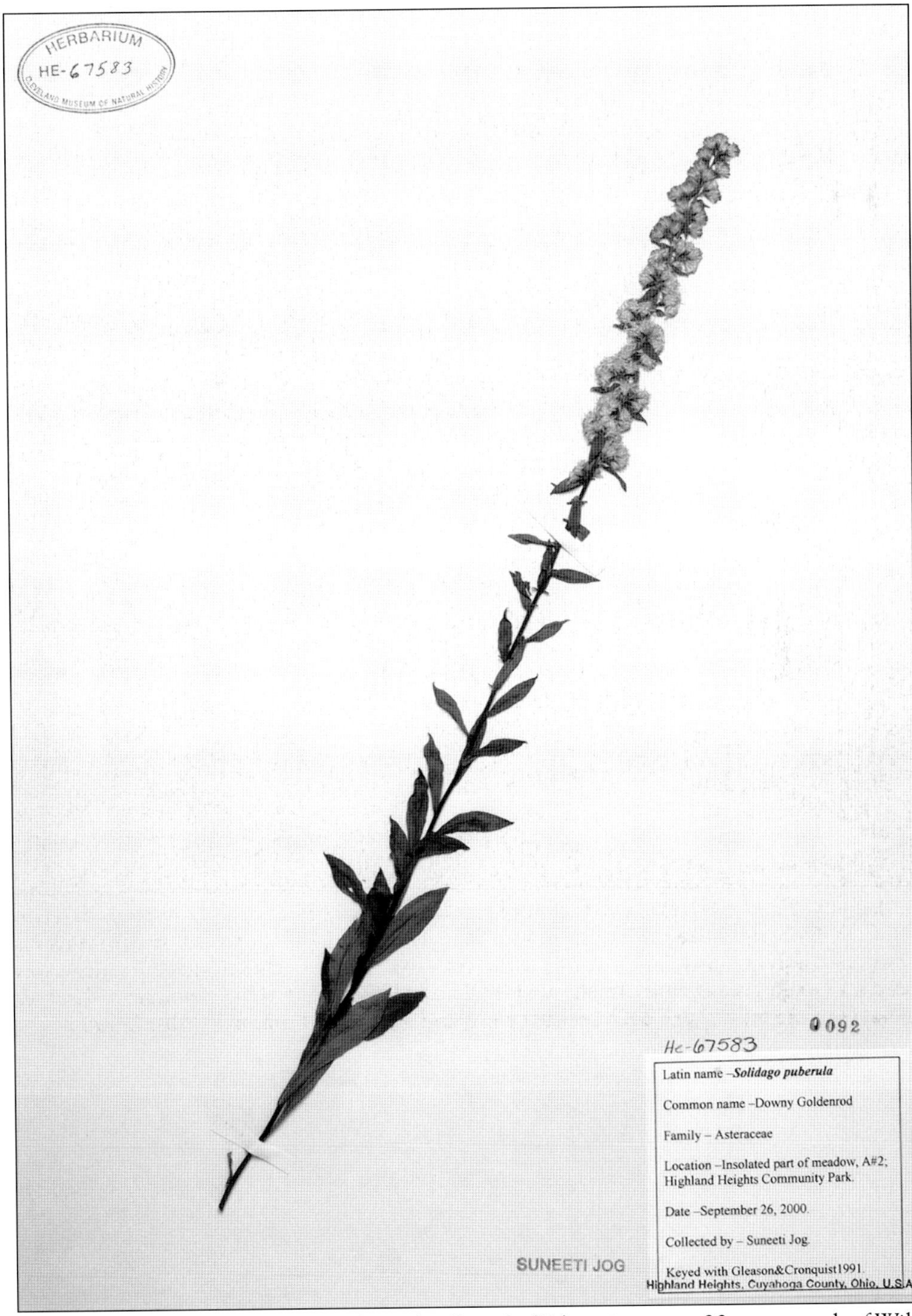

DOWNY GOLDENROD. The Highland Heights Board of Education owns 30-acres north of Wilson Mills Road. The wetland portion contains many water-loving plants, including downy goldenrod (*Solidago puberula*), now a very rare form in northern Ohio. As of spring 2005, the City of Highland Heights had a $600,000 grant to restore the wetland, but the board and city had yet to agree on the project. (CMNH.)

BIBLIOGRAPHY

A Pictorial History of the City of Mayfield Heights. City of Mayfield Heights, 1997.

Johnson, Crisfield. *History of Cuyahoga County, Ohio*. Euclid Township: D. W. Ensign & Company, 1879.

Keidel, Helen, ed. *Golden Anniversary, Richmond Heights Ohio, 1917–1967.* Richmond Heights Kiwanis Club, 1967.

Lake, David J. *Atlas of Cuyahoga County, Ohio*. Euclid Township, 1874. http://www.clevelandmemory.org/ebooks/.

Larick, Roy, and Craig Semsel. *Euclid Township, 1796–1801: Protest in the Western Reserve*. Western Reserve Historical Society publication.

Lyndhurst: A Pictorial History. City of Lyndhurst, 1994.

Morris, Jeffrey. *Beechwood: The Book*. 1997.

Schuemann, Nancy L. *On the Threshold of a New Century: The City of South Euclid, 1967–1999.* City of South Euclid, 1999.

Telshaw, Helen, ed. *History of Highland Heights*. City of Highland Heights, 1976.

Urban, Mrs. George J., ed. *The Proud Heritage of South Euclid, Ohio (Golden Jubilee, 1917–1967)*. City of South Euclid, 1967.

Williams, John. *A History of the City of Euclid*. Euclid Historical Society, 2003.

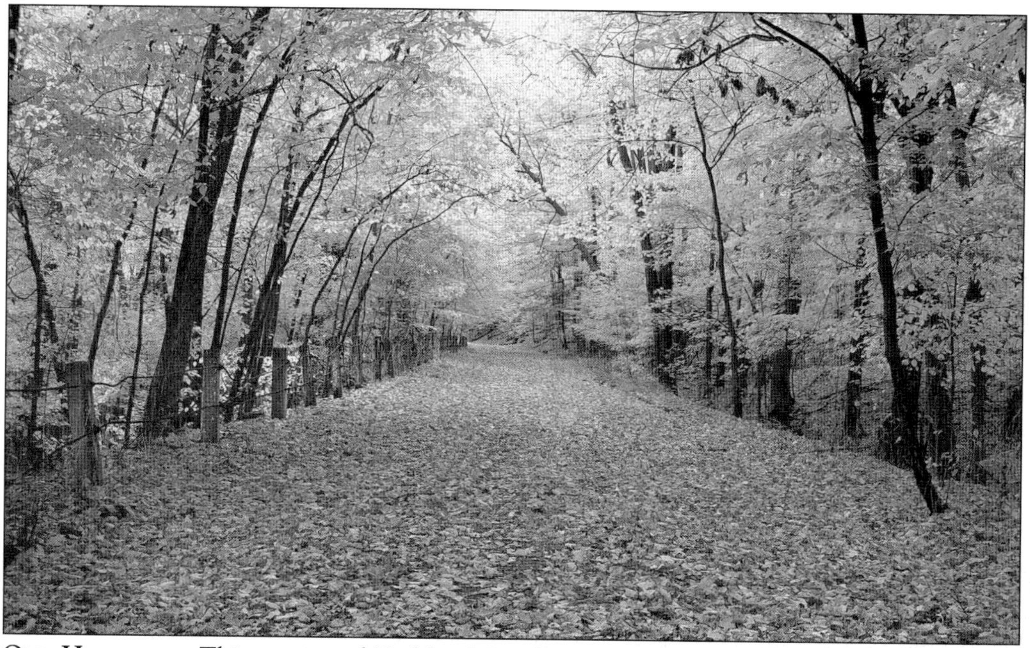

OLD HIGHLAND. This section of Highland Road is part of the prehistoric Native American trail that mounts Euclid Creek's center branch. The road was abandoned in 1965 with the construction of new Highland. Monica E. Daugherty captured this image to win a prize in the Friends of Euclid Creek 2004 watershed photography contest.